KISHTWAR CAULDRON

The Struggle against the ISI's Ethnic Cleansing

KISHTWAR CAULDRON

The Struggle against the ISI's Ethnic Cleansing

Maj Gen (Dr) G D Bakshi SM, VSM (retd)

Foreword by

Lt Gen S K Sinha PVSM (retd)
Former Governor J&K and Assam

PENTAGON PRESS

KISHTWAR CAULDRON
The Struggle against the ISI's Ethnic Cleansing

Maj Gen (Dr) G D Bakshi SM, VSM (retd)

ISBN 978-81-8274-736-4

First Published in 2013

Published by
PENTAGON PRESS
206, Peacock Lane, Shahpur Jat,
New Delhi-110049
Phones: 011-64706243, 26491568
Telefax: 011-26490600
email: rajan@pentagonpress.in
website: www.pentagonpress.in

Printed at Avantika Printers Private Limited

"Be nice to the people: Be nasty to the terrorists!"

9 Sector RR Slogan

*Dedicated to all ranks – past and present of the "**Mystic**" **9 Sector Rashtriya Rifles** and **6th Battalion the Jammu & Kashmir Rifles**, that I had the honour to command in the years of intense struggle in J&K. Their heroism, valour, and tremendous sacrifice was instrumental in saving the state from **ethnic cleansing** and worse.*

Contents

Foreword *ix*

Preface *xix*

List of Abbreviations *xxv*

1. Prologue: An Indian Doctrine for Low Intensity Conflict 1

The Era of Low Intensity Conflict 1

A Literature Survey 3

Fourth Generation Warfare 9

The Indian Context 9

An Indian Doctrine for LICO 10

Protecting the People versus Kinetic Factors 13

A New Counter Terrorist (CT) Model: The Hinterland Variant in Kishtwar 14

Counter Terrorist (CT) Operations: The Proactive Model 16

The Ethnic Cleansing Factor 18

2. Assignment Kishtwar 24

3. Historic Backdrop: The Insurgency in Kashmir 39

Backdrop 39

Onset of Jihadi Insurgency: Operation Tariq Anwar (TOPAC) 41

Roots of Jihad 43

The Attrition Curve 48

4. The Spread of Jihadi Insurgency in Doda 52

Overview of Operations in Kishtwar 56

5. Sector Commander Kishtwar: Energising an Organisation 59

Reception 59

Overcoming the Morale Problem 60

The Jama Masjid Episode 70

Non-Initiation of Combat Operations (NICO) 72

6. The Road versus the Hinterland Controversy 74
   Perils of a Staff Screen 78

7. Ending Ethnic Cleansing: The Need to Deter 83
   Ethnic Cleansing 88

8. Heliborne Operations at Navapachi 98
   Heliborne Operations in Warwan 102
   Slithering or Low Hover 103

9. Advantages of an Offensive Mindset: The Kishtwar Experience 106
   The Highest Award: Ashoka Chakra 113
   Miracle at Machail 116

10. Winning Hearts and Minds 120
   Navapachi Reconstruction 122
   Educational Infrastructure 123
   Turning Black Areas to White 124

11. Operational Research and Statistical Analysis (ORSA) 131
   ORSA in Kishtwar 132
   ORSA Applications 134

12. Lessons Learnt 135
   Macro Lessons Learnt: The Indian Context 145
   Issues for Debate 146

13. Demographics as Destiny: The Road Ahead 153
   Demographic Dimensions of Internal Security 154
   Military Manpower Conundrum in India 157
   The Indian Civilisational Trajectory 159
   The Gen Malik Era: Search for Quick Fixes 160
   The Path Ahead in J&K 166
   Issues of Governance 168

Post Script 171

Select Bibliography 173

Index 177

Foreword

Major General G D Bakshi has written an interesting book on the theory of low intensity conflict and has given the reader the benefit of his long and varied experience of dealing with this type of warfare. His book provides a good insight into the ongoing conflict in Kashmir, which has been festering for decades. He has done this in an admirable manner. This should also be of great help in understanding the different dimensions of the Kashmir problem. As Governor of Jammu and Kashmir, I interacted with him when he was Brigadier General Staff (Information) at Headquarters Northern Command. He used to brief me of developments in Kashmir every week. I also used to get weekly briefings from the Intelligence Bureau and Research and Analysis Wing (RAW). I found his briefings of much use. His views were largely in line with my thinking. As mentioned by him in this book, I used the term psychological initiatives rather than psychological warfare. This underscores the fact that we are not at war with our own people but are trying to win their hearts and minds, and bring them back to the national mainstream. This has to be achieved not only through economic development but also with an emotional content in psychological initiatives to neutralise the main reason behind the people taking up arms against the State. This strategy succeeded very well in Assam. We not only isolated the ULFA in Assam but won over the people by suitably addressing the root cause of militancy, namely unabated illegal migration into Assam from Bangladesh encouraged by the Congress Governments for vote bank. Militancy was crushed and at the same time the Robin Hood image of the militants vanished. A large number of people now started viewing them as criminals. Gradually, we succeeded in bringing about a total change in the situation. There were several instances of the people in rural areas apprehending the militants and handing them over to the Security Forces. In some cases they even lynched them.

In Assam there was a feeling of neglect and discrimination by the Government at Delhi and also exploitation of the resources of the State of oil and tea. The immediate cause was of Government encouraging illegal migration from Bangladesh. The Election Commission identifying presence of 70,000 illegal Bangladeshi voters ignited militancy in the State. My 42 page printed report to the President on illegal migration took the people by storm giving me a people friendly image. This was supplemented by my attempts to use history to make the people of Assam proud of their unique past and rest of India proud of Assam. All this combined with successful military action against militants brought about the desired results. Our installing one lakh shallow tube wells in the Brahmaputra Valley in a year turned Assam from a rice deficit to a rice surplus State.

By the end of my six years tenure in Assam, I was being referred to as a true son of the soil of Assam. On leaving Assam I started being called an NRA (Non Resident Assamese). Over a decade has elapsed since I left Assam. I am still treated as NRA. I have been frequently getting invited to public functions in Assam. It was very satisfying to find that Dr Ema Simmons in her monograph on Counter Insurgency Operations for National War College in the USA, has referred to our handling of militancy in Assam as one of the success stories of such operations in the Twentieth Century. I am mentioning this in all humility and not trying to blow my own trumpet. I am doing so to high light how this strategy succeeded in Assam. This can be a guide for dealing with such operations in other theatres, suitably modified to suit local conditions.

I tried to apply the strategy developed in Assam modified to conform to local requirements for restoring normalcy and peace in Jammu and Kashmir. In Jammu and Kashmir religious fundamentalism with Jehadi violence and very pro active terrorist operations conducted by Pakistan from across the border, was our big problem. This has been getting a fillip from the pusilanimous approach of the Central Government in pursuit of its policy of appeasement. I have been actively associated with Kashmir from Day One, that is 27 October 1947. I landed at Srinagar airfield with the first lot of troops to rescue the people of Kashmir from the tribal invasion launched by Pakistan forces in overwhelming numbers. They had reached Baramulla and Srinagar lay defenseless. The Maharaja and his administration had fled from Srinagar to Jammu. Yet despite all odds, there was a silver lining. Kasmiriyat, the much admired Kashmiri tradition of a fully integrated society without any religious divide, continued in the Valley when the rest of the Sub Continent was in the grip of communal holocaust of Partition. The Valley was a small island of communal amity in a sea of senseless communal orgy. Though Srinagar faced an imminent threat of being overrun like Baramulla which had been razed to the ground suffering most brutal rapine and plunder, Srinagar was calm with no communal violence or communal tension. The popular slogan of the people in the city with young men carrying only *lathis* for protection was, *Hamlewar Hoshiyar, Ham Kashmiri Hindu Muslim Sikh Tayyar.* Mahatma Gandhi had then said, I see a ray of light only in Kashmir.

When I took over as Governor of Jammu and Kashmir in 2003, the conditions in the State had changed drastically from what they had been in 1947. The Kashmir of Maqbool Sherwani had become the Kashmir of Maqbool Bhat. The former was a truly a secular patriot. He tried to mislead the raiders to gain time for the defence of Srinagar. When the enemy realised this, they brutally killed him crucifying him on a Cross. We liberated Baramulla and found his hands and feet nailed to a wooden cross near the Bramulla Convent. Maqbool Bhat was a criminal who laid the foundation of terrorism. He plundered banks and killed the Hindu minority. He was hanged after a due process of law. In 2003, terrorism was rampant in the State and frequent violations of the LOC were taking place with artillery duels on the LOC. From Zulfikar Bhutto's threat of a thousand years war, Pakistan was now actively pursuing Zia-ul-Haq's strategy of thousand cuts. Jammu and Kashmir was the main theatre for this. An average of ten people was being killed due to terrorist violence every day. The most popular tourist destination in India was now having a mere 28, 000 tourists a year. Hindu pilgrims going to Amarnath were being frequently attacked and killed by terrorists. Ethnic cleansing of about 4 lakh Kashmiri Pandits had taken place with the commencement of terrorism in 1990. These unfortunate people were living in most atrocious improvised conditions in camps in Jammu and Delhi. Nearly a hundred Hindu temples had been vandalised. This ethnic cleansing was downplayed and called migration. Both the Central and State Governments called the evicted Kashmiri Pandits as migrants. This implies that they moved out of the Valley of their own will. The separatists even claim that the Government had deliberately encouraged their moving out of the Valley to give a bad name to their "freedom struggle." They are agreeable to their returning to the Valley provided they join them in their "freedom struggle" against the Indian State and take up arms along with them. The Government has not been taking due action to facilitate their return. They are officially called migrants and not refugees. The latter terminology makes them eligible for assistance from UN Refugee Funds.

I tried to apply the three point strategy of unified command, economic development and psychological initiatives developed in Assam, with suitable modifications in Kashmir. The unified command presided over by the Chief Minister was incomplete as the Army Commander was kept out of the loop although the two Corps Commanders were part of it. It was strange that DGs of Para Military Forces at Delhi who exercised no operational control over their forces in the State were included in this set up. Even when the Prime Minister or the Union Home Minister presided over meetings of the Unified Command, the Army Commander was not included. Against opposition from the PDP Chief Minister Mufti Mohamad Sayeed, we managed to have the Army Commander included. The Chief Minister was non co-operative with what we were trying to achieve. Fortunately after the first over two years of my tenure, a Congress Chief Minister, Gulam Nabi Azad took over. With his co-operation we made much progress. We had been bringing down heavy artillery fire to suppress Pakistani firing from across the LOC. By the end of 2003 Pakistan proposed a Cease Fire on the LOC. We readily agreed. We put up a 700 km long electrified wire fence near the LOC in a little over a year, to curb terrorist infiltration. We also went slow on cordon and search operations. We concentrated more on surgical strikes based on good intelligence. The daily average killing due to terrorism came down from 10 to 1 and near normalcy restored, giving a boost to terrorism from 28,000 to over 4 lakhs. As for economic development, like shallow tube wells in Assam, we installed one thousand micro hydel projects, each producing 8 to 10 Kw of electricity. This provided 30 to 40 light points in villages which had not seen electricity before. By day this asset was used to operate looms and grind corns.

Our psychological initiatives took into account the very diverse population in the State. Some 45 per cent were Kashmiri speaking Muslims, 20 per cent were non Kashmiri Muslims like Gujjars and Bakherwals and some 30 to 35 per cent Hindus, Sikhs and Buddhists. We tried to address the problems of each of these segments. The non Muslims nurtured a feeling of neglect. We arranged for greater devolution of authority for development to the Regional Council in Ladakh. A Centre for Buddhist Studies was started in Jammu University. We established a teaching technical University for 2000 boarders with donations received by Mata Vaishno Devi Shrine Board without any assistance whatsoever from the Government. Management graduates passing out from this University started getting hundred per cent placements. Statues of the Dogra icon and one of India's great military heroes, General Zorawar Singh, were put up at key locations in Jammu and Reasi. A modern state of the art auditorium for 2,000 was constructed in Jammu University and named after him. This was done to remove any feeling of neglect or discrimination against them. Apart from this, 1000 micro hydel projects whose beneficiaries were Gujjars and Bakherwals, the Army arranged mobile schools for their small children of these tribes going up the mountains for grazing their animals and schools at their bases. Free hostels were also arranged for their older children When I went up to the last hydel project completed by the Army by road in the mountain, I saw all villages en route having the national flag fluttering and the villagers lined up with paper flags on the side of the road near their villages. This showed the extent to which we had been able to win them over. As for the Kashmiri Muslims we tried to promote Kashmiriyat and wean them away from fundamentalism, separatism and terrorism. The Kashmiri Muslims are primarily affected by these anti-India activities. The other Muslims like the Shias in Kargil and others are not affected. We used the Amarnath Shrine Board and also the Kashmir University for winning over Kashmiri Muslims. At the commencement of Amarnath pilgrimage every year, I would go to perform the opening *Pooja* at the Holy Cave and from their fly direct in a helicopter to Charar-e-Shareef to place a *Chadar* on the grave of the patron saint of Kashmir Sheikh Nooruddin equally revered by the Hindus who called him Nund Rishi. The Shrine Board started a three days Sufi music festival to coincide with the commencement of the Yatra. For the first time Pakistani Sufi musicians were invited to perform in Kashmir and they started coming every year for the Sufi music festival. As the years went by, we made the festival more elaborate inviting Sufi musicians also from Egypt, Uzbekistan and Libya besides of course Indian Sufi musicians. This festival became highly popular in Kashmir. We also established an Institute of Kashmir Studies in Kashmir University, to promote study of Kashmiri culture, arts, cuisine, history, religions, traditions and so on to promote Kashmiriyat. We organised international seminars on Kasmiriyat and historical connections with Central Asian States. Scholars from Pakistan and some Central Asian States attended this seminar. The latter had been part of the Soviet Union affected by Communist thinking and have kept themselves away from religious fundamentalism. They are opposed to terrorism. We worked on exchange programme between Kashmir University and Tazakistan University. A seminar on Kashmiriyat was successfully held in Kashmir attended by scholars from Pakistan and some Central Asian Republics. The high water mark of our efforts at promoting Kashmiriyat was reached in the last week of May 2008. We held an international conference to promote Kashmiriyat which stands for harmony between religions and promotion of peace and understanding. High level delegations from all the eight

South Asian countries including Pakistan and Afghanistan attended the conference in Kashmir University which used to be the hotbed of terrorist activities. The President of India inaugurated the conference at the newly built Kashmir University auditorium. Despite the boycott call given by the separatists and the PDP which was part of the Coalition Government in the State, there was enthusiastic participation by the students and the auditorium was overflowing. The following day we got the Junoon Sufi Pop Music Band from Pakistan to perform in the open near the Dal Lake. Despite the boycott call several thousand youth and others were enthralled by the musical show. The leader of the band from Pakistan in his opening remarks stated that he had come from Pakistan on a musical Jihad to promote peace. The leading English daily of Pakistan had an editorial the following day on 28 May 2008 stating that music knew no boundaries. The people of Kashmir had an opportunity to express their anger against religious terrorism. My five year tenure was finishing on 4 June 2008. I was happy that I could not have finished my assignment in Kashmir on a better note.

The separatists including the PDP were rattled at our success in promoting peace and amity. They decided to launch a communal typhoon on a totally non issue to retrieve their lost ground. As the President of the Shrine Board I had requested for the 100 acre of barren land at Baltal, traditionally used as a base camp for pilgrims going on the short route to the Holy Cave. We wanted to put up temporary prefabricated shelters and environment friendly toilets for pilgrims. This request was examined by PDP Minister in charge Forest for three years. The proposal was ultimately unanimously approved by the Cabinet soon after the highly successful international functions on Kashmiriyat. There was a little delay in the name of my relief being announced. I had gone on a long tour to Jammu region on farewell visit to my old battalion and army formations which had co-operated with me so well, as also to some civil organizations in Jammu. The highly co-operative Congress Chief Minister, Ghulam Nabi Azad was in Mumbai for some time due to a serious illness in his family. A baseless canard was started that in pursuit of an RSS agenda, I had the land at Baltal allotted to the Shrine Board on the eve of my departure. The facts that this land was to be leased to the Board on payment of 2.51 crores and ownership to remain with the State Government were ignored. So was the stipulation that the Board was to use the land for construction of temporary prefabricated shelters only, and for no other purpose. The separatists spread a baseless propaganda saying that like Israel changing the demography of Palestine, India was setting up a Hindu township at Baltal with a view to ultimately reducing Muslims to a minority in the

State!. The land at Baltal remains covered with snow for about nine months in a year when it is unapproachable and uninhabitable. The State laws forbid any non citizen of the State to acquire land in the State, was also ignored. Communal frenzy rapidly began overwhelming the Valley. Clarifications issued by the Board were blacked out. The State Public Relations Department did not have a full time Director and remained mute. The anti India media in the Valley supported with funds from Pakistan had a field day. The national media ignored the storm building up in the Valley. In one or two incidents the Police had to open fire. The Chief Minister returned from Mumbai and was confident that he would hold a Press Conference to clarify matters and the situation will be brought under control. This did not work. I left Kashmir on 25 June. The situation started getting from bad to worse. The Valley was now engulfed in large scale massive public demonstrations as had happened in the holy relic of the Prophets hair was found missing at Hazratbal in 1963. Massive demonstrations on those lines a week or so after my departure from Kashmir. Over 50 people were killed due to Police firing. The PDP whose Ministers who were a party to the Coalition Cabinet's unanimous decision for transfer of the land at Baltal, joined the band wagon of the separatists. The Centre and the State Governments panicked, rescinded the Baltal land allocation order and virtually decided to wind up the Amarnath Shrine Board restricting its function to rituals at the Holy Cave with responsibility for management of the Yatra to be taken over by the State Government. There were now rumours in Jammu that like the Amarnath Shrine Board, the Mata Vaishno Devi Shrine Board would also be wound up. Unprecedented widespread disturbances broke out spontaneously in Jammu. Omar Abdulla, then a MP during the debate on nuclear co-operation with the US, participated in the debate with his speech, which was much applauded. His irresponsible emotional outburst, *Jan Denge Par Zamin Nahin Denge* referring to the Baltal land was in no way relevant to the nuclear debate. It acted as a fuel to the fire raging in Jammu. One agitator immolated himself in Jammu which was now engulfed in large scale agitation for three months, the like of which had not happened in the country. Some fifty people were killed in Jammu as a result of firing by Security Forces. The supply route to the Valley remained closed for some time by the virtual blockade in Jammu region. The Government was forced to yield and rescind the order cancelling the transfer of Baltal land. The Amarnath Shrine Board was allowed to function as before. Status qou ante was restored. The summer madness of 2008 cost the State a hundred lives and an estimated loss of a thousand crores to the economy. Maulana Mohammad Madani MP addressing Islamic clerics in November 2008 rightly stated, "Transferring of land from the Forest Department to the Board did not harm Muslim interests. There was nothing to oppose. It was unnecessarily made into a political issue by all sides." Pakistan took advantage of the communal divide and in the following two years engineered disturbances in the Valley. The stone throwing operation in the following years financed by Pakistan in the Valley cost many lives. It is significant that stone throwing remained confined to the Valley and did not spread to other parts of the State.

I have deliberately elaborated on the incidents of 2008 to 2010 so that the present generation and the future draw appropriate lessons from them. My ambitious plans for restoring peace ultimately floundered for three reasons, neglect to curb rumours, no media policy and feeble governance.

I can with a full sense responsibility state that the Government of India has been committing repeated follies from Day One in Kashmir in pursuit of policy of appeasement. This has made the solution of the Kashmir problem very difficult. We have been scoring repeated self goals most of the time. We have no road map on how to resolve the Kashmir issue in our best national interests. We only parrot that Kashmir is an integral part of India and that a solution would emerge through dialogue with Pakistan and separatists. We only try to react to situation rather than pursue a plan which will enable us to resolve issues on our terms. As a case in point we have taken no interest whatsoever in the agitation often erupting in violence in Gilgit Baltistan region. The frequent agitation of the local Shias against their colonial masters in Islamabad has been brutally suppressed. We have never provided any moral support to the people in the region. They have been periodically launching agitations. Not only have they been denied basic human and democratic rights, deliberate attempts are being made by Pakistan to change the demography of the region by settling in this region, their Sunni population of Pathans and Punjabis from mainland Pakistan. Baroness Ema Nicholson MP of the European Parliament sent to study the ground situation in Jammu and Kashmir and report to that Parliament. She visited Pakistan Occupied Kashmir, Northern Areas and Indian Administered Kashmir. In her report she has stated that democracy does not exist in POK, the Northern Areas are the only surviving colony in the world and has been appreciative of democracy functioning in Indian Administered Kashmir. We agreed to the opening of Srinagar Muzaffrabad Road without pressing Pakistan to simultaneously open Kargil Skardu Road. Yet we continue to claim that Jammu and Kashmir including Gilgit Baltistan, is an integral part of India. Today, China has a military presence in this region and declines to have dialogue with us on the 2000 mile long Ladakh-

Tibet border without Pakistan being a party in that dialogue. They now want India China border talks to be confined to the remaining 2000 mile border with us!

More than a generation separates me from General Bakshi. And so does his association with Kashmir, Directorate of Military Operations, the Kashmir issue and experience of combating low intensity conflicts. I have also had the advantage of dealing with such conflict from a political level in two different States afflicted by this malady, for eleven continuous years, six years in Assam and five years in Kashmir. He joined the Army nearly thirty years after me. There may be variations in our thinking on dealing with low intensity conflict but there is no difference in our basic approach towards this type of war. My association with insurgency in the North East started with the first shots fired by Naga rebels in Naga Hills district of Assam (now Nagaland) in 1956, when I was a company commander. Subsequently I served at all level of command in the North East from company to division. Similarly my association with Kashmir began on Day One, that is, 27 October 1947 when I was a Major, General Staff Officer Operations. I landed in Srinagar on that day with the first lot of troops. I served thereafter in every rank from Major to Major General in that State.

Low intensity conflicts cover a variety of operations like insurgency, terrorism, intrusions across the border and so on. There is a difference between insurgency and terrorism. The former is a conflict against this State by a popular leader pursuing a noble ideal and inspiring the people to follow him in pursuit of that goal. Adopting guerilla tactics, the insurgents wear down the security forces and secure a haven in which they can develop conventional military strength to defeat security forces in conventional battle. Shivaji was the first person to develop this type of warfare. His example was followed by Mao se Dong in China and Ho Chi Min in erstwhile Indo China. Terrorism on the other hand tries to wear down the State by attacking soft targets including innocent women and children in pursuit of an aim devoid of normal human values. The Naga rebellion has been primarily an insurgency movement. Both in Brahmaputra Valley and in Kashmir we faced a combination of insurgency and terrorism. This combination has been more pronounced in Kashmir fueled by Jihadi fanaticism. Another connected aspect in Kashmir has been ethnic cleansing of Kashmiri Pandits. They were evicted in the first few days of Pakistan implementing Ziaul Haq's strategy of thousand cuts. They constituted a minuscule minority and have no martial tradition. The attempts at ethnic cleansing in Kishtwar Doda region have not so far succeeded and the aim of the separatist to have a Greater Kashmir remains unfulfilled. Dogra Hindus in this region are over thirty per cent of the population and have a martial tradition. Many of them have served in the Army. Thus the Village Defence Committees have been able to foil the bid for ethnic cleansing. The author has elaborated various factors affecting our military operations in the area. The terrain is difficult with high mountains and valleys intersected by several water channels merging with the Chenab which originates from this region. The area is several times more than the area covered in Kashmir Valley. There has been paucity of troops. The Village Defence Committees are equipped with the old Enfield 303 rifles while the militants have modern automatic weapons. Moreover, we have failed to develop communications with neighbouring Himachal Pradesh which can be profitably used for integrating this region. Yet Government provided 1000 crores to develop the Mughal highway from Poonch to Shopiyan in the Valley at great cost to the environment cutting 10,000 trees and shifting a 25 square kilometer game sanctuary to integrate Poonch region with the Valley providing fillip to the concept of Greater Kashmir. Like Kishtwar-Himachal road link, developing a land route between Ladakh and Himachal Pradesh remains a low priority. The author has given various details of successful tactical operations carried out by him in this region. Very recently there has been an outbreak of communal violence on Eid Day in Kishtwar as yet another way of attempting ethnic cleansing. It is a matter of grave concern that a Cabinet Minister of Jammu and Kashmir who was present in Kishtwar on that day perhaps deliberately did not take any action to check the violence for some time till the Army was called out to restore order. The Minister concerned has been made to resign. A judicial enquiry has been ordered.

I compliment Maj Gen G D Bakshi the author of this book for his illuminating work and recommend this book to the readers. It provides a useful addition to the literature on Kashmir problem and a valuable record of the author's long experience of combating low intensity conflict.

New Delhi, **Lt Gen (Retd) S K Sinha**
10 September 2013

Preface

From 1990-onwards the Indian nation state has waged a grim Counter Terrorist campaign to retain the state of Jammu & Kashmir (J&K). In an asymmetric conflict scenario, Pakistan felt it had checkmated Indian conventional escalation threats by playing the nuclear card. As Michael Kreepon had said, *"Nuclear weapons can generate risk taking because they presumably provide an insurance policy against escalation."*

The Afghan War was waged against a Nuclear Power—the former Soviet Union. Pakistan, with the backing of USA and China, acted as the surrogate regional destabiliser. Assurance of American support in the event of escalation caused her to indulge in a very dangerous and high risk enterprise. The Afghan experience highlighted to Pakistan the possibilities of Fourth Generation Warfare. The Pak-Afghan border became one vast armed camp with hundreds of Madrassas that soon formed the global Factory of Jihad. The Soviet collapse in Afghanistan was primarily economic. Militarily, the USSR had stabilised the situation. It was only when Mikhail Gorbachev pulled out the economic plug that Najibullah's regime fell in Kabul. The optical illusion of success against a superpower gave heady delusions of grandeur to the Pakistani military elite. The air in Islamabad was rife with a strident triumphalism. This prompted her to launch and then intensify her Proxy War in J&K. The narrative on the Indian side is fixated somehow on the discourse, that it was only the alleged electoral fraud of 1988 in J&K that triggered the onset of the Insurgency in that state. This is a patently false premise. At the very start of the decade of the 1980s Gen Zia-ul Haq had invited the leaders of the Jamat-e-Islami (JeI) in J&K, over to Pakistan clandestinely and asked them to prepare for the Jihad in Kashmir. This was no spontaneous uprising triggered by Indian self goals. This was a well crafted and meticulously prepared asymmetric warfare campaign to prise J&K lose from India's grip that had been in the making in Pakistan for almost a decade.

The Stability-Instability Paradox—Amongst the nuclear theorists there were two divergent schools of thought. Kenneth Waltz and other nuclear optimists felt *that offsetting nuclear capabilities are stabilising because they make war too costly.* Waltz claimed that when faced with almost certain destruction, military miscalculation becomes unlikely among nuclear powers. Indian Security Planners tended to go along with the Waltzian paradigm. They had hoped that nuclear symmetry in South Asia would usher in stability. Pakistan, suffused in the triumphalist afterglow of Afghanistan, however really began to push the envelope. It was reckless in the risks it took—especially before Kargil in 1999 and before Op Parakram in 2001. Its irrational behaviour seemed to prove the nuclear pessimists of the Scott Sagan school right. Sagan had claimed that the potential dangers of nuclear weapons outweigh any stabilising effect they might have. It was only consistent, determined and credible Indian conventional responses to both provocations that caused the euphoria in Pakistan to evaporate and reigned in somewhat the irrational triumphalism in Islamabad.

These exploratory forays to test the deterrence envelope in South Asia engendered the ugly Stability-Instability Paradox between India and Pakistan. Pakistan persisted with her dangerous Proxy War in J&K for well over two decades. It is often forgotten that the Proxy war in J&K came after a decade of Pak sponsored terrorism in the Punjab. This has led to one of the most large scale Counter Terrorist campaigns in human history. This book is an eyewitness account—especially of the penultimate closing phases of the Low Intensity Conflict Operations (LICO) when the campaign was in its most intense phase.

I was singularly fortunate to get a ringside view of these conflicts from 1985-2006 and saw combat at every rank from Major upwards:

- From 1985–mid-1987, I commanded a company of Sikh troops in CT operations in the Punjab in the wake of Operation Bluestar. It was a most challenging assignment and I owe a debt of deep gratitude to my boys who rose so magnificently to the occasion
- From mid-1987–1990, I had served in the prestigious Military Operations (MO) Directorate at Delhi, first as a GSO-2 (Operations) and then as a GSO-1 (Operations). I dealt with CI in the North East; with Terrorism in Punjab and later with the onset of Terrorism in J&K. This was also the period of Op Pawan—India's

intervention in Sri Lanka and it kept our noses to the grind for almost two years.

- I later commanded my own battalion(6 JAK RIF) during very major skirmishes in an area of intrusion in the Kargil sector from 1990-1991 which was largely blanked out of the media to save the huge embarrassment to the government of the day. My unit saw extensive combat along the Line of Control (LC).It was a grim period of fighting and my unit suffered some six killed and 21 wounded and inflicted four times that number of casualties on the Pakistani Army units deployed opposite. This will give an indication of the intensity of the conflict. My unit won, one Vir chakra (posthumous), three Sena Medals, and twenty other lesser awards. Our unit was awarded the Chiefs citation for our stellar performance and I was personally awarded the VSM.
- I later commanded 9 SECTOR RASHTRIYA RIFLES' in Kishtwar in J&K from 2000-2002 for a period of close to two and a half years. It was a most memorable tenure and saw the elimination of a record number of terrorists in that district. I also had to wage a very grim struggle against the Inter-Services Intelligence (ISI) tanzeems attempt at ethnic cleansing in that area whose unvarnished aim was to force an exodus of the entire minority Dogra community from that mountainous district. This book is primarily devoted to the operations in Kishtwar.
- After a one year sabbatical at the National Defence College (NDC), I found myself back in J&K.
- This time I served as the Brigadier General Staff (BGS) (Information Warfare) at HQ Northern Command in Udhampur.
- In September 2004, I took over Counter Insurgency Force ROMEO as a Major General. This was the centre of gravity of our Counter Terrorist campaign, South of the Pir Panjals; and in the wake of the famous Operation Sarp vinash, the operations were then at a very critical juncture. We succeeded in virtually decimating the terrorists in this area. Thus, from the year 2000-2005, I spent three consecutive tenures in J&K (of which two were outright combat assignments).
- In 2005, I was moved to HQ Eastern Command to contribute my experience to the ongoing CI operations in the North East. I finally hung up my spurs from a teaching assignment at the prestigious National Defense College in New Delhi where I had a

good opportunity to reflect upon our collective experience in J&K and hear the best minds in the country on the vital issues of national security.

I can therefore claim to be a firsthand witness to this critical phase of LICO in J&K and got ample opportunity to deal with this genre of conflict, both, at the Staff and at the Field levels where I personally led operations. It gave me invaluable, hands-on combat experience of countering the Fourth Generation of Warfare, which demands skilful synchronisation of not just Military and Civic operations, but also Psychological and Information operations. I do believe I have learnt valuable military lessons, which would be of considerable interest to future generations of soldiers, who will be frequently confronted with this new form of war. They will have to deal with asymmetric warfare far more often than they will have to deal with regular/conventional conflict.

The Indian Army has one of the richest funds of combat experience in the Post World War-II phase of history. Unfortunately, we have failed to exploit it for the simple reason that we have not recorded it in detail. This book is an exercise in recording our recent military history and personal narratives of combat. I was lucky enough to have not just fought these campaigns but survived them to recount the tales. I am now doing my duty by writing them down for posterity, so that future officers of the Indian Army do not have to reinvent the wheel with each new conflict.

This is the first of a triology of books to record my extensive operational experiences in J&K. It deals in specific with my command of a Brigade (a Rashtriya Rifles Sector) in the most rugged and mountainous region of Kishtwar. It was a most momentous period when the Counter terrorist campaign in J&K was reaching its operational peak (in fact the maximum number of terrorists were eliminated in J&K in the year 2001). The struggle in Kishtwar however was unique. The population of the Hindu minority here is almost 40 per cent. The ISI backed tanzeems had unleashed a concerted program of ethnic cleansing. It had a clear cut operational design—to cause an exodus of the minority Dogra community from that region and thereby set the stage for a Pakistani takeover of the whole of J&K that would, at long last, give it the direct control of the waters of all the rivers that flowed through its length. This involved a horrific series of massacres of the hapless minority who began to flee the state in droves, much like the Kashmiri Pandits had done almost a decade ago. Some 400,000 Pandits are still languishing in the refugee camps of Jammu and Delhi. Ethnic cleansing is a crime against humanity. The world has not heard the last of the ethnic cleansing carried out in Serbia and Bosnia. But not a word is said of the horrific ethnic cleansing that drove out the Kashmiri Pandits from their homeland, nor the attempted ethnic cleansing of the Dogra minority that the ISI had unleashed in Doda-Kishtwar. I saw those horrific massacres at first hand and will never be able to forget them or erase those memories. We must end this conspiracy of silence. Some senior officers of the Pakistan Army and ISI deserve to face the International Court of Justice for ordering the ethnic cleansing of the minorities from J&K. We need to speak up—for ethnic cleansing is too horrific a crime to be brushed under the carpet. The professed quest for peace is laudable but it cannot be at the cost of basic principles. Crimes against humanity cannot be condoned and such evil forces must be fought against. Compromise and pusillanimity are no solutions. They only invite more mayhems. Narratives of victimhood are spun out by the spin-masters of the ISI on the subject of Kashmir. I fail to see any reason for the conspiracy of silence on our part for not talking about the ISIs ethnic cleansing in J&K. That is clearly an outrageous crime against humanity. The Pakistani ISI and its Jihadi cohorts were clearly guilty of ethnic cleansing in J&K and it is time that the accusation was leveled squarely and unequivocally. Anything less would be moral cowardice of the worst order.

In the evening of my life I owed it to my men who laid down their lives under my command, to record their tremendous bravery and sacrifice. One of them, Naik Rambir Singh Tomar of 26 RR went on to win the nation's highest gallantry award of the Ashok Chakra—posthumously. This book is dedicated to the sacred memory of those men. It is also dedicated to the meek and unfortunate victims of ethnic cleansing in J&K and Kishtwar, in the pious hope that their suffering at least deserves to be made known to all human beings—so that the world can raise its collective voice against such insensate brutality. Wars will always have to be fought—at least for as long as such mass murderers remain. But can we not pursue these wars with at least a modicum of decency and not make unarmed civilians—especially women and children the chief targets? The way we fight—shows us who we really are. The notable fact was that the local Kashmiri boys who had taken up arms were rarely involved in such horrific massacres. By and large, they still retained that basic decency that comes from being Indian. Most of these massacres were perpetrated by the foreign terrorists. The Jihadi fanatics unleashed by the ISI in J&K who perpetrated such massacres of the innocents were debased criminals and the scourge of mankind. They had to be fought against and eliminated ruthlessly. I'm so glad to record that my boys of the 11 and 26 RR as also the Sikh Li, the Gurkhas, and the Rajputs and Mahars put up such a heroic and brave fight against such evil forces. Their countless deeds of valour—

so much above and beyond the call of duty—leave me deeply humbled. It was an honour to command such men—an honour that I will cherish to the end of my days. This is my humble tribute to the gallant men of the Mystic Ninth Sector of the Rashtriya Rifles. Sometimes I do wish I could do more, especially for the brave boys who laid down their lives and their poor families who struggle on without their breadwinners. Its not just old soldiers like me, but this nation that has the duty to remember these men and their enormous sacrifice, nor forget the families they left behind. If J&K remains firmly with the Indian Republic today, it is entirely due to the tremendous sacrifices made by these men.

Maj Gen (Dr) G D Bakshi SM, VSM (retd)

List of Abbreviations

AC	Ashok Chakra
AoR	Area of Responsibility
AFSPA	Armed Forces Special Powers Act
AVSM	Ati Vashisht Seva Medal
BGS	Brigadier General Staff
BJP	Bhartiya Janata Party
BPJs	Bullet Proof Jackets
BPP	Bullet Proof Patka
BSF	Border Security Force
Cas evac	Casualty evacuation
CBMs	Confidence Building Measures
CI	Counter Insurgency
CIA	Central Intelligence Agency
CO	Commanding Officer
COAS	Chief of the Army staff
CPOs	Central Police Organisations
CRPF	Centre Reserve Police Force
CT	Counter Terrorist
DC	District Commander
DGMI	Directorate General of Military Intelligence
DGMO	Directorate General of Military Operations
DO	Demi Official Letter/Duty Officer.
DQ	Deputy Adjutant and Quartermaster General
DZ	Dropping Zone
FT	Foreign Terrorist
GDP	Gross Domestic Product

GMD	Guo Min Dang
GOC	General Officer Commanding
GS	General Staff
GSO	General Staff Officer
GSQRs	General Staff Qualitative requirements
GWOT	Global War on Terror
HE	High Explosive
HEAT	High Explosive Anti Tank
HM	Hizbul Muzahideen
HQ	Headquarter
HR	Human Rights
HuA	Harkat-ul-Ansar
HUJI	Harkat-ul-Jihad-e-Islami
HUM	Harkat-ul-Mujahideen
humint	human intelligence
IAF	Indian Air Force
IB	International Border
ICT	Information Communication Technologies
IEDs	Improvised Explosive Devices
IM	Indian Mujahideen
INSAS	Indian (5.56 mm) Service Assault Rifle
ISI	Inter-Services Intelligence
ITBP	Indo Tibetan Border Police Force.
IW	Information Warfare
IWT	Inland Water Transport
JAG	Judge Advocate General
JAK RIF	Jammu and Kashmir Rifles
JCO	Junior Commisioned Officer
JeI	Jamat-e-Islami
JeM	Jaish-e-Mohammed
JKLF	Jammu and Kashmir Liberation Front
JS	Joint Secretary
KRA	Key Result Area
LC	Line of Control
LeT	Lashkar-e-Toiba
LICO	Low Intensity Conflict Operation
LMG	Light Machine Gun

LTTE	Liberation Tiger of Tamil Elem
MA	Mountain Artillery
MBT	Main Battle Tank
MCC	Maoist Communist Centre
MHA	Ministry of Home Affairs
MNA	Mizo National Army
MO	Military Operations
NATO	North Atlantic Treaty Organisation
NDC	National Defence College
NGO	Non-Governmental Organisation
NH	National Highway
NICO	Non-Initiation of Combat Operations
NLI	Northern Light Infantry
NSG	National Security Guards
NTR	Nothing to Report
OGWs	Over Ground Workers
OODA	Observation, Orientation, Decision and Action
Op	Operation
ORBAT	Order of Battle
ORSA	Operational Research and Statistical Analysis
OT	Operation Theatre
PAP	People's Armed Police (China)
PGLA	People's Guerilla Liberation Army
PLA	People's Liberation Army (China)
POK	Pakistan Occupied Kashmir
PoW	Prisoners of War
PVSM	Param Vishisht Seva Medal
PWG	Peoples War Group
QRT	Quick Reaction Team
RAS	Rear Area Security
RLs	Rocket Launchers
RMA	Revolution in Military Affairs
RMO	Regimental Medical Officer
RMP	Recruitable/Recruitment Male Population
ROP	Road Opening Parties
RPGs	Rocket Propelled Greanades
RR	Rashtriya Rifles

RSS	Rashtriya Swayamsevak Sangh
SAF	Small Armed Factory
SAM	Surface to Air Missile
SF	Security Forces
SIMI	Student Islamic Movement of India
Sitrep	Situation Report
SMEs	Small & Medium Enterprises
SOP	Standard Operating Procedure
SPOs	Special Police Officers
SSG	Special Services Group
SSP	Senior Suprindentant of Police
TA	Territorial Army
303	Three knot three
UAVs	Unmanned Aerial Vehicles
UBGL	Under Barrel Grenade Launchers
UJC	United Jihad Council
VDC	Village Defence Committee
VSM	Vishisht Seva Medal

CHAPTER 1

Prologue: An Indian Doctrine for Low Intensity Conflict

The Era of Low Intensity Conflict

Doctrinal Evolution. In the wake of the Second World War, the symmetric nuclear scenario between the two super powers led to a standoff that precluded the chances of any major conventional conflict. Such a conflict between nuclear armed adversaries could have easily spun out of control and led to a global thermo-nuclear exchange with catastrophic results. In any case, the combatant nations of Europe were exhausted by two debilitating World Wars. As such, this symmetric scenario led to conflict being confined to below the threshold of conventional operations. Low Intensity Conflict Operations (LICO) waged by superpower surrogates in the peripheral areas of the third World, became the prime form of conflict in the post war decades. The Chinese Communist Armies had laid the ground work for this transition to Low intensity conflicts in their civil war with the Kuomintang that started in the 1920s and culminated in the establishment of the Peoples Republic of China in 1949. Mao had formulated the theory of 'People's Revolutionary War' with three clear cut stages:

(a) **The Strategic Defensive.** In this phase, the guerillas commence preparation for armed struggle. They build up the organisational support base and try to harass the civil administration and police forces by small scale terrorist actions.

(b) **The Strategic Stalemate.** In this period, the guerillas form platoon, company and then battalion sized bands to engage in hit and run guerilla actions using raids and ambushes to harass and tie down the regular armed forces. This phase is stretched out for one to two decades or even more, to tire out and exhaust the government forces and erode their will to fight. This is the classical guerilla war—the 'death by a thousand cuts' phase.

(c) **Strategic Counter Offensive**. Having sufficiently worn down the regular army, having eroded its morale and sapped its will to fight, the Guerilla bands effect the switch from irregular to regular warfare. The Guerilla forces now form regular fighting formations, the divisions and Corps that will effect the switch to regular, conventional warfare and deliver the coup de grace. This is what Mao did after the Second World War and by 1949 had conquered the whole of China in a major civil war.

This pattern of Communist Guerilla warfare later resurfaced in Malaysia, Philippines, and Indo-China in the decade of 1950s and sixties. The Vietnam War transformed the current paradigm of conflict. Vo Nguyen Giap's Viet Minh guerillas wore out the French forces in Indo-China. They effected the switch to regular combat and inflicted a humiliating defeat on the French at Dien Bien Phu in 1956. The Americans thereafter intervened in South Vietnam to prevent what was then deemed the 'domino effect'. After over a decade of protracted guerilla warfare in the rice fields and dense forests of Vietnam, the US armies were thoroughly demoralised and home-sick. Anti-war sentiment against the Vietnam conflict snowballed in America. Despite throwing in massive amounts of airpower and technology, the Americans suffered a humiliating debacle. Gens Giap and Van Tien Dung's forces entered Saigon in triumph. Subsequently, Communist regimes also came up in Cambodia and Laos. In most of these case studies—Wars of National Liberation leveraged upon communist dogma and Peoples War theory and practice to successfully wage Asymmetric conflicts with the erstwhile colonial powers. With progressive experience, they were able to humiliate even a superpower like America. The emotive fuel for these successful wars of national liberation—however, came not from the ideology of communism, but plain and old-fashioned nationalism. The new Paradigm of Conflict was well-established. It was the classical defense by an Agricultural civilisation against an Industrial Power. *An Industrial Power mobilises all its resources for a quick victory. The guerillas seek to deny them that quick victory by stretching out the war in time and space. This was done by presenting no viable targets and using stealth and mobility and rugged terrain. 'WILL' was another component of this asymmetric conflict. The Asian nations were able to display a vastly superior will and ability to mobilise the people to take punishment and lengthen out the conflict.* This seemed to exhaust the materially superior and industialised enemy.

A Literature Survey

A vast amount of literature was generated by the American and other Western Armies on this new genre of conflict based upon their experience of this type of war in Indo-China, Algeria, Malaya and Kenya, etc. The classical authors of CI doctrine were Tranquier, Galula, Mc Cuen, Thomson, and Kitson. It would be essential to recount the essence of their writings to understand the evolution of the doctrine and practice in the field of Low Intensity Conflict Operations.

1. **Roger Trinquier (1964).** Roger felt that an insurgent organisation must be destroyed through offensive action. He emphasised adoption of counter strategies to support insurgency in the territory of the external sponsor nation. Much of what he wrote has relevance in this day and age and specifically in the Indian context. It highlights the painfully reactive and defensive approach of India in CI/CT operations. We have failed so far (despite 30 years of provocation) to carry out any offensive operations across the borders or even the Line of Control (LC), to raise the costs for Pakistan for its support first to the terrorists in Punjab and then those in J&K and the rest of India.
2. **David Galula (1964).** Around the same time as Trinquier, Galula outlined his famous principles of a CI Campaign. He suggested an approach based on an understanding of Communist revolutionary war theory and practice. He highlighted the fact that "the population will only extend its support to the Counter-Insurgent if the latter demonstrates the will, the means and the ability to win." Galula highlighted a step by step approach. He emphasised that *effective military-police operations must precede political, social and economic action.* The Counter-insurgent, he emphasised, must always negotiate from a position of strength. What Galula said then, sounds almost prophetic today in the Indian context. A foreign-funded NGO led orchestrated lobby is today suggesting a novel approach based only upon socio-political and economic measures to solve the Maoist insurgency. Despite some 15,000 heavily armed Maoist cadres free floating in the jungles and the tribal human terrain, they refuse to acknowledge it as a Security and a law and order problem. Some of these Liberals have taken to calling the Maoists—"Gandhians

with guns". It is one of the most ridiculous oxymorons ever invented. It is essential that we read Galula and understand the relevance of what he said in the 1960s to our context today.

3. **John Mc Cuen.** Mc Cuen highlighted the imperative need for unity of effort in CI operations. Like Tranquier, he laid great stress upon counter-organising the local population. Contrast his advice with the outcry in India against the Salva Judam. The Indian Army has always used rival gang and pseudo-gang operations as a very successful tactic. This new liberal outcry that nothing must be done to defeat the insurgents/terrorists and the country should quietly disintegrate to show its commitment to lofty human rights and universal values, is a bit unnerving. Mc Cuen outlines some of the principles of Communist Revolutionary warfare as under. (Please note their clear echo in the operations of the Maoists in contemporary India.) The principles are:

   - **Preserve yourself and Annihilate the enemy**. The actions of the Maoists in the dense jungles of Dantewada, highlight this aspect so graphically.
   - **Establish Secure Base Areas**. The Maoists have established such base areas now in the densely forested tracts of the Indian states of Chattisgargh, Orissa and Maharashtra. They are expanding these base areas towards the western Ghats as also the jungles of the North East.
   - **Mobilise the Masses.** The Maoists today are doing it by extensive propaganda, subversion and coercion of the tribal population.
   - **Seek Outside Support**. A strange canard is being spread about the Maoists that they are great patriots and Robin hoods fighting purely for the down trodden. The actual fact is that today the Maoist literature openly talks of aligning with the Sub-nationality struggles with the terrorists in J&K and the insurgents in the North East. Not only that, they are in touch with Chinese intelligence agencies and the ISI and have already started receiving AK-47 and other weapons and military grade explosives from China and Pakistan, through the insurgent organisations in the North East.
   - **Unify the Effort**. As part of this drive for unity, the Maoist Communist Centre (MCC) and the Peoples War Group (PWG) merged in 2004 to become the Communist Party of India (Maoist).

Roger Thompson (1966). Thompson highlighted the five basic principles of a government approach to Counter insurgency operations. He listed these as:

- **Clear Political Aim.** Thomson listed this as the sine qua non for success. Once again, I would like to emphasise that the Indian approach to the Maoist problem highlights the total lack of clarity, not only in the aim *per se* but equally in the means to be used to address this problem. Instead of a whole of government approach, we find different state organs and the ruling party speaking in many different voices that serve to create dissonance at the functional level and results in inchoate and inefficient operations with consequent loss of lives and operational initiative. There is a painful absence of coordination between the various states and above all, between the state and the centre.
- **Overall Plan.** An overall plan naturally stems from a properly conceived political aim.

  It encompasses the kinetic and psychological operations as also the socio-economic development plans of the region.
- **The CI Forces must Function in Accordance with the Law**. The converse is also true. Legal cover must be provided to the forces sent in to operate against the insurgents/terrorists. Archaic laws/ legislations may have to be amended to match the ground realities.
- **Need to Build Democratic Process from the Grassroots Level**. This also implies that the state affords proper protection from the grassroots Panchayat level upwards. In recent months, there have been instances in the Indian context of the killing of Panchayat members in J&K and in the Maoist affected areas.

Julian Paget (1967) and Frank Kitson (1971). Both Paget and Kitson endorse the views of Thompson. Kitson additionally lists the four aspects that constitute the essential framework of a CI campaign. These are given below. I have adduced comments alongside on their current status in the Indian context:

- **A Coordination Machinary**. Due to the extensive Indian experience with this genre of operations, we have evolved a workable Unified Command Mechanism, with the state Chief Minister/Governor in charge and all components (Army, Police, Intelligence and Civil Agencies) reporting to him.
- **Appropriate Political Atmosphere**. This is conspicuous by its

absence in the Maoist Context in India today. There is dissonance and lack of coordination between the centre and the states as also between the states. Battles of turf serve to severely degrade such operations. Most successful Maoist strikes have come at the junction of two or more states.

- **Proper Intelligence**. This surely is the sine qua non for success in such operations. Such intelligence comes largely from human intelligence sources. As such, it is imperative that the people be the Centre of Gravity of our operations.
- **Strict Adherance to Law**. Kitson reinforces Thompson's insistence on the legality of our operations. The Security Forces must never be asked to operate without due legal cover and should never resort to illegal methods as these erode the credibility and good faith that characterise these operations.

Robert Cassidey and David Kilcullen (2008). With Cassidey and Kilcullen, we approach the new era of CI characterised by the Iraq and ongoing Afghanistan Conflicts. A whole body of literature on CI has emerged from American sources during these conflicts and constitutes the second generation of writings on this subject. There is a distinct and definitive shift in this phase from Kinetic operations and destruction of the insurgent organisation to protection and control of the Civil population. Gen Petraeus was instrumental in formulating this new doctrinal approach to CI operations and practiced the same during his campaigns in both Iraq and Afghanistan. In essence it sought to go beyond the body count approach of the Vietnam war and shifted the focus more to the protection of the population. This tension between the two key components of any CI strategy has always been there and is often dependent on the personal orientation of the commanders on the ground. Some are gung-ho and aggressive and tend to emphasise actual attrition on the insurgent organisation as the only true index and objective measure of success. The theory goes that only if you have good intelligence will you gain live contact with the insurgent. Only if your tactical skills are good will you be able to convert such contacts into "kills (attrition)". So the touch stone of the objectivity of such operations are the number of contacts gained and kinetic events generated leading to actual elimination of terrorists/ insurgents.

There is equally the other school of thought in all armies, that pure attrition is not the end aim of such operations. The actual aim is to restore peace and normalcy in that area. These proponents emphasise winning the hearts and minds of the population, civic actions and a softer approach generally. Which of these is the correct approach to CI operations? My extensive personal experience indicates that the answer possibly lies in between the two approaches. Too exaggerated and exclusive an emphasis on any one particular approach can be counter-productive. The necessity for actual attrition on the insurgent ranks cannot be wished away. How else can you protect the population from such terrorist depredations and violence? How else do we deter him from entering the population centres and intimidating the populace? However, too obsessive a focus on kinetic events alone can be rather counter-productive. It often ends up in excesses and a near total alienation of the population. Intelligence about the elusive terrorist/insurgent can only come from the people amongst whom he tries to hide. Without precise humint (human intelligence), most operations usually degenerate into futile jungle-bashing. Hence, the population simply has to be won over and weaned away from the terrorists. However, I have also seen the other extreme wherein some units, (on the pretext of avoiding any kind of Human Rights violations), have failed to dominate their areas effectively and not been able to generate contacts and kinetic events with the terrorists in their area. Overtime this emboldens the terrorists who begin to roam freely over the territory and coerce the population into complete submission. This starts a vicious cycle in which all humint dries up completely and further severely degrades that unit's operations. The answer, to my mind is a correct mix of both. Only live contacts with the terrorists test the truth of our operational estimates and assessments. Kinetic events thereafter, are a true index of our tactical effectiveness. Contacts and kinetic events crystallise our situational awareness of the battle field. Yet contacts will only come with accurate intelligence and that can only come from the people of that area. This is the current debate and this inherent tension between the two approaches has always existed for Counter-Insurgent forces at all times. Based on recent experience the US Rand corporation has recently summed up the new American approach to CI operations in its five doctrinal steps:

- **Isolating the Insurgent from the population**. In practice this entails, to my mind, area domination, patrolling and ambushes and above all effective operations that eliminate terrorists who approach/ come to the population centres.
- **Adopting an Operational Grid for the Deployment/Employment of Forces**. This is the basis of our CI operational philosophy in the Indian Context ever since the initial insurgencies in the North East. This Grid (of usually company sized posts), serves to secure the lines of communication of the Force as also the key civilian

population centres. This constitutes the backbone architecture of our operational design in such situations. This serves to protect the population and provides the base for launching operations into the interior areas beyond the basal grid.

- **Physical Domination over Area of Operations**. This is self-explanatory and is a mandatory condition for protecting the population. This implies complete freedom of movement for own troops and concomitantly restricting the movement of the insurgent/terrorist groups and their logistics.
- **Restraint on the Use of Force**. Initially the US troops (in Vietnam, Iraq and Afghanistan) tended to rely excessively on offensive Air Power, Tanks and heavy caliber weapons (like medium and heavy artillery, Multi Barrel Rocket Launcher systems, etc.). Over a period, they found that this resulted in heavy collateral damage to the civil population and was rather counter-productive in terms of getting reliable humint (human intelligence), as it thoroughly alienated the population and incensed them into supporting the terrorists. This caused US commanders to put significant restraints on the use of air power and heavy caliber weapons in Iraq and Afghanistan. However, by and large Fighter Ground attack aircraft and bomber support was usually substituted by Attack Helicopter support and even this curtailment drew howls of protest from the troops operating in these areas. The weapons usage levels by the US and NATO troops have been, and still are, far higher than the weapon usage profiles of the Indian Army in such operations. The Indian troops have always been confined to the use of small arms and straight legged infantry. Indian operations therefore have been far more discriminate, humane and people friendly. Yet the paradox is that while we have hardly heard many Human Rights (HR) violation charges against the US and NATO forces, the Indian Army remains swamped with a barrage of HR violation accusations. In hindsight, most were deliberately and falsely manufactured by local Over Ground Workers (OGWs) and some Foreign funded NGOs to stymie the Indian Army operations and put it on the backfoot.
- **Military-Civic Action for Winning Hearts and Minds.** This now receives as heavy an emphasis in the US Army as it does in the Indian Army. Operation Sadbhavna in J&K and Operation Good Samaritan in the North Eastern states has seen the expenditure of millions of dollars worth of civic action projects like building

schools, hospitals, roads, and bridges, etc. for the local population (with local resources) and holding medical/veterinary camps for the people and their livestock. The Indian and American doctrines now, are more or less aligned in theory and in practice. However, the Western weapon usage profile continues to remain far more lethal. The emphasis is now increasingly shifting to the use of Armed Drones/UAVs.

Fourth Generation Warfare

By the 1990s, Communism as an ideology, had lost the battle for the minds of men. Its demise came primarily from an unviable economic system. The Soviet Union's collapse was not military but economic. In China, Deng Xiao Peng understood the psychology of the peasant far better and started economic liberalisation within the existing system. The nation-state system had emerged with the Treaty of Westphalia in 1648. The only global challenge to the nation state was Communism. It sought to play down national frontiers and horizontal boundaries for the global spread of an ideology based on vertical class conflict. It asked the workers of the world to unite. It sought to remind them that they had nothing to lose but their chains. Communism however had lost the ideological battle decisively by 1990. *It was however soon replaced by another archaic global ideology—the ideology of Jihad. Militants and extremist Islamists sought to divide the world into a Dar-ul-Islam (where the faithful ruled) and Dar-ul-Harb (the rest of world which became the Land of War). Jihad ideology was the motivational fuel that powered the rise of Fourth Generation warfare.* Osama Bin Laden and his cohorts who had been nurtured by the Afghan war now started staging a series of tactical terrorist acts which had a huge strategic impact. 9/11 and the destruction of the Twin Towers (World Trade Centre) demonstrated the lethality of Fourth Generation warfare. A terrorist has to defend nothing. He focusses only on attack—and in his attack, he choses primarily soft and undefended civilian targets. He leverages the latest in technology and combines it with unremitting fanaticism to produce a dangerous cocktail of nihilism and destruction. *His primary advantage is his asymmetry of will over his more decent opponents.*

The Indian Context

Having taken a doctrinal overview of the evolution of the new forms of Low Intensity Conflict at the global level, let us take a closer look at how LICO has evolved in the India context. A rash of tribal insurgencies had started in the Indian North Eastern states in the early 1950s. The Indian

Army was called upon to tackle these tribal insurgencies in Nagaland, Manipur, Mizoram and subsequently in Tripura and Assam. The Indian Army initially borrowed its counter insurgency techniques from the British Templar Model of Malaya. It chiefly relied upon the Frank Kitson model of establishing a CI grid based upon securing key population centres and communication infra-structure and launched manpower intensive operations. Over the years, it was able to refine its LICO techniques and a highly successful Indian model emerged that was able to pacify and play out the tribal insurgencies. In most cases, it set the stage for a political resolution of the conflict based upon creating the conditions for a resumption of dialogue and accommodating the rebel forces into the democratic mainstream. Mizoram and Tripura were clear cut successes. The insurgency in Nagaland and Manipur however, sputters along. Another notable and decisive success was the Punjab. The Indian success at LICO provided a stark contrast to the French, American and later the Russian failure in this genre of combat. Both the superpowers had gone in for a technology intensive approach that was in sharp contrast to the Indian manpower intensive model. The critical aspect was that the Indian approach had succeeded time and again, where the superpowers themselves had failed.

An Indian Doctrine for LICO

Based on years of experience in this genre of conflict, first in the North Eastern states and later in Punjab, Sri Lanka and Kashmir, the Indian Army has formulated and perfected its unique style of LICO. *Inspirations from the Templar model of Malaya and Frank Kitson's CI grid model have been incorporated and modified to suit Indian conditions*. Though the Indian Army has not promulgated this aspect as formal LICO doctrine as such, it's essential contours can be summed up in the succeeding paras:

(a) **A Manpower Intensive Approach**. Trained manpower alone can be discriminate in approach and distinguish between the innocent civilian and the armed terrorist/insurgent (this cannot be done by B-52 bombers flying at 50,000 ft or more). As such the Indian LICO approach has been characterised by a heavy committal of well-trained military manpower. *The Indian operations have therefore been infantry predominant and small arms based. They have eschewed any recourse to lethal heavy firepower of area weapons* (like mortars or artillery) and in specific have not exploited offensive airpower (except for logistics, command and control and reconnaissance aspects).

(b) **People Friendly Operations**. The manpower intensive approach has ensured people friendly operations. These stem from high level of training and discipline of the Indian Army. Being a professional standing army has been critical in this aspect. Besides the Indian Army's heavy emphasis on Civic Action Programs has served to project this people-friendly image and in many cases contributed towards reducing the popular angst and resentment against the government.

(c) **Sustained Force Committal**. Being a large army, the Indian Army has been able to ensure sustained committal of force levels for prolonged periods of one or two decades or more in the insurgency/terrorism infected states. Regular turnover of battalions and lately the employment of the Rashtriya Rifles have ensured that the Army copes well with the aspect of combat fatigue due to sustained operations.

(d) **Psychological Tiring Out of Terrorists/Population**. This sustained force committal and extended operations lasting a decade or more, have served to inflict a high rate of attrition on the insurgent/ terrorist organisations and above all, these have served to psychologically tire out the civilian population and terrorist groups involved. In a sustained struggle—the Indian Army has displayed a tenacious asymmetry of will. Its large size has enabled regular turnover of troops and a willingness to take and inflict sustained casualties that eventually led to the psychological exhaustion of the insurgents/terrorists and the populations involved.

(e) **Creating Conditions for Dialogue**. In almost all cases, this psychological tiring out of the population and the severe attrition imposed on the terrorist/insurgent armed wings, has created the conditions for a dialogue and political resolution of the problem. Elected state governments have been installed in all the states that were affected by insurgency/terrorist violence. The military operations act as a catalyst for the resumption of the democratic/ political process. The grievances that led to the rebellion are thus played out and the insurgents accommodated via the dialogue process. However, before this happens, it becomes essential to inflict heavy attrition on and wear down the insurgent hard core by concerted military operations.

(f) **The Area Grid System**. At the tactical level, the Indian Army has refined the CI Grid model evolved by Templar in Malaya and used it as the basis of its intelligence and operational efforts in CI/CT environments with great success.

(g) **Behavioural/Cognitive Objectives**. In most cases the Indian Army objectives have not so much been "Attritional" as Behavioural/ Cognitive. Lalthan Hawla, the then commander of the Mizo National Army (MNA), explained to his Indian interlocutors (after surrender) that the attrition inflicted on his cadres in a decade-long campaign had not been very significant. However, constant cordon and search operations exhausted and wore down the civilian population. Successive years without any success drained out the insurgent groups psychologically. The psychological breakdown/crumbling came much before the physical decimation. *The prime objectives in a counter insurgency/counter terrorist campaign therefore are primarily Cognitive and Behavioural*. The centre of gravity of our operations is the hearts and minds of the people.

It was my personal good fortune to have served for nearly five years in the prestigious Directorate General of Military Operations (DGMO) at New Delhi first as a Major, a Lt Col and then as a Colonel. My first tenure from 1987-90 enabled me to deal closely with the ongoing CI operations in the North East, in Punjab, Sri Lanka and J&K. I also dealt with Internal Security and Aid to Civil Authorities at the macro level. This entailed close interaction with the Home Ministry and the Para Military Forces and Central Police Organisations [viz., the Assam Rifles, Border Security Force (BSF), Central Reserve Police Force (CRPF) and Indo Tibetan Border Police (ITBP)]. I had a very educative apex view of these operations. These tenures enabled me to deal with the staff and higher command aspects of such operations first hand as also do a lot of conceptual work on this genre of operations and prepare doctrine papers for the same. It also enabled me to study our hands on operational experience in various sectors in the realm of LICO.

ORSA Approach. The Indian Doctrinal approach based upon a super saturation of the concerned area with manpower seems to be the answer to this problem of LICO. *Based on the Operational Research and Statistical Analysis (ORSA) approach we had drawn up quantitative models of our operations in the North East. We had worked on the Force ratios required to contain and roll back insurgent/terrorist movements. An analysis of a vast amount of statistical data highlighted that it needed a force ratio of 20:1 to contain an insurgent/terrorist movement at the existing level. Whenever we were able to achieve force ratios of 30:1 and above (between offensive CI forces and the terrorists), we were able to inflict a significant level of attrition on the insurgent armed hard core and force it to seek a political resolution*. Such force ratios had in fact, been achieved just prior to Shillong Accord in 1976 and the Mizoram Accord in 1986. A massive super saturation of Punjab (at one time almost 600,000 Army troops were stationed there) had enabled the Punjab Police to deliver a death blow to the vicious terrorist movement in that state. The Force ratios were in terms of offensive CI Forces (read Army Battalions) versus the number of hard core/armed insurgents/terrorists. Considerable work had been done to draw up these force ratios over the years for Nagaland, Mizoram, Manipur and later Tripura. I was involved with the exercise while at the MO Directorate and later was able to follow up this theoretical work at the Staff College in Wellington.

I came back for a second tenure as a Director MO-5 at the Military Operation (MO) Directorate in 1998. I was fortunate to serve at the apex level during Op Vijay, the Limited war in Kargil. It was professionally a most educative experience. I later served for two years and two months as the Sector Commander of our Rashtriya Rifles Sector in Kishtwar. I got a year break in the National Defence College. I was thereafter posted back to Headquarter (HQ) Northern Command as the BGS—Information Warfare (IW), a newly created test bed organisation that proved to be a 'very stimulating challenge'. This organisation dealt with media interaction, Psychological operations, Deception and Open Sources Analysis. The then Army Commander (Lt Gen Hari Prasad PVSM, AVSM, VSM was very keen to develop this expertise) and gave me a free hand to experiment and launch sustained and proactive Information Operations. The then Governor of J&K, Lt Gen S K Sinha also took a deep interest in what he called as Psychological Initiatives to win over the people. Their success was highlighted by the panic reactions of the United Jihad Council (UJC) in Pakistan Occupied Kashmir (POK) to our initiatives. In September 2004, I was pulled out from this vital slot and sent to command the prestigious Counter Insurgency Force Romeo that was deployed in the Rajouri and Punch districts, West of the Pir Panjals. It was the centre of gravity of our CI/CT campaigns and the famous operation Sarp Vinash had just been concluded here. In fact, *I thus had three consecutive operational tenures in J&K in the critical five years when the fighting was at its peak and we broke the back of the terrorist tanzeems in that vital border state.*

These successive Staff and Field tenures at the MO Directorate and then in the Field in J&K have more than qualified me to record the events of a most critical military campaign in the Republic's history and draw pertinent lessons for the future.

Protecting the People versus Kinetic Factors

At the end of the day we still have the professional debate on whether CI/CT campaigns are won by a strategy of body counts and kinetic events or by providing protection to the people as Gen Petraeus and the US forces have concluded recently. When I look back on my personal experience of these operations, I can recall instances of both. *Kinetic events and kills may not be the sole deciding factors in a campaign but are a part of protecting the people from heavily armed terrorist groups.* However, I can equally recount instances where what tilted the scales were not the kills we inflicted on the terrorist hard core but the area domination and population control that we exercised by frequent operations and high visibility in an area where the terrorists had staged violent incidents. At the end of the day what mattered was not how many of the armed terrorists we killed but how safe and secure the civil population felt and *who they perceived as the winning side*. To do that you have to have a combination of both, kinetic and protective elements in your campaign. *An army's ability to generate kinetic events is a direct function of its capability to obtain intelligence about an elusive quarry and thereafter, its professional skill and competence generate a contact and ensure a kinetic event that results in a kill/ elimination of the armed terrorist*. Good intelligence results in contacts with an elusive foe and good tactical skills result in physical elimination of the target. Only once the armed terrorists are eliminated can the people be made to feel secure. Yet an exclusive focus on the kinetics alone can lead to alienating the people. That in turn will turn off the flow of intelligence and degrade operations. What works is a judicious combination of both aspects?

A New Counter Terrorist (CT) Model: The Hinterland Variant in Kishtwar

Based on an overview of our Army's prolonged involvement in CI operations, I had, over the years, become a firm adherent of the manpower intensive approach to CI operations. It was a simplistic model but it worked. It served to leverage our considerable human resources for winning such conflicts. In October 2000, I moved on promotion to command a Rashtriya Rifles Sector in Kishtwar (a Brigade level formation of Light infantry specifically configured for CI/CT operations). The next two years proved to be a revelation. I was given a vast area of 7,500 sq kms of the most arduous and difficult mountainous and jungle terrain to control in J&K. I initially had three battalions for this task. The problem was that this area was deep in the Kashmir hinterland. In those days, the overall strategic design was to focus maximum resources on the LC and its immediate depth to stop or prevent (to the extent possible) any trans-border infiltration. It was a sound strategy and a welcome change from the earlier approach of the Gen Zaki era (1990-92), where the focus was on tackling the terrorists in the interior and keeping the LC quiet so that we could focus on CT operations in the rear. This was a reactive and purely defensive stance forced on us by the sheer paucity of troops to task. This eased somewhat with the first tranche of raising of 35 Rashtiya Rifles battalions in Gen Joshi's tenure. The new approach thereafter was sound and practical. The mountain terrain is difficult and porous, it is very difficult to prevent infiltration. Hermetically sealing the border is a virtual impossibility. Yet, that by itself was no excuse for not attempting to raise the degree of difficulty in the process of infiltration. When the terrorist movement started in 1990, the Indian Army's first reaction was that it should not be held accountable for preventing infiltration across the LC—for a hermetical sealing of such a mountainous frontier, was virtually impossible. Subsequent years were to prove this pessimistic observation right. However, there was simply no getting away from this task. *We had to either deter infiltration by the threat of retaliatory military action across the LC (the more sensible and cost-effective option) or just attempt the impossible—a virtual, hermetical sealing of a border in a terrain that resembled Dante's Inferno.* The initial, marked hesitation of the Indian Army for this task sprang from a clear "fear of failure" syndrome. The Army was pessimistic about being able to seal the border in such terrain. However, in the absence of any proactive strategy there was no option but to do this. The strategy was accordingly revamped to suit the ground realities. In the late nineties, the earlier flawed approach was corrected and maximum emphasis was laid on stopping the terrorists at the First and Second tiers along the LC itself. In 2003, the work on the LC fencing was commenced on a war footing and completed by 2005. It was a herculean task but it was highly successful and brought down the levels of infiltration by almost 70-80 per cent. Above all it curtailed the inflow of ammunition and arms and this proved to be a significant component of the defeat mechanism. It reinforced what we had learnt in the Punjab where the border Fencing had equally proved to be a turning point.

The second priority in J&K was allocated to keeping the life line of the National Highway (NH-1A) from Jammu to Srinagar, secure for unimpeded flow of civilian and military traffic to and from the valley. This meant that the vast hinterland in Doda and Kishtwar was unfortunately at priority three for force levels and resources. The terrain here was very difficult and mountainous. It impeded and slowed down the flow of information and intelligence and consequently our reactions. It was a very demanding task and a major personal challenge to conduct CT operations in the peculiar tactical conditions of the hinterland in Kashmir with very low troop levels.

Facing Ethnic Cleansing. A few months after my arrival in Kishtwar, my Force HQ decided to focus more resources on the main road. It proposed to take away another battalion from my Order of Battle (ORBAT). I was horrified. I would be left with just two units to control 7,500 sq kms of the most rugged terrain in J&K. I protested that this lowering of force density would lead to massacres of the minority community in my area. I was overruled in the larger interests of the theatre strategy. My dire predictions however came true a few months later when the terrorists took full advantage of the voids created to strike at the minority community in remote hamlets and grazing grounds out of reach of even the police posts and the Village Defense Committees (VDCs). The situation was grim and there was an outcry in the Press and Ministers helicoptered down in droves to berate the Security Forces. The decision to thin down force levels in this area had been a conscious strategic decision in pursuit of the revised overall priorities. The Corps Commander Lt Gen JBS Yadava had visited my headquarters and personally explained to me the overall situation. He sympathised with my plight but told me that in the interest of the overall strategy we would have to innovate in the hinterland. *We would have to do a lot more with much less than the optimal.* It was a challenge to me and my formation and he wanted us to measure up to it. "This is not a situation wherein like Motgomery we seek unlimited resources", he said, "I would like you to emulate Rommel and try and optimise your resources to do more with much less. There is virtually no other option in the hinterland", he said. My third battalion was taken away and I was left with just two units to hold a vast area of the most rugged terrain in the world which contained such formidable peaks like the Nun Khun and the Sickle Moon.

Counter Terrorist (CT) Operations: The Proactive Model

I thought long and hard over the problem. It was a daunting professional challenge. I gathered my team of COs and spoke to them at length. There are two ways of protest—the standard way of bitching and carping and adopting the "I told you so" approach. The other is the Japanese approach of keeping quiet and simply redoubling our efforts. The low force to space ratio made our situation precarious. Our only salvation lay in hitting out—in turning purely proactive and offensive. Our guiding credo for survival would be *"Create situations for him faster than he can create them for you."* Get inside his OODA (Observation, Orientation, Decision and Action) loop. Seize the initiative and retain it for all times. I worked on a proactive model of CT operations with my Commanding Officers. Though overall, our force levels were low, the trick was to focus resources on the point of contact; to side step troops to increase the grid density in the specific area where we sought a decision. In purely quantitative terms it meant that of the 12 companies of the Rashtriya Rifles that I was left with, I should be able to focus at least two to three companies wherever major contact was made with the terrorists or we had to react to a massacre of the minority community.

Over the next two years, we were able to actualise this aggressive and proactive model. I was lucky with my units. Both 11 RR (Dogra) and 26 RR (Kumaon) had hill troops totally suited for this terrain. I was singularly lucky in as much as both my commanding officers were dynamic and professional officers. They led cohesive and well-motivated battalions. Both Rajesh Sahai (CO 11 RR) and Anil Khosla (CO 26 RR) later earned the Sena Medal for distinguished service when they left. Both later rose to be Brigadiers. At the cutting edge the operations were led by a crop of excellent and motivated company commanders. In the year 2001, we intensified our CT operations and achieved a record number of 54 kills in our sector area. Keeping in view the terrain and environmental difficulties, the highest tally in this area had been 51 in 1998 when five army units were deployed there. That year, in 2001, with just two Army units we had raised the "kills" figure to 54. This was also the highest score in CI Force Delta that year. Considering the very arduous nature of the terrain these figures were unprecedented for that area (operations are far easier in the flat terrain of the valley or the lower hills. In the case of Kishtwar, the valley floor was 6000 feet with the adjacent ridges over 14,000 feet and more). The other sectors in Delta Force, with three and four battalions each had eliminated 47 and 37 terrorists, respectively, in that year. Our proactive "Israeli model" had worked; If we got contact in a given area, we quickly rushed our troops by road from both the battalions to the focus areas. This way up to 10-15 columns were brought to bear upon the decisive point/area from both my units. We had taken a metaphorical leaf from Rommel's book (as the Corps Commander had suggested). Though overall we were low on force levels, wherever we sought a decision, we were able to focus superior resources at the Sector level. I experimented with the idea of creating a series of MI-17 capable helipads at critical points in my area of operations. Overall it was a great operational and professional challenge but the boys of the "Mystic Ninth" proved more than a match. Thus, we were, over the course of two years of unrelenting operations, able to largely pacify the Kishtwar region. At that stage, the Army

Commander Northern Command, the redoubtable Gen Rustom Nanavati, sensed the magnitude of our attrition effort. Kishtwar was fast heading towards pacification and to give this process a decisive push, he allocated to me two more infantry battalions and an ITBP battalion. I got another infantry battalion for a few months. This huge force accretion served to completely pacify the area. Most of the terrorist tanzeems simply fled the area and sought refuge in the neighbouring sectors and remote hideouts where they decided to lie low. I now changed my emphasis on a massive effort to win over the civilian population by large scale civic action programs and in this I got the whole hearted support of my Force Commanders Gen Mono Bhaghat and later Gen Choudhury.

The whole saga of operations of the Mystic Ninth in Kishtwar, therefore throws up a plethora of very valuable hands on military lessons that will be of immense use to all commanders and troops engaged in such operations. A new model of how to achieve more with less can enable us to generate reserves for more proactive employment elsewhere. Is there another approach apart from the pure manpower intensive approach of our Army? Can tactics be refined to generate greater mental mobility and efficiency? Based on my experience as a Sector Commander I do feel it is possible. My boys were able to achieve these results on the ground. I have tried to record our experience for posterity so that others can gain from this tactical experience. This is an unfortunate area of great weakness in our Army. *We have, in the post war period, one of the world's richest fund of combat experience. Unfortunately, we have done precious little to record this legacy for posterity. In not recording it, we waste our experience. This is a tragic mistake. We must remember that in the modern day context, winning organisations are learning organisations*. To grow as a professional organisation, we must document and meticulously record our operational experience for posterity. Only then can we analyse it and learn from it.

The Ethnic Cleansing Factor

There is one facet of the CT operations in Kashmir in general and Kishtwar in particular, that has escaped the public notice completely. This is the painful aspect of Ethnic cleansing and genocide that Pakistan's ISI adopted very deliberately as a policy tool to influence outcomes in J&K and shape a solution in its favour by mass killings of unarmed civilians that induced the exodus of inconvenient minorities from the areas it was targeting. The ethnic cleansing of the Kashmiri Pandit community from the Kashmir valley is one of the most sordid chapters of recent human history. The great pity is that the Indian state itself tamely accepted this atrocity as a fiat accomplis of sorts. It acknowledged its helplessness in protecting the minority community in the valley and tacitly accepted that they be driven out of their ancestral homes to rot in refugee camps in Jammu and Delhi for decades. Even after the terrorist tanzeems have largely been wiped out from J&K, the state has not facilitated the return of these refugees. What is even more reprehensible is the curtain of silence it drew over this horrible attempt at genocide and ethnic cleansing by Pakistan. The world has heard no end of the ethnic cleansing in Bosnia and Serbia. As late as July 2013, Radovan Kavadzic is being tried by a war crimes tribunal in the Hague for the genocide and ethnic cleansing of Muslim serbs. By the same logic a number of the heads of Pakistani ISI equally deserve to be tried for the crimes of genocide and ethnic cleansing against the Kashmiri Pandits and Dogras. The ethnic cleansing of the gentle and docile Kashmiri Pandits however was blanked out of the Indian media itself. The world therefore could not care less for these hapless victims of Pakistan's Proxy War. This has been a horrible crime against humanity. The Indian state has been complicit in this conspiracy of silence. This tragedy needs to be recounted in detail, not to add to mutual recriminations, but simply to ensure that such a deliberate crime against humanity is not repeated again. The Indian state failed to protect its people in the valley, which is the essence of CI operations. It connived in their tragic flight and till date has not summoned the political will to highlight their plight to the world or send those hapless people back to their ancestral lands. What happened in the valley in 1991-1992 was a ghastly tragedy. The world has a duty to remember—for only if it remembers this tragedy will it exert itself to prevent the re-occurrence of such episodes of ethnic cleansing and genocide.

Though the Jammu and Kashmir Liberation Front (JKLF) initially put on the façade that it was fighting for "Azadi" or Independence—its communal intent soon became clear in February and March 1990, when it started a systematic ethnic cleansing campaign to kill, terrorise and drive out the entire 400,000 strong community of Kashmiri Pandits from the Valley of Kashmir. A systematic campaign of persecution was commenced. Over 20,000 houses of Kashmiri Pandits were burnt, some 105 of the Pandit Educational Institutions were destroyed and 103 Temples razed to the ground. Over 1100 Kashmiri Pandits were tortured and killed. Between February and March 1990 some 140,000 to 160,000 Kashmiri Pandits fled the Valley. This was followed by high profile killing of senior Hindu officials, intellectuals and prominent citizens. This resulted in a complete panic and a total exodus of some 400,000 Kashmiri Pandits (or 95 per cent of the entire K P population) from the valley. These hapless Pandit families largely fled to some eight major refugee camps in Jammu (around 300,000 people) and some 14 refugee camps around Delhi (some 100,000 refugees). They still live there in abysmal conditions with five to six families huddled into small rooms and tents. Unused to the heat of the plains, some 2000 of them died of heat stroke. The pity is the conspiracy of silence about this horrible genocide. It is one of the largest single cases of ethnic cleansing in the Post World War II era. The whole world knows about the pitiful case of the ethnic cleansing of Muslim Serbs in Serbia and Bosnia. Former Yugoslav political leaders, like Slobodon Melosovic have been tried and sentenced to jail for this crime of genocide and ethnic cleansing by the International Court of Justice. Yet, not a whisper is heard about the even more horrific ethnic cleansing of Kashmiri Pandits from Kashmir. There is a deep conspiracy of silence to completely black out this news of the ethnic cleansing of the Kashmiri Pandit Community from J&K. The Indian govt itself has gone to great lengths to blank out this news from the electronic and print media. And so for the past 20 years and more, the hapless community of Kashmiri Pandits, continues to live in the miserable conditions of the refugee camps, uprooted from their traditional homes and mountain landscape to swelter in the hot plains. When they tried to go back they were threatened with dire consequences. Some Kashmiri Pandits decided to brave it out and tried to return to their homes. In response, there were targeted massacres of the Kashmiri Pandits. Eight were killed in Budgam on 22 March 1997 and another 26 were killed at Wandama, a hamlet in Ganderbal area of the Valley on 25-26 January 1998. There was another killing of some 26 Pandits in Prankote on 21 April 1998. Another attempt was made to send the Kashmiri Pandits back in 2003. This resulted in yet another massacre of 24 Kashmiri Pandits in the Nadimarg village of Pulwama district on 23 March 2003.

Nothing highlights the rabidly communal agenda of the separatist movement in Jammu and Kashmir than this orchestrated and deliberate ethnic cleansing of the hapless Kashmiri Pandit population of the Valley. Whatever claims they may make to the moral high ground by their so called "Intifada", the naked truth is highlighted by this horrible ethnic cleansing perpetrated by the ISI tanzeems in concert with the Jamat-e-Islami (JeI) cadres.

Ethnic cleansing in Kishtwar. The genocide and ethnic cleansing of the

Kashmiri Pandits was not the sole instance of such butchery by the ISI sponsored tanzeems. Having driven the Pandits out of the valley, the ISI next set its sights on the Dogra Hindu population in the mountainous district of Doda and Kishtwar. This pogrom was triggered in 1995 and intensified in 1998 when there was some talk in the backchannels of reviving the Owen-Dixon Plan of partitioning the J&K state between India and Pakistan along the natural faultline of the Chenab river. To claim the whole state as it were, the ISI ordered the ethnic cleansing of the minorities from Doda and Kishtwar. It is noteworthy that the population ratio here is broadly 60:40 between the majority and minority communities. It was our misfortune to serve in this region when the ISIs ethnic cleansing drive in Kishtwar was at its worst phase. Gen Petraeus and Kilcullen emphasise that the essence of CI operations is to protect the population. Could we just sit back and allow some 40 per cent of the population here to be massacred and driven out? Would that not have highlighted the complete impotence of the state and a failure of our CI efforts?

A distinct feature of the Counter-Terrorist campaign in Kishtwar was the grim struggle we had to wage against the ISIs strategy of deliberate ethnic cleansing in the Kishtwar region. This stemmed from the nature of the human terrain in this district. The population of the Hindu Dogra community was 39.3 per cent. As a very cold blooded strategy, the ISI tasked its terrorist tanzeems here to carry out ethnic cleansing by way of deliberate and targeted massacres of the minority community. These were designed to trigger a mass migration of the Dogra population from this area, much like the Kashmiri Pandits had been driven out of Kashmir. What was the ISIs design behind such ethnic cleansing? One school of thought felt that it was because they suspected the minority population of aiding the Army and wanted to drive them out. It later transpired that the effort here was far more deliberate and linked to Pakistan considering the Owen-Dixon plan to partition J&K along the Chenab river, as one of the likely solutions of the Kashmir conflict. This proposal was actually dusted out and spoken of at the turn of this century and what followed was the ISIs deliberate attempt to drive out the Dogra population from the Doda-Kishtwar region and deliberately alter the demographics and human terrain of this area to ensure its inclusion in Pakistan. It was a nightmare for the minorities of this area. Initially they had begun to migrate in large numbers. What saved the day was the grit of this community. The government decided to arm the Village Defense Committees (VDCs) with World War I Lee Enfield rifles. This helped them to keep attackers at bay till the Army came in. The ISI now devised a more diabolical plan to strike outside the villages in the high Alpine pastures where in the summers the old citizens and children took the live stock out to graze. What we had in my tenure were a series of such horrific massacres in the pastures where old people and young children were specifically targeted and slaughtered in droves. It was a horrific crime against humanity. However, very strangely, the Indian state reacted to this horrific ethnic cleansing with a curtain of silence. It was a grim struggle.

Fortunately, the boys of 9 Sector RR rose to the occasion. So did the Dogras who formed Village Defense Committees and fought grimly to save their hearth and homes and their children. They were clear that if they fled once they would never be able to return. So they waged a grim struggle with the antiquated 303 rifles that the state government gave them. My superior HQs told me it was beyond my capacity, that it was the job of the Police to protect these people; that the Army could not take on this defensive and reactive task. True, there was no way that my Brigade could defend each village, hamlet and pasture. However, I decided instead on not defending each hamlet but upon a more proactive approach of targeting ruthlessly the tanzeems and groups that had carried out these massacres. It took us months of a major effort. My troops scoured the high mountains, sometimes at heights near 15,000 feet. It was a herculean effort and needed superlative stamina and dedication. But the boys did not flinch. Months of painstaking efforts paid off and we finally gunned down those terrorists guilty of such horrible massacres of the innocent. In fact, the main group fought desperately when cornered and had to be eliminated by using the Russian Thermobaric weapon. That put a searing end to this horrific campaign of ethnic cleansing in Kishtwar. What happened in the valley was not repeated in the mountains and hamlets of Kishtwar. We had won the war against ethnic cleansing. It was a superlative effort but the boys of the Mystic Ninth sector of the RR had risen to the challenge. It was a grim struggle. We lost many good men. One of my boys, Naik Ram Bir Singh Tomar of 26 RR got the nation's highest gallantry award, the Ashok Chakra, posthumously.

This book then is the Saga of the Mystic Ninth Sector of the Rashtriya Rifles and its CT operations in the Kishtwar region of J&K through the eventful years 2000-2002 when the struggle in J&K was at its grimmest peak. This experience is unique in that it represents the struggle of decency against horrific crimes like genocide and ethnic cleansing. It was a grim struggle but the boys were able to protect the population despite all odds of terrain and the brutal nature of the enemy. It is a grim saga that teaches and uplifts. This book is my personal tribute to the magnificent boys of the Mystic Ninth that I had the honor to lead in battle. It is vital that as a nation we do not forget the sacrifices made by our boys. What is more important is that we record our experience and learn our lessons for the future. This initial chapter is designed to set my account in a larger professional and theoretical context that will facilitate an understanding of tactical events as they unfolded in my tenure. Let me therefore recount the narrative in its chronological order.

CHAPTER 2

Assignment Kishtwar

September 2000, I was serving as Director MO-5 in the prestigious Directorate General of Military Operations (DGMO) at Delhi reaching the conclusion of a very eventful tenure. It had been a very hectic and eventful tenure. We had burnt much midnight oil through the months of Operation Vijay. It had been a significant limited conflict fought against a nuclear backdrop and had thrown up its rich harvest of lessons. The Pakistani intruders had been thrown back by a very methodical and bloody operation involving about two divisions plus of the Army in offensive operations in very difficult high altitude mountain terrain. Since the theatre of operations was localised, we had been able to marshal resources very methodically. There was an initial period of confused, probing attacks and knee jerk reactions by the local formations and the Leh based 3 Infantry Division in early May 1999. However, these served to locate and fix the enemy and thereafter the Indian Army methodically concentrated another Division and a Para Brigade. It staged a deliberate tactical cum logistical pause to build up our gun density to almost a hundred tubes supporting each battalion sized attack. Then yard by bloody yard, our infantry men (led by intrepid young Subalterns and Captains) had pushed back the Pakistanis. Tololing was the turning point. Then came Tiger hill and Yaldor. The Indian Air Force (IAF) had entered the fray in end May after frenzied lobbying by the Army. It persisted initially with the Lo-Lo attack profiles of the 1960s and 70s vintage and paid a steep price (two MiGs and a M-17 helicopter gunship). Thereafter it shifted the attack profiles beyond the shoulder fired Surface to Air Missile (SAM) and Air Defence Gun envelope and switched (like the Americans in the Gulf War) to attacks from the high and mid altitudes. These effected accuracy of the strikes as we did not have adequate Laser/Precision Guided Munitions. The Air Force however innovated and soon had added strap on GPS guidance kits to conventional gravity bombs. Despite strident arguments to the contrary, the Air Force contribution was effective. The salient gain was that it dominated the air space over Kargil and prevented Pakistani helicopter resupply to the Northern Light Infantry (NLI) troopers stuck on the dizzy heights. Lack of food and water proved to be their nemesis. Kargil was an audacious gamble by Pakistan. Having gained nuclear parity, it was confident that it could deter a major Indian conventional response. Within the backdrop of the nuclear threat, it decided to stretch the Indian thresholds of tolerance and probe the limits of its elasticity. The concept had been around for years. Pakistani officers had articulated it to Stephen P. Cohen as far back as the 1980s. Contingency plans had been drawn when Gen Pervez Musharraf was the DGMO. What experts called synchronity perhaps played a major role in shaping events. As a Colonel, Pervez Musharraf had been handpicked by the ISI boss Lt Gen Javed Nasir for the Special Services Group (SSG). He served in the Afghan War and understood the cost effectiveness of low-intensity operations that could bleed even a superpower white. He commanded the Siachen Brigade and later was the Force Commander Northern Area. As such, his entire service profile veered around J&K. No wonder the moment he became the DGMO, he had set in motion planning for the Kargil intrusion. As Pakistan's Chief of the Army Staff, therefore, he was a man with a single-minded mission. He would unfreeze the status quo in Kashmir. Was Kargil a strategic effort to unfreeze the status quo in J&K and force the world to intervene by creating a crisis (much like the Egyptians had attempted on the Suez in 1973)? Or was it merely a tactical ploy to pay back the Indian Army for its very effective interdiction of the Neelam Valley road? It is still difficult to say. But the fact is that an old plan overruled by Gen Jehangir Karamat was dusted out and put into action the moment Gen Pervez Musharraf became the Chief.

Kargil was a vast gap in the defence lines on the LC. Logistical and terrain constraints had forced both India and Pakistan to accept this vast stretch as a void. Unfortunately for us, the NH-1A road from Srinagar to Leh, ran in the shadow of this void. This vital communication artery ran parallel to the unheld LC and provided a tempting target to the Pakistanis. When Musharraf took over as a Chief he dusted out these pre-existing plans and decided on a very high risk gamble to unfreeze the status quo in Kashmir. The NLI troopers would infiltrate in the guise of militants and establish posts to bring the Leh-Srinagar highway under the fire of direct firing weapons. The existing nuclear standoff, he was certain, would checkmate any Indian conventional response. It would be a fiat accomplis.

The threat of a nuclear holocaust would cause the Americans and the rest of the world to cry a halt and Pakistan would be left free to consolidate its gains. This was what Gen Pervez had hoped for.

The levels of subjectivity have traditionally been inordinately high in the Pakistan military hierarchy. Their military planning and analysis are uni-dimensional and one sided. They usually fail to think things through and factor in the responses of the adversary. A psycophantic military hierarchy does not dare to question the wisdom of its Chief and therefore does not factor in the likely enemy reactions.

India carried out a partial mobilisation of a large part of its forces in the Western Theatre in the instant case. It also mobilised its Air Force and Navy to pose serious threats in being. Pakistan's anchor premise that it would remain a very localised affair was thus knocked out at the very outset. India pushed the envelope between an all out Nuclear/Conventional Conflict and a low intensity conflict to launch a limited war. Limited Wars have been the natural response option in situations of nuclear symmetry. Wars can be limited in terms of Aims and Scope, geographical area (space limitations) and limitation of time. We chose to limit the response in space. We also undertook to fight on our own side of the Line of Control (LC). This limitation brought us a great deal of diplomatic mileage for maturity, restraint and responsibility. However, in hindsight, it proved to be an error of judgement. Probably we should have used the Kargil provocations to cross the LC (albeit in a limited manner). Our strategy of Defensive-Defence was unfortunately to feed Pakistani delusions of grandeur. It gave them very wrong signals about our ultimate political and military resolve. Deterrence as per the Israeli analyst Zaeev-Maoz is based upon a triad of three factors.

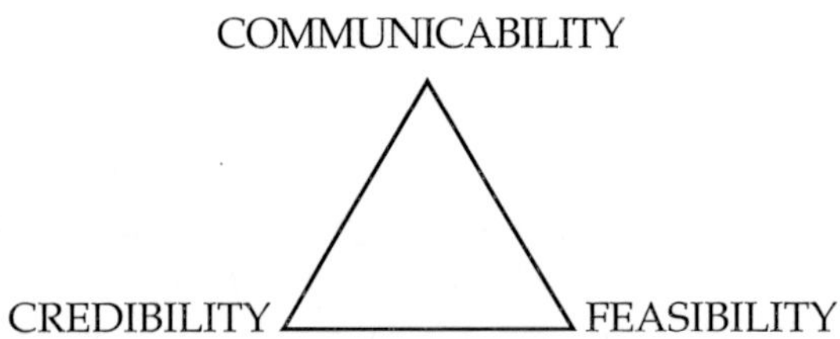

Communicability. It is imperative that our actions clearly communicate to our likely adversaries the following:

(a) Existence of a threat (of Nuclear or Conventional Retaliation).
(b) Conditions under which the threat will be carried out.
(c) Political, economic and military consequences of carrying out that threat.

Credibility. The far more critical aspect is the credibility of that threat. India has a credible nuclear arsenal and more important, strong conventional armed forces that overmatch Pakistan's by an appreciable margin. However, this threat can become credible only if we have (like Israel) a *reputation for resolve. Credibility therefore is an amalgam of Capability and Intent*. It was perhaps our failure to communicate an intent to cross the LC in 1999 that led to Op Parakram a mere two years down the line after Op Vijay.

Feasibility. The last factor of this triad of deterrence is Feasibility. This defines the extent or degree to which a nation that seeks to deter can respond to a given violation of the status quo. This usually fails when the violations are low order threats to the status quo. That was the case in Kargil.

Op Vijay had mixed results. It was an unqualified success in as much as we threw the Pakistanis out of this critical space overlooking the vital communication artery in Kargil. The operation did turn out to be a disaster for Pakistan. Nawaz Sharief was forced to flee to Washington for succour. He was forced to back down. The Pakistani army conveniently pegged all blame on his ostensible pusillanimity and lack of resolve. A few months later Nawaz Sharief was overthrown and Pervez Musharraf took over in a bloodless coup. Despite the sea change in the global scenario due to 9/11, Musharraf had clearly drawn the wrong lessons from Kargil. A feudal military order is not given to objective evaluation of its own performance. It conveniently projects its failures on to a civilian establishment, which has served as its traditional "whipping boy" in Pakistan.

The Indian Armed Forces had displayed tremendous grit and valour in Op Vijay. The sacrifices of our men and intrepid young officers had saved the day. The Infantry had displayed tremendous stoicism and pressed home attacks in impossible terrain with steely resolve and determination. It had shown the stomach to absorb fairly high casualties and press on undaunted. However, at the end of the day, we had to return to our Counter Terrorist (CT) grids in Kashmir. The concerted focus on the LC had led to a reprieve for the terrorists in the hinterland. They had hit out against our sources and intelligence network and reasserted their sway. Though Op Vijay was a significant success in conventional operations, from the Counter Insurgency (CI) operations aspect, the terrorists had gained a major reprieve. The diversion of troops and resources to Kargil had caused a setback to our CI effort in Kashmir—especially in the hinterland.

Conventional operations had ended. The CT operations would have to be resumed with redoubled vigour in Kashmir. Being in the Military Operation (MO) Directorate for a second tenure (I had earlier been there as a Major and then a Lt Col during the Punjab Terrorist movement and then Op Pawan—the intervention in Sri Lanka) had been a tremendously enriching experience. I was awarded the Chief of Army Staff's Commendation Card for my work at the MO Directorate during this exciting period of our history in Op Vijay.

I had been sitting approved for the rank of Brigadier almost for the last three years. The deferment of retiring ages (post the nuclear tests) had put a brake on promotions. By mid 2000, these were removed and all of us from the star crossed batch of 1971 began to look forward to our next assignments (our course incidentally had been commissioned just a month before the 1971 War of Bangladesh and had paid the steepest cost in live and limbs).

Déjà vu. I came one day in September 2000 to find a Poetry Magazine called "Chandrabhaga" on my table. It had just come in by post. Somehow the name fascinated me. I could not take my eyes off its cover. For some reasons, the name kept resurfacing in my consciousness over the next few days and weeks. I had a curious experience of *Déjà vu*. The place I am going to will have high mountains and Pine trees—I told my family and friends. I could not shake off these feelings of *Déjà vu* as it were. It was curious. On 16 September 2000, I finally got my promotion and posting orders after a long wait. I was headed for 9 Sector Rasthriya Rifles. A quick look at the Operations Map indicated that it was in Kishtwar. The Chandrabhaga or the Chenab River ran through its centre. The river course neatly bisected my area of responsibility. The feelings of *Déjà vu* had been right all along. I was to take over by 20 October 2000. I had two Rashtriya Rifles and one regular Infantry battalion on by ORBAT (Order of Battle). My area of responsibility encompassed the Kishtwar Sub-Division of Doda district as also the Tehsils of Thatri and Gundoh. It spanned 7,500 sq kms of the most rugged and difficult mountainous terrain in J&K. The force to space ratio was low but being the deep hinterland, it was all that could be spared. The region itself was fascinating. I tried to read as much as I could on this area over the next few days and the ongoing operations in that region. Being in the MO Directorate helped and I was able to gather a mass of information. One of the traditional perks of being in the MO Directorate is a foreign trip to some seminar etc. Since I was nearing the end of my tenure, I was offered a trip to Sweden to attend a UN Conference on Banning of Anti-Personnel mines. It did not strike me as an enterprise

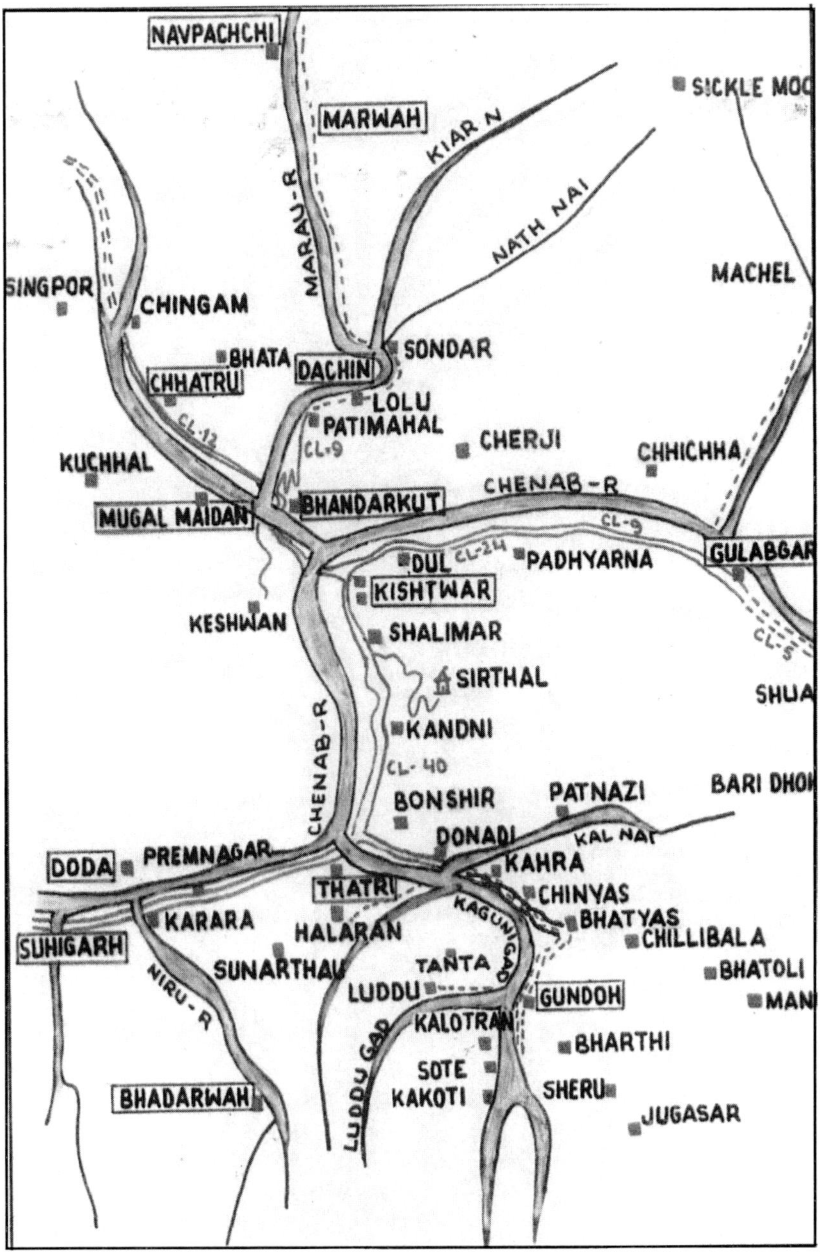

Map 1: Kishtwar—Water Courses and Communications

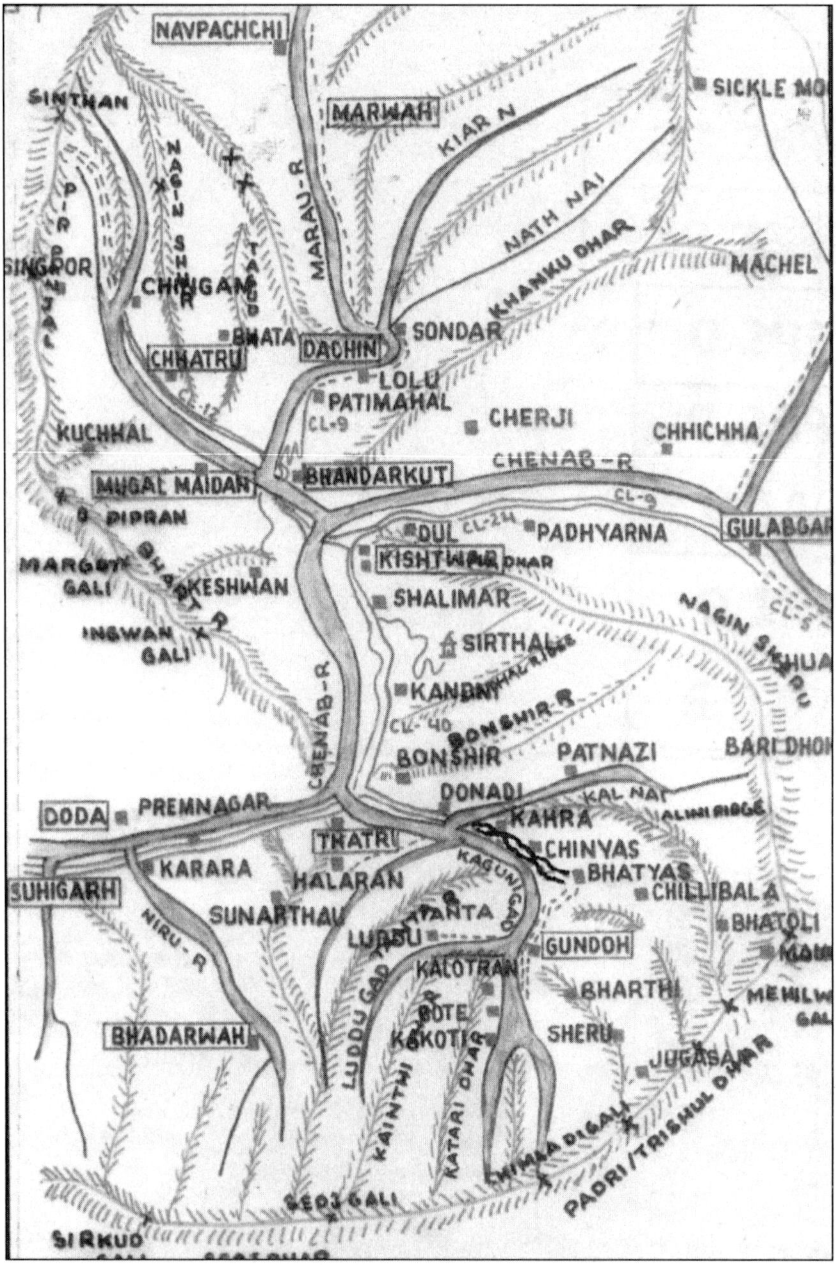

Map 2: Kishtwar—Major Ridgelines

where I would learn much professionally, so I requested to be excused for this trip for personal reasons. I decided to focus instead on my forthcoming field assignment. My giving up a prized foreign trip amazed my collogues but I do think the craze for "phoren" needs to be tamed a bit in our context. Brig Behel (my predecessor) had come down to Delhi for a spot of casual leave. I sought him out and requested him to give me an initial briefing and send reading material, which would help me prepare for my command assignment. He had had a long and extended tenure in Kishtwar and it had taken a toll of his health. His wife was the one person most delighted to see me for my posting as relief meant that her husband could at last come back home. Brig Behel took the trouble to brief me in detail. I also sought out Brig (later Lt Gen) Gangadharan, who had earlier commanded this Sector and he also gave me a great deal of valuable inputs and background that was invaluable for me in the days ahead.

Kishtwar was a fascinating realm. My area of responsibility was bounded by the Great Himalayan range in the North and North West. At its extremity lay the 7,135 meter high Nun Khun peak. Closer to my area where the famous Sickle Moon peak (6,574 m) and the Brahma I to V series of jagged peaks (6,100 m and more). These had once been the favourite haunt of mountaineering expeditions. The Chandrabhaga (or the Chenab river) is the main morphological feature of this region. It flows in an East-West direction through the famous Gulabgarh valley. At Dul it turns Southwards sharply and flows past the plateau of Kishtwar to Thatri at the bottom of the deep gorge. There it turns westwards again to flow onto Doda and join the Chenab Main near Chanderkot. The main tributaries of the Chandrabhaga are:

(a) *The Maru River.* This is an ancient stream and finds mention in the Nadi Sukta of the Rig Veda as the Marud Vridha River. It is said that many of the verses of the Atharva Veda that deal with medicinal and psychotropic plants were composed on its banks. It arises in the wide glaciated bowl of Marwaha valley, which is famous for its Rice and Rajmah (kidney bean) crop.

(b) *The Chhatru Nala.* This rises from the Pir Panjal range and joins the Maru River near Bhandarkut. Both streams join and flow into the Chandrabhaga.

(c) *Kagune Gad.* The Kagune Gad arises from the Seoj Dhar ranges in the South. Its tributaries are the Jai Gad (that flows in from Bhadarwah) and the Kal Nai that flows in from the glaciers in the Bari Dhok region. This stream joins the Chandrabhaga at Thatri.

These rivers and streams have carved steep gorges in the mountains. The communication system naturally follows the course of these streams. The main artery is the National Highway 1-B, which runs along the Chandrabhaga course. Bhandarkut to Chhatru-Mughal Maidan and the Sintan Pass on the Pir Panjal that provides connectivity with the Anantnag portion of the Kashmir valley. Feeder roads are the ones from Bhandarkut to Patimahal and the Keshwan Marwah valley. Another road leads via Dul-Gulabgarh to Himachal Pradesh. A third artery winds down the Kagune Gad to Gundoh.

Ridge Lines. The Great Himalaya towers in the North and North West serve to separate the region from Ladakh. The other important ridge lines are:

(a) *The Pir Panjals*. With an average altitude of 4,000-4,100 metres, these constitute the divide between the Kashmir and Kishtwar valley and the Doda region. These get 5-6 feet of snow in winter (December-March). These are numerous gallies which are important choke points for the movement of terrorists. The Pir Panjals have three major offshoots:

(i) *The Bharat Ridge*. This ridge tapers down from the Southern Singpore area via the Agash Mandal to the Chandrabhaga river near Thatri. It serves to separate Doda from the Kishtwar valley. It has about 10 major gallies or passes. Large number of Bakarwals and Gujjars migrate to its alpine in spring and summer pastures with their flocks of sheep-goat and cattle and provide sustenance bases to the terrorists, who climb up to the ridge lines in their wake.

(ii) *The Nagin Shur Ridge*. This ridge tapers down from the Phamber area towards Chhatru and Mughal Maidan.

(iii) *The Tagud Ridge*. This is another outrider of the Pir Panjals that slopes down towards Bhata and Bhandarkut.

(b) *The Khanku Dhar*. This massive range serves to divide the Maru river basin (the Marawaha-Dachin area) from the Gulabgarh valley formed by the gorge of the Chandrabhaga. This is a steep and precipitous ridge with only a few crossing points formed by the Cherji and Chichha nalas.

(c) *The Seoj Dhar*. This massive range serves to divide the Doda area from the Chhamb area of Himachal Pradesh. Its average altitude varies from 3,400 to 4,000 metres plus. In winters, it receives some

5-7 feet of snow. It has massive offshoots that snake into the Kishtwar region. The main ones are:

(i) *Nagin Sheru*. This ridge emanates down from the Seoj Dhar and slopes down towards the Kishtwar plateau via the Dul Dhar range.

(ii) The Alni Ridge.

(iii) The Khakri Ridge.

(iv) The Kilari and Katari Dhars that converge on to the Tehsil of Gundoh, provide connectivities from the Bhadarwah area. Interestingly, this area is a very close terrain analogue of the Panjshir valley in Afghanistan.

Demographics. The demography of this region is peculiar and had a major influence on the operations being conducted in this region. The 2001 census gives the following population breakdown:

(a)	Muslims	:	53.26%
(b)	Hindus	:	39.33%
(c)	Scheduled castes and tribes (Gujjars/Bakarwalas/etc.)	:	6.64%
(d)	Others	:	0.77%

This is expressed in Fig. 1.

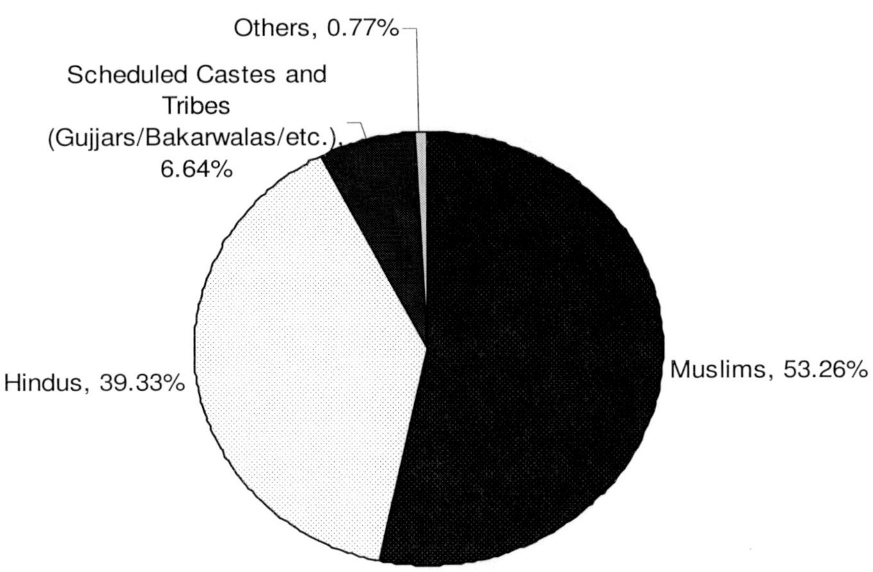

Figure 1

The Hindus are mainly concentrated in the river valleys and major population centres and are mainly Dogras—an ethnic group famed for its martial qualities (see Fig. 2).

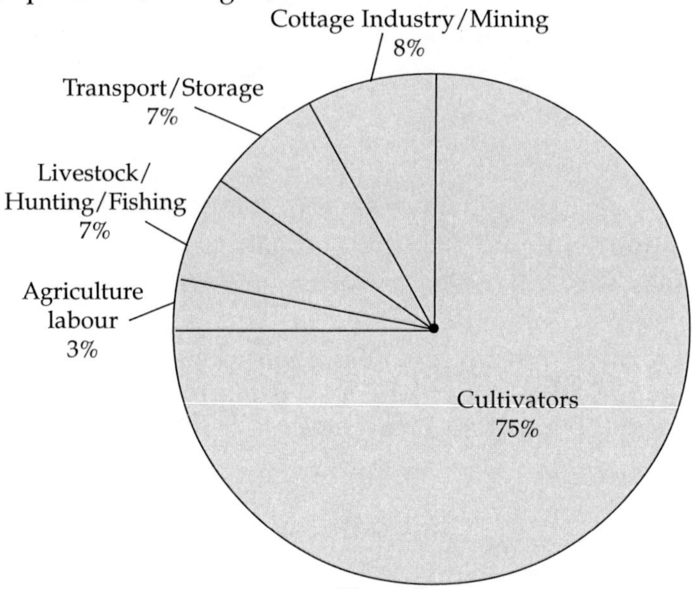

Figure 2

Employment profile. The above pie chart gives an idea of the employment profile in this area. The bulk of the population is engaged in agriculture and pastoral pursuits. A critical 7 per cent is involved in hunting, fishing and collection of forest produce (medicinal herbs, Guchhi mushrooms, etc.). This segment traditionally used to provide guides for hunting expeditions in the pre-partition days. This breed is adept as trackers and hunters and at living off the land. As such, some of the most dreaded local terrorists of this area have come from this population segment. Unlike the Kashmiris of the valley, they are used to moving in mountainous terrain and have a flair for field craft and are adept at living off the land. They therefore make natural insurgents/terrorists. The terrain provides them ideal forest cover and rugged mountains with caves and Khuds. The countryside is a guerilla fighter's dream.

Historical Background. I hurriedly went around the various libraries in Delhi to soak up as much material as I could on Kishtwar. The region had a very rich and remarkable history. Kishtwar finds mention in the Mahabharata epic as the Lohit Mandal. Lohit incidentally means saffron and Mandal is Canton or region. It was even in those hoary times famous for its saffron. To this day saffron is grown in Kishtwar. It is a prized variety with short red carpels. From the month of August onwards, the saffron fields form an enchanting and unforgettable landscape of Mauve and Violet. Kishtwar's history stretches back even earlier to the Vedic period. Portions of the Atharva Veda are said to have been composed on the banks of the Maru River. This is an ancient stream that finds mention in the Nadi Sukta of the Rig Veda as the Marud Vridha alongside such famous Indian rivers as the Ganga, Yamuna and Saraswati; and the Asikioni and Vyath (Beas).

In the Buddhist period, Kishtwar was made famous by one of its brilliant scholars called Naga Sen. He lived in the Nagseni pargana around the Second Century BC (in the picturesque Gulabgarh valley). It is said that he had engaged Menander, the Indo-Greek King of Sakala (present day Sialkot) in a great philosophical debate that lasted over a week. He had converted him to Buddhism. Menander was renamed Milinda. Nagasena came back to his monastery at Sayadraman in Kishtwar and recorded that debate for posterity in a great Buddhist text called "Milinda Panaha". (How Milinda came to the faith) In Kishtwari it is called Milind Pano and copies of this ancient text are still available today. It is one of the most famous texts of Buddhist sacred literature.

Kishtwar fell prey to Muslim invasions in later years. The locals put up a fierce resistance. There is a place called Mughal Midan near Chhatru where ostensibly a large number of Mughal troops were slaughtered by the local armies in a major ambush in the sixteenth century.

A Sufi saint from Baghdad came to Kishtwar in the 16th Century. He is credited with many miraculous feats and converted a large number of people to Islam. It was however a very syncretic and tolerant version of Islam. The local Hindu rulers who converted, retained their original names. Thus, the last ruler of Kishtwar was Mohammed Tegh Singh. The name itself is evidence of the traditional harmonious relationship between the two communities in this mountainous region.

The Era of Zorawar Singh. Kishtwar shot to fame during the rule of Dogras under Maharaja Gulab Singh. Gulab Singh appointed one of his most illustrious generals, Zorawar Singh, as the Military Governor of Kishtwar in 1824. Zorawar Singh was a visionary soldier. He set about raising and training a formidable Dogra Army with which he would launch spectacular campaigns of conquest towards the heartland of Central Asia.

In 1834, he assembled a 7,000 strong army and marched via Dachin-Marwaha region to the Warwan valley and of thence via the Bhot Kol Pass to Lankartse and Ladakh. He conquered Ladakh and made it a principality of his ruler in Jammu. He returned to quell numerous rebellions in this unruly province. In 1837 he made a daring march via Gulabgarh and the 5,431 meters high Umasi La Pass at the height of winter to surprise the rebels in Ladakh. He totally crushed all rebellions and consolidated his hold in this strategic province. In 1840 he set about to capture Baltistan. He captured Skardu and Khapalu (the Pakistani base areas for the ongoing war in Siachen Glacier). He again crossed the Umasi La for the last time in 1841. This time he launched a breathtaking invasion of Western Tibet. He penetrated as much as 700 miles into Tibet and defeated the combined Chinese and Tibetan Armies on the banks of the famous Mansarovar lake. He was only defeated by the Tibetan Winter which took a severe toll of his troops. He was killed in battle and his forces lost heart and retreated. The Chinese came up in pursuit and laid siege to Leh. The Dogra armies hit back the next year and routed the Chinese and drove them back to Tibet. If India has a window into the strategic heartland of Asia today, it is all due to one of its most intrepid and able Generals—Zorawar Singh. Zorawar Singh is incidentally one of the founding fathers of my Regiment (the Regiment of Jammu and Kashmir Rifles [JAK RIF]). Another illustrious soldier of Kishtwar was Mehta Colonel Basti Ram, a tactician par excellence and the first battalion commander of the oldest unit of my Regiment, the Fateh Shibji or the Fourth Battalion of the JAK RIF. That played a stellar role in the invasion of Tibet and in fact captured the famous Chinese Mantalai flag. Col Basti Ram also played a stellar role in the invasion of Baltistan and the capture of Skardu.

Departure for Kishtwar. One was busy and in such a flurry of activity that one had no time to think. The handing taking over at MO Directorate over I packed my bags. 13th of October 2000 I found myself on the Delhi Railway station. My wife and daughter had come to see me off. As the train streamed off my daughter started crying. It hit me for the first time then. I was going into clear and present danger.

I had had the good fortune to command my parent unit—6th Battalion the Jammu & Kashmir Rifles (JAK RIF), into which I had been commissioned in November 1971. As the Commanding Officer (CO) I had led the battalion through very intense and major skirmishes with the Pakistanis at a place called Dalunang in the Kargil sector. These entailed heavy fire of artillery, mortars, anti-tank and anti-aircraft guns. The unit had performed superlatively but we had to pay a steep price. We had lost six men killed and 21 wounded. The enemy of 29 Baluch and 3 Northern light infantry had suffered four times these casualties and had their battalion Headquarter (HQ) in the villages of Shaqma and Thanus destroyed. I was lucky to be awarded a VSM for leading these skirmishes. The unit had won 20 awards (including a posthumous Vir Chakra) and the Chief's Citation. I had later commanded the unit again in Lucknow and had earned the Army Commander's Commendation Card. I owed my promotion and decorations to this very intrepid unit and its gallant Dogras. Luckily the unit was then stationed at Jammu. It was most appropriate that I put on my rank badges in the unit *mandir* (temple). I had requested the CO (young SK Varni) and he had been delighted. Accordingly, I put on my rank badges in the unit temple at a gracious ceremony with all officers and men. Then I was invited to address the Sainik *Sammelan*. Coincidentally while I was headed for the killing fields of Kishtwar, the unit was headed for the Northern Glacier—the highest battlefield in the world. I gave them what advice I could. I reiterated the lessons we had learnt the hard way in Kargil and was happy to see the boys in very good heart.

The ceremony was over, we headed off for Kishtwar. The Staff Officer who had come to receive me politely pointed out that in view of the threat of terrorist ambushes/IEDs enroute, the current practice was to avoid star plates and flags. I thanked him for the prudent advice but pointed out that I had slaved for 30 years to earn this star plate and flag. I was damned if I was going to take it off for fear of a terrorist attack! On this somewhat defiant note we set off for my new and very challenging assignment at Kishtwar.

Udhampur lies enroute. It is a small mofussil town that has grown over the years because of the massive Army presence here. The Headquarters of the Northern Command of the Indian Army are located here. My father, had been the Chief Education Officer of the J&K State Forces in the times of Maharaja Hari Singh. He had subsequently been posted as Financial Advisor to the 15 Corps Headquarters at Udhampur from 1953-59. I had thus spent my early childhood in Udhampur. From Udhampur one looks eastward to the massive Pir Panjal ranges and the mountains of Bhadarwah and Kishtwar. These had formed the hills of my childhood horizon. Each day as a child, one had seen the sun rise majestically from behind the towering ranges of Bhadarwah. I honestly thought the line where the mountains met the sky, was the edge of my childish universe. It is strange coincidence, that I was now heading for the hills of my childhood memories. I felt a powerful wave of nostalgia and asked to be driven through the town. I stopped to see the house where we had stayed as children in the early 1950s. That multi-storied building had seemed so massive and huge to me as a child, for some reason seemed rather commonplace and diminished in size now. We grow up, our memories remain frozen. The nostalgic diversion was over we sped off to my new action field. Kishtwar lay at the end of a seven hours journey along winding mountain roads through grottos of Pines and stately Fir trees.

We had to turn off from Batote and drive along the NH-1B with the Blue-Green stream of the Chandrabhaga as a constant companion. The gorge gets narrower as you approach Doda and then Thatri. The hills were singularly bare and Khaki. Doda is not an inspiring landscape for the newcomer. From Thatri the Chandrabhaga river takes a sharp almost right-angled turn. The road begins a gradual ascent that grows steeper as you approach the plateau of Kishtwar. The whole valley suddenly opens up to a lovely amphitheatre as one enters the lush green plateau of Kishtwar. Its verdant landscape and Saffron fields are such a marked contrast to the barren-ness and dryness of Doda. The sector HQ is located outside the town in a lush and verdant patch. That was to be my action field of the next two years.

CHAPTER 3

Historic Backdrop: The Insurgency in Kashmir

Backdrop

An analysis of the counter insurgency (CI) operations in Kishtwar must perforce be prefaced with a broader analysis of the Jihadi Terrorist Movement in Kashmir *per se*. A study of the historical backdrop therefore is essential to place the CI/CT operations in Kishtwar in their correct context and perspective.

Pakistan made its first abortive bid to annex Kashmir in 1947 itself. Akbar Khan Bugti and others have offered an insight into this failed putsch. About 10,000 Afghan tribesmen led by Pakistani Army officers in Mufti were launched into Kashmir to seize this strategic state. As Pakistan's representative, Zafrulla Khan was to recount later in the UN General Assembly, Pakistan's prime motivation for seizing Kashmir was not ideological but strategic. Three of Pakistan's six major rivers emanate from Kashmir (the Indus, Chenab and Jhelum). These water sources are critical for Pakistan's agriculture based economy. Pakistan wanted to seize their source—Kashmir and also remove a strategic threat to its capital region of Islamabad-Rawalpindi via the old Mughal route.

This naked geo-strategic ambition has been cloaked in reams of ideological justification and a hypocritical concern for the rights of "self determination" of the Kashmiri people. The simple fact is that in 1947-48, the tribal lashkars let loose such a mayhem of loot, rape and pillage in Kashmir that they served to totally antagonise the local population.

Subsequent Pakistani military narratives lamented the loose discipline of the tribal lashkars, which alienated the population. The Indian Army was flown in; it fought back doggedly and soon had the Pakistanis on the run. Just as we had gained the upper hand militarily—the then Indian political leadership (in its first flush of naiveté and pacifism) took the case to the UNO. It was a strategic blunder, for which we are still paying a steep price.

The river waters sharing dispute was closely linked with the Kashmir dispute in the 1950s. In the hope of resolving both issues, we gave away our bargaining leverages with the Indus Water Treaty in 1961. In the meantime, Pakistan sought to offset her military and material inferiority by invoking extra regional powers—in specific the USA. It joined the SEATO and CENTO alliances and reaped a major windfall of military assistance by renting out its territory for foreign bases. In fact, by 1965, it had not only acquired parity but a discernible edge in armour and artillery and the number of frontline fighter aircraft over India.

India had faced a major politico-military humiliation at the hands of Chinese in 1962. A shaken nation was still reeling under the shock. The sudden and massive expansion process of the Indian Army had commenced and generated a great deal of systemic turbulence. Existing formations had been milked of experienced officers and men to raise new units and formations. The process of the modernisation of the Indian Armed Forces was proceeding apace. Pakistan reckoned that 1965 was its last chance to seize Kashmir by force before the post-1962 expansion process of the Indian Armed Forces was taken to its logical conclusion.

The maverick but brilliant Pakistani officer, Maj Gen Akhtar Hussain Malik had concieved the plan of *Op Gibraltar* and sold it over the head of his Army Chief (Gen Mohd Musa Khan) to Field Marshal Ayub Khan. The plan was an unintended spin off of the Cuban Foco theory of revolution. In the Pakistani estimate, the Kashmiri population was restive and seething under Indian rule. All it would take was a few thousand Pakistani infiltrators to instigate a major rebellion against the Indian regime. Eight columns of Mujahids (with fancy Islamic names like Salaudin, Ghori, etc.) were infiltrated into Kashmir all along the porous gaps in the Line of Control (LC). Three columns were to converge on Srinagar, join the emotive crowds protesting the theft of Hazratbal relic, seize the radio station and key installations, proclaim *'freedom'* and ask for Pakistani assistance. The whole plan was subjective and based on inaccurate assumptions that were far removed from ground realities.

A Gujjar grazier warned the Indian troops of the presence of these infiltrators. Major operations were launched to intercept and destroy these groups. The Kashmiri people showed complete indifference to this invasion cum liberation exercise. In a bold response, India upped the ante by launching tactical level operations to seize/seal off the routes of infiltration. A two brigade sized operation succeeded in capturing the Haji Pir Pass. Pakistan now responded with a grandiose Operation Grandslam to cut the Indian jugular in Akhnur with an Infantry division accompanied by an ad hoc armoured brigade. The operations made a rapid initial progress. India responded by throwing in its Air Force and then in a major surprise move, by attacking across the International Border (IB) towards Lahore and Sialkot in the West Punjab heartland. Pakistan was forced to recoil from Kashmir and fight a battle for its own survival. Its major riposte at Khem Kharan with its First Armoured Division proved to be a major fiasco. Even though the war ended largely as a stalemate, the Pakistani plan to seize Kashmir by military force, lay in smoking ruins.

The Indian military juggernaut completed its build up with Soviet assistance thereafter. Pakistan had lost its last chance to grab Kashmir. In the 1971 War, it courted complete disaster. The country was cut in two and 93,000 Pakistani military personnel surrendered in Bangladesh. Pakistan was now a battered and traumatised nation. Bhutto signed the Shimla Agreement in 1972 (which had unwritten clauses to freeze the existing LC into a permanent border). The Kashmir dispute seemed close to resolution. To avoid a "Versailles" mentality, we once again gave away our bargaining lever of 93,000 Pakistani Prisoners of War (PoW) in the hope for perpetual peace in Kashmir. As subsequent events were to prove, our magnanimity was badly misplaced and the gesture had gone in vain. In fact, it was sadly exploited by Pakistan to get her prisoners back even as it refused to return ours.

Onset of Jihadi Insurgency: Operation Tariq Anwar (TOPAC)

The security scenario in South Asia has undergone a series of dramatic paradigm shifts post 1971. After 1971, the USA and USSR acknowledged India as the pre-eminent South Asian Power. Pakistan was defeated militarily and marginalised geopolitically. All that however changed overnight with the Soviet invasion of Afghanistan in 1979. The decade of the 1970s had been a critical period that saw much ferment in Islamic societies across the globe. In 1973, the Arabs used oil as a weapon and gave the world its first oil shock. The flow of petro-dollars was used to ignite a fundamentalist Islamic revival. The Iranian Islamic Revolution overthrew the Shah of Iran and threw up Ayatollah Khomeini as a new icon of Islamic revivalism. Then came the Soviet invasion of Afghanistan. In a shortsighted tactical move, the American Central Intelligence Agency (CIA) sought to use Islamic Jihad to bleed the Soviets in Afghanistan (in revenge for Vietnam). Pakistan now enthusiastically rented out its territory and border population and became a key frontline state for this Jihad. American military and economic aid poured in. All the gains of the 1971 war were thus neutralised in this decade in one fell swoop. The rise of strident Islamic revivalism had led to politics of fear and appeasement in Kashmir, which unintentionally planted the seeds for a violent Islamic insurgency in the state. Flush with CIA arms and funds, and petro-dollars, Gen Zia-ul Haq of Pakistan anointed himself as a new Islamic Caliph all set to wage Islamic Jihads not just in Afghanistan but even beyond in Soviet Central Asia and more ominously for us in Kashmir. The Pakistani Inter-Services Intelligence (ISI) became a formidable covert action agency. It started terrorism in Punjab and when that petered out, it turned its full attention to Kashmir. Zia-ul Haq had drawn a plan code named Tariq Anwar (The Rock of Gibraltar) for a systemic jihad in Kashmir. The Indian media was awash with its fictionalised version called Op Topac Amru. The plan was unfortunately a sinister reality and not just media hype. In fact, as M J Akbar recounts in his well-researched book, "Tinder Box: The Past and Future of Pakistan" that in 1980 itself Gen Zia-ul Haq had called the Jamait Chief in POK, Maulana Abdul Bari and outlined his plan to him. He clearly told him that Afghanistan was the smoke screen behind which Pakistan would carefully prepare for a more significant battle in Kashmir. "How could the Americans stop us from waging Jihad in Kashmir when they were themselves waging a Jihad in Afghanistan?"

Zia had argued thus to convince the highly skeptical Bari and asked him to establish contact with the Jamait leaders in the Indian Part of J&K

- Bari thereafter met his counterpart in Indian Kashmir—Maulana Saidudin Taribali in a village called Ajis. His message was simple—the Pakistan Army would not start a war but it would pay all the bills for a massive armed uprising in J&K.
- In Sep 1982, writes Akbar, Jamait leaders from Indian Kashmir were taken on a secret visit to Pakistan (via Saudi Arabia—which was their official destination) and briefed in detail about the plan.
- The Jamait leaders were understandably nervous. In 1983 therefore, to convince the latter of Pakistani support, a direct one on one meeting was organised between Gen Zia and Maulana Saidudin.

- This worked and the Jamait cadres set to work to spread venom and rouse the people in J&K for a Pakistan sponsored Jihad. To help them, the ISI had infiltrated its agent provocateurs in the garb of some 2500 displaced Kashmiris who were sent back by Pakistan in the early 1980s. Propoganda material and venomous tapes were freely circulated and Mosque congregations fully made use of to disseminate the virulent diatribes meant to incite communal passions and undercut the syncretic Sufi culture of Kashmir.
- When the first group of Jamat volunteers crossed the LC to get military training in Pakistan Occupied Kashmir (POK), Maulana Saidudin's own son was among them
- The initial batches were trained at the Khalid Bin Walid, Al Faraooq and Abu Jindal camps. The Harkat-ul-Mujahideen (HUM) trained large number of volunteers at the camps in Afghanistan whereas the ISI largely focussed on the camps in POK and Pakistani Punjab itself. To aid deniability for Pakistan and give it the trappings of a so called freedom movement, this phase had focussed on the slogan of Azadi and was led by the Jammu and Kashmir Liberation Front (JKLF).
- The simple fact is that to date the Army has recovered over 80,000 AK series of rifles, some 1300 machine guns, 2000 Rocket launchers, some 63,000 hand grenades and some 37.000 kgs of Explosives in J&K. This is enough to equip almost two corps of the Army. This was what was recovered by the Army. The ISI had sent in much more than this. This then was a war and had to be fought as such. Many of our bleeding heart liberals have simply no idea of what we were up against in J&K. With its abundant supply of weapons and well trained cadres, the ISI had turned J&K into a full fledged war zone.With this factual backdrop, the story that the electoral malpractises of the 1988 elections in J&K were the root cause of the insurgency is something of a joke.

Roots of Jihad

The roots of the current terrorist movement in J&K can thus be traced to the success of the Islamic Revolution in Iran in the 1970s and the Afghan War in the 1980s (in which the ISI became the bridgehead for covert action against the USSR). Gen Zia-ul Haq diverted a large quantum of US arms for Afghan Mujahideen into J&K. Another contributory factor for the growth of militant communalism in the valley was the return of 2,500 displaced Kashmiris from Pakistan in early 1980s. The ISI exploited these to induct a large number of trained agent provocateurs who began to spread the agenda of a virulent and anti-secular interpretation of Islam. The Mulla-Khwaja (trader) combine in the valley promoted fundamentalism and feudalism and provided over-ground support for the nascent terrorist movement. Rubaiya Saeed was kidnapped in 1989. The timid response of the State and Central government gave a major fillip to the terrorist movement. The best way to understand the course of the Kashmiri insurgency is to summarise its annual progression from 1990 to the present time. The annual landmark events of this rebellion have been listed below to provide the overview of our counter proxy war effort in Kashmir. This overview is critical for understanding the basic nuances of our CI/CT campaign in J&K.

(a) ***1990***. The ISI agent provocateurs had slipped in with the 2,500 returning displaced kashmiri persons and started preaching the gospel of hate and intolerance in this placid valley. There was a large scale exodus of J&K youth to Pakistan for arms training in camps in POK and elsewhere. This was the buildup phase of the terrorist movement. Some 1250 terrorists infiltrated into J&K and some 550 were killed by the Security Forces (SF).

(b) ***1991-92.*** These indoctrinated youth were trained in ever increasing numbers and reinducted to start a large scale terrorist movement, which was then spearheaded by the Jammu & Kashmir Liberation Front (JKLF). This was the first heady and romantic phase of this movement. The dream of independent Kashmir (Azad Kashmir) seemed but a short struggle away. There was an unreal sense of *Déjà vu* and euphoria. The marching tune then was "*Tez chalo sathiyo, saamne manzil hai* (move fast comrades, the goal is near)". It was a goal too far. The initial practice was to cross the LC in large bands. In December 1990 a group of 100 terrorists had been intercepted in Uri. In March 1991 a group of 80 terrorists was killed after crossing over in Dubli in Chaokibal. This trend was to continue till 1993. By then however 760 kms stretch of the Kashmir LC was greatly strengthened,. Despite this due to the extreme ruggedness of the terrain and overall paucity of troops some 1400 terrorists infiltrated in 1991 and some 3045 in 1992.

(c) ***1993.*** The J&K Police Revolt occurred in 1993 and was successfully quelled. Concerted Army CI operations began the process of inflicting severe attrition on the terrorist groups. A record number of some 3045 terrorists entered J&K that year. The Pakistani ISI

Author at his Sector HQ in Kishtwar

Authors convoy enroute to an operation near Kishtwar

Commanders escort on move

Mi-17 Helicopter landing at Navapachi

Khankhu Dhar backdrop

Kishtwar in Winter

On way to Gulabgarh-Machail

now started a fratricidal struggle between the Hizbul Mujahideen (HM) and the JKLF. The pro-independence slogan and ideology of the JKLF just did not suit them. The fratricidal conflict between these groups helped the Indian Army. The JKLF was virtually wiped out over the next two years. The ISI also stepped in to starve it of funds and resources. After Hazratbal, the Harkat-ul-Ansar with its Afghan alumni began to cross over. They shifted their routes of infiltration southwards to the Rajouri-Punch sector. The size of infiltrating bands had come down to 10 or less.

(d) ***1994-96.*** A bomb blast in Badami Bagh Cantt killed eight officers including the Directorate General of Military Intelligence (DGMI) designate in 1994. Concerted CI operations by the Army in 1994 and 1995 led to very heavy attrition on the terrorist tanzeems (in specific, the JKLF). From a peak terrorist cadre strength in 1993 (all groups), the figure *was brought down drastically. Some 1596 terrorists were killed in 1994 and another 1332 the next year* (see Attrition Fig. 3). What must be understood however is that the bulk of the attrition inflicted was on the independence seeking JKLF cadres. Pakistan's ISI was not happy with this group as it was showing signs of independence and autonomy. It covertly abetted with its elimination and encouraged the rise of pro-Pakistan Hizbul Mujahideen and other Jihadi groups. Even as the JKLF was wiped out, some 3200 cadres of the Hizbul Mujahideen and other Jihadi tanzeems were infiltrated in 1995. This period therefore marks the end of the indigenous Kashmiri struggle for independence and the rise of Pakistan instigated Islamic terrorism in Kashmir. Increasingly this struggle was taken over by Pak-sponsored foreign militants and the ISI's recruits from the Afghan jihad. The face of "militancy" in the valley was transformed forever. The Indian Army had crushed the "Azadi rebellion". The J&K struggle would have ended here had it not been for the Pakistani intervention in a very major way of inducting 3200 fresh cadres in 1995.

(e) ***1996.*** The very serious attrition imposed on the terrorist tanzeems brought their numbers to a manageable level that permitted the successful conduct of the Parliamentary Elections in May 1996 and the Assembly Elections in September 1996. An elected State Government was installed in office in October 1996 in J&K. This was a significant turning point in the Counter-Proxy War, for which the lion's share of the credit must go to the Indian Army's 15 Corps, then led by Lt Gen S Padmanabhan (who subsequently rose to be the Northern Army Commander and then the Army Chief).

(f) ***1997.*** The terrorist strength was further decimated in 1996 and in 1997. Pakistan now decided to extend the arc of terrorism to South Kashmir, to the Rajouri and Punch area and intensify terrorism in Doda and even Jammu. The reliance had by now shifted entirely from JKLF to HM and other Jihadi tanzeems (pro-Pakistan) with a large Foreign Terrorist (FT) content. In fact, the terrorist content had reached almost 60 per cent.

(g) ***1998.*** Lok Sabha polls were successfully completed in 1998. This was a major feather in the cap of the Counter Insurgent Forces. Possibly in prepration for Kargil a record number of 3720 terrorists crossed over in this year

(h) ***1999.*** Pakistan tried to internationalise the Kashmir issue by exploiting the nuclear card to stage massive infiltration in Kargil. Op Vijay succeeded in throwing out the infiltrators and causing a major set back to Pakistani efforts. However, the large scale disruption of the CI grid gave another lease of life to terrorism and caused a set back to our counter terrorist drive in the hinterland.

(i) ***2000-2001***. Despite continual attrition the terrorist strength in J&K had stabilised at a level of 2,500-3,100. In 2000-2001 the Indian army raised some 36 additional battalions of the RR and inducted more troops to intensify operations in J&K. The highest levels of attrition were inflicted in this year. Extensive efforts at infiltration tended to make up losses suffered at the hands of the Security Forces (SFs). Pakistan under Gen Musharraf made an all out attempt to up the ante and the levels of infiltration really shot up in 2000-2002. There were 2040 terrorists who came in the year 2000. In 2001 these numbers shot up to 3486 (to make up for the record number that were killed in the year 2001 as the Indian Army increased its force levels and intensified its operations). A major turning point now came with Al Qaeda's terror bombing in New York in September 2001. America declared *Global War on Terror* and Pakistan was forced to abandon the Taliban. This brought about a major paradigm shift in the situation. Attacks on the J&K Assembly in October 2001 and the Indian Parliament in December 2001 succeeded in crossing the Indian tolerance threshold and Op Parakram was launched to force Pakistan to retract overt/covert support to the terrorist movement in J&K. This mobilisation was partially successful and for a time forced Pakistan to call off overt military support to the terrorist tanzeems. However, covert funding and support continued. The next year-2002, the Pakistanis infiltrated a record number of 3543 terrorists (to make up for the highest attrition level of 2020 terrorists killed in the year 2001 in J&K) even as troops were mobilised for Op Parakram and taken off from CI operations to ready for possible conventional operations. The years 2000-2001 therefore were the phase of the peak of attrition in J&K and one was fortunate to be a part of this most intense phase of operations. The Indian army in J&K was then led by a very professional soldier, Lt Gen Rustom Nanavati and the highest levels of attrition were inflicted on the Jihadi tanzeems in his watch. The figures of terrorist casualties and Infiltration clearly highlight that this was the grimmest phase of the fighting when both India and Pakistan intensified operations and infiltration in J&K to seek a final resolution of sorts. Over 2000 terrorists were killed in 2001 but as per the pattern, Pakistan simply infiltrated that many more into J&K to keep the Proxy war going. Finding the troop density too high in J&K, Pakistan also tried to spread the terror attacks into the rest of India—especially on iconic targets like the Parliament. What was becoming obvious was that the infiltration tap would have to be turned off—either through coercion/ raising the costs by escalating to the conventional level or as was attempted from 2003 onwards, by fencing the LC itself. The threat of conventionalising the conflict worked for some time in Op Parakram and forced Musharraf to make some placatory noises initially. However, as India failed to actualise its threat of a limited war, the Pakistanis were gradually emboldened and the pressure wore off. A mere threatening deployment not accompanied by any actual operations was not enough to coerce Pakistan and that left the purely defensive option of fencing the LC alone. This was finalised by Gen Vij as the Chief in 2003 (the Punjab precedent proved quite useful) and it succeeded in reducing infiltration to the extent of some 60-70 per cent and more. This choking of infiltration was the real turning point of the J&K campaign and by 2005 the back of the terrorist tanzeems in J&K was quite decisively broken. I once again had the good fortune of being a part of this intensive phase now as General Officer Commanding (GOC) of Romeo Force in Rajouri and Punch. Notwithstanding this analysis—the crucial fact is that the first instalment of the drop in infiltration came in 2003—before the Fence was completed. The final drop came in 2005 after the fence was in place. What was the first drop due to? The intense attrition imposed on the Jihadi Tanzeems in 2001-02? Or was it due to intense American pressure on Pervez Musharraf to stave off an Indo-Pakistan War? It seems a combination of both. However, US pressure on India and Pakistan to negotiate peace over J&K really increased after 2004 when the UPA regime came to power.

The Attrition Curve

A quantitative overview of Counter Terrorist (CT) operations in J&K is provided by the annual attrition curve of the terrorists. This gives a very accurate index of the effectiveness of our operations over the years and highlights the efficacy of the attrition principle in CT operations. This graphical representation in effect sums up the historical course of the Indian Army operations in J&K and is critical to its understanding (see Fig. 3).

Thus, two clear peaks of attrition appear in the years 1993-1995 when the JKLF was decimated and then again from 2000-2003 when very severe attrition was imposed on the Jihadi tanzeems by significantly raising troop levels. Once the fence was completed in 2006, we find a steep decline in infiltration and concomitantly on attrition (see Fig. 4).

The SF casualties also rise appreciably in the years 2000-2003 when the fighting was at its most intense level. These decline sharply after 2005 once the fence was completed (see Fig. 5).

The peak of infiltration first came in 1992-1993 to make up for the decimation of the JKLF. From 1995 to 1999 the infiltration was maintained at a level of over 3000 a year to make up for the rates of attrition and widen the arc of terrorism to south of the Pir Panjals. There is a final burst of infiltration in the years 2001-2002 before it falls steeply in 2003 to below 2000. The construction of the fence was started in that year but completed only in 2005. Hence, the major drop in 2003 could also be attributed partly to Pakistan perhaps scaling down its infiltration due to intense American pressure.

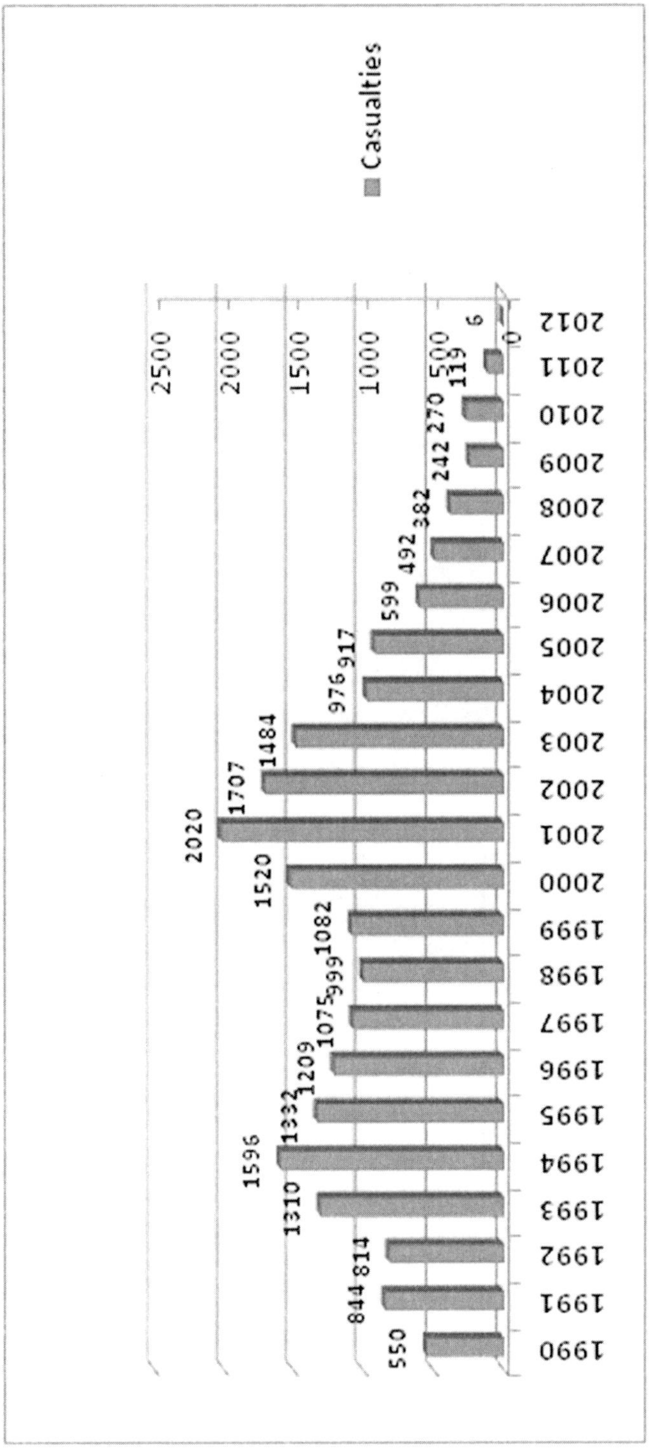

Figure 3 Terrorist Casualties

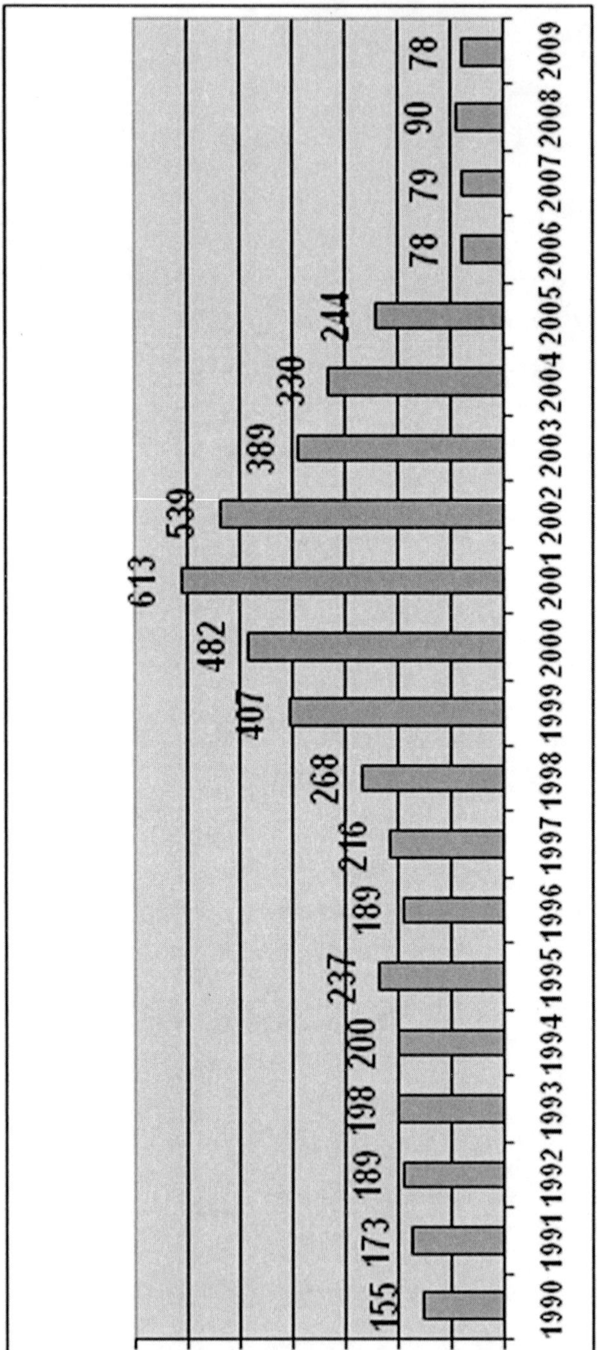

Figure 4 Security Forces Casualties

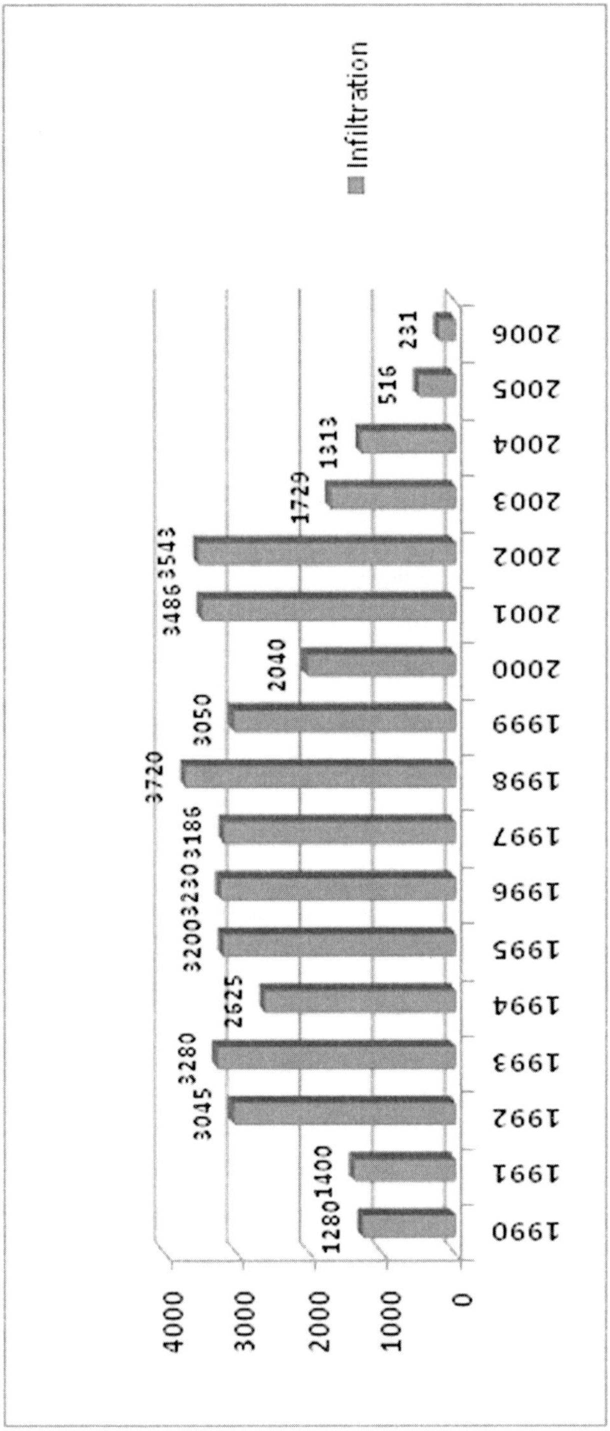

Figure 5 Infiltration Profile: J&K

CHAPTER 4

The Spread of Jihadi Insurgency in Doda

The spillover of Jihadi insurgency from the Kashmir valley to the vast and sprawling hinterland of the district of Doda can be studied in two phases:

(a) Phase One - 1990-1994
(b) Phase Two - 1995-Present

Phase One

Doda is a huge and sprawling district, in fact the second largest in the whole of India. It encompasses an area of over 11,691 sq kms of the most difficult and rugged terrain in the whole of J&K. It spreads out to Himachal Pradesh in the South and to Ladakh in the North and West. In the East the mighty Pir Panjals serve to separate it from the Kashmir valley. Kashmiri terrorists first came into Doda to escape the pressure of Indian Army operations in the valley. They used its higher pastures as a safe haven and sanctuary. They often sought shelter with the Gujjars and Bakkarwals in their Dhoks and alpine pastures. They used this area initially for rest and recuperation and later for training. The first such groups had begun to slip into Doda in 1991 itself.

1992. The ISI soon realised the vast potential of this unheld Doda region as a classical guerilla base area. It decided to spread the insurgency to this remote region that had no Indian military presence. Pakistani ISI agents were inducted in an advisory role and Saidulla Tantrey, a Pakistani trained militant of the Hizbul Mujahideen (HM—the military arm of the Jamat-e-Islami) was made the Chief Area Commander of Doda district. The terrorists started their depredations on a minor scale and soon made their presence felt. The Army had its hands full in the valley and did not want to be sucked into the vast hinterland. It was felt that this would take it well away from the LC and would hamper a rapid transition to conventional operations when needed. As such, the government rushed in two Border Security Force (BSF) battalions to Doda to assist the civil administration and the beleaguered police. On 16 August 1993, the terrorists carried out a massacre of 14 Hindus in a bus near Hasti (close to Kishtwar). It sent shock waves over the whole country. The intention was clear—to carry out an ethnic cleansing of the Hindus of Doda and force them to migrate like the Kashmiri Pandits. Later, there were whispers that this ethnic cleansing drive was to block an actualisation of Owen-Dixon Plan, which called for a partition of J&K between India and Pakistan along the Chenab-Ravi faultline. This ethnic cleansing took on an ominous form during my tenure as Sector Commander. The Owen-Dixon Plan had actually been discussed in back channel diplomacy prior to the Kargil Conflict. However, in the 1990s there was a spate of killing of prominent citizens, arson of government buildings and police stations and local temples. Initially some units of an Infantry Brigade located at Udhampur had been inducted into this area temporarily for specific operations. After the Hasti massacre, however, Headquarters 16 Corps was given full responsibility of the Doda district for CI operations.

1994. By 1994, the Islamic insurgency in Doda had achieved full blown form. The civil administration was totally paralysed. The number of Jihadi terrorists went up to almost 800-900 (led by an initial batch of some 20-25 Pakistani militants). 800 Dogra families migrated to Himachal Pradesh. In response to this crisis situation an Infantry Brigade was deployed in Doda. These were—partial knee jerk responses. Ultimately in September 1994 CI Force Delta was raised to bring this area under control. Its first GOC was Maj Gen Behel of the Gurkhas. It had four Rashtriya Rifles (RR) Battalions, six BSF Battalions and some 35 companies of CRPF were allocated to it. Intensive Counter Insurgency operations were launched and the remote hills and jungles with their numerous caves and khuds combed extensively. 9 Sector Rashtriya Rifles was raised in August 1994 and after initial moving around settled in Kishtwar to take charge of operations here. It was raised by Brig Bhuman Rajan of the Armoured corps and since then, a large part of its rituals and ceremonials followed the traditions of our Cavalry.

Phase Two

1995. Major successes were achieved by CI Force Delta in 1995. The ISI had diverted a number of its Sudanese volunteers from the Afghan Jihad into Kashmir and Doda. These Sudanese groups had become active in the forested areas of Thatri-Tanta-Halaran and the Jaigad forests in Bhaderwah. They had set up so called liberated zones. Relentless pressure by the security forces now began to cause significant attrition on the militant tanzeems. A number of liberated zones were cleared. To prevent mass migration of the Dogra minority, the Village Defence Committee (VDC) Scheme was revived and some 330 villages were brought under the protection of VDCs by issuing weapons to the local Hindu youths and ex-servicemen of these hamlets.

1996. By early 1996 the intensive CI efforts began to pay off. A large number of key terrorist leaders were killed. These included Zulkar Nain, a District Commander (DC) of the Lashkar-e-Toiba (LeT), Raja Daud Manhas, District Commander of the Harkat-ul-Ansar (HuA), Javed Qureshi, the Provincial Commander of HM. The terrorist tanzeems were shaken by these leadership kills. The situation was stabilised to a large extent. In fact, such a lull descended on the area that the government was emboldened to go in for Lok Sabha elections and then Assembly elections. In desperation, the terrorists responded by three massacres of Dogras—16 were killed in Barsohala; 10 in Kam Lein and 13 in Saruwa. Despite these killings the Lok Sabha elections were held on schedule. There was a 62 per cent voter turnout (which was the highest in the whole of J&K state). Encouraged by this the government went ahead and held the Assembly elections in September 1996. There was 50 per cent turnout and a popularly elected government was installed in J&K. This lull in terrorist activities led to a false sense of complacency. Six BSF Battalions were now de-inducted from the Doda district in end 1996. It was a tragic mistake. Concerted CI operations in an area tend to drive away the terrorists to remote hideouts or neighbouring districts for their survival. This leads to a situation of relative or apparent calm and no 'terrorist nutrilisations'. This can be very deceptive. In such circumstances it is essential to retain SF presence for an extended period to ensure full migration/elimination of the terrorists. To take an analogy, the process is like forcibly drowning a man. An initial struggle is needed to push him down below the water. He then has to be kept down there till the last bubbles stop emanating from his mouth or nose. Any premature withdrawal of pressure can cause him to leap back. This "premature withdrawal syndrome" was to prove the bane of CI operations in the Doda district.

1997. Unfortunately this withdrawal of Six battalions from Doda coincided with a change in ISI strategy in Kashmir. The ISI now deliberately decided to enlarge the arc of terror and spread its Islamic insurgency focus to the

Rajouri-Poonch, Doda and Jammu region. A large number of locals had been recruited and sent across for training. Some 60-70 foreign terrorists were now inducted into the Doda area to restart the militancy. The rejuvenated terrorist tanzeems struck back in 1998 with vicious massacres of the Hindu minority. Three horrific killings took place as part of the diabolic design of ethnic cleansing in this area. A documentation of these attempts of ethnic cleansing provides some horrifying details:

(a) ***19 June 1998***. 25 Dogras were massacred in a place called Chepnari

(b) ***19 July 1998***. 23 Dogras were killed in Kalaban in neighbouring Chamba

(c) ***27 July 1998***. 16 Dogras were killed in Horna/Keshwan adjacent to Kishtwar itself

Additional troops were now rushed in a largely reactive, knee jerk response. Five additional battalions of the RR/Army were now sent to 9 Sector to launch concerted CT operations. This was the peak military strength ever inducted in Kishtwar and a record number of 51 terrorists were killed in the year 1998. Another 15 were apprehended and some 24 surrendered. Operation Vigil—groups comprising of Army personnel from the local areas were raised to energise, motivate and train the Village Defence Committees. There were signs of hope that the worst was over and the Doda-Kishtwar region had been pacified.

1999. However, the very next year, Op Vijay caught the country by surprise. All the troops of 9 Sector were now rapidly taken out of Kishtwar and redeployed for Rear Area Security duties in the Rajouri-Poonch area to cater for any Pakistani attacks in this area. The Pakistani attacks never materialised. However, the entire CI grid had been removed from Kishtwar. The terrorists took the fullest advantage. They brutally murdered a large number of the sources and informers of the Indian Army. Some of them were skinned alive. The entire intelligence grid that had been built up so laboriously was badly disrupted overnight. No rear area threat materialised in Rajouri but the CI grid in Kishtwar was badly destabilised. On 20 July 1999, the terrorists massacred 15 Hindus at the Liyota village. The situation was deteriorating rapidly. This shocked the hierarchy into action. 9 Sector was now rushed back with just two Rashtriya Rifles Battalions and later 5 Sikh Light Infantry was also sent in. The overall force level in Kishtwar was now scaled down from its peak level of five Army units to just three. Despite this disruption, the units set to work with a will. They tried to piece together the severely disrupted intelligence set up. The terrified sources asked then—was the Army going to stay or would it again leave them at the tender mercy of the terrorists? The RR did its best to reassure them. Slowly intelligence started trickling in again. A total of 43 terrorists were killed in this year despite the diversion of troops for Op Vijay for over three months. One of the Infantry battalions of 9 Sector RR (5 Sikh Li) was taken away and redeployed along the National Highway.

2000. 9 Sector resumed its relentless operations in Kishtwar. The terrorist leadership came under intense pressure. They soon retaliated by targeting the minority in a major way. In the year 2000, they carried out a total of six mass killings of the Hindu minority as under:

(a) 01 August 2000 : 5 Dogras were killed at Murlakot
(b) 01 August 2000 : 12 Dogras were killed at Kunda
(c) 01 August 2000 : 4 Dogras were killed at Dhammota
(d) 02 August 2000 : 8 Dogras were killed at Kiar
(e) 21 November 2000 : 4 Dogras were killed at Khanpura
(f) 24 November 2000 : 5 Dogras were killed at Patimahal

This was when I joined the struggle in Kishtwar at the end of the year (Oct) and tried to re-energise the operations. It took a major effort but soon we were inflicting significant attrition upon the terrorist. The HM's field commander Mazid Dar offered an abortive ceasefire in July 2000. This was, however, countermanded by his supremo Salauddin ensconced in Muzaffarabad. On 29 November 2000, the Indian government launched its own peace initiative in the form of an offer for Non-Initiation of Combat Operations (NICO). This was supposed to set the stage for a political dialogue with the militants and the Hurriyat. It was a well intentioned offer but unfortunately the terrorists tried their best to take advantage of it to get a reprieve from military operations and used this period to rest, regroup and bring in more trained cadres across the LC. A total of 43 terrorists were eliminated in the year 2000 by the SF in the Kishtwar Area.

Overview of Operations in Kishtwar

Ethnic Cleansing: The salient feature of the Jihadi terrorist campaign in Doda-Kishtwar was the blatant emphasis on ethnic cleansing of the Hindu minority. The peculiar ethnic composition of this region (53.2 per cent Muslims; 39.3 per cent Hindus) encouraged the terrorists to undertake this blatantly genocidal campaign. The world has heard no end of the horrors of genocide of Bosnia. There was no cogent reason why our response to these massacres should have been so muted and played down.

Secularism does not imply that we accept ethnic cleansing of any community in this day and age. Our information warfare strategy should have hinged on fully exposing Pakistan and her terrorist zealots for this horrible genocide. The Kashmiri Pandits had already been driven out of the valley and have been languishing in refugee camps for over two decades. The ISI strategy in Doda-Kishtwar was blatantly premised upon carrying out an ethnic cleansing exercise designed to cause a mass migration of the minority community from this scenic region. Possibly the overall design was to strike South of Chenab to cause a migration of the Dogras population and thereby change the demographic pattern. This was possibly being done to gain advantage in any projected negotiations based on a possible partition of Kashmir along the Chinab river, that may be mooted by the international community at any later stage. It was a cold blooded and cynical exercise. It is a pity that this ethnic cleansing design was actually carried out. Thus, from 1993-2001 a total of 229 Dogras were systematically massacred in a cold blooded exercise of ethnic cleansing within the Kishtwar area. There were specific acts of mass killing directed against the minority community and this figure does not include the hundreds of other civilians (both Muslims and Hindus), who were killed in other specific incidents of terrorist related violence (e.g., Killing of sources/informers). The chatteratti of Delhi and the keepers of the world's conscience (the Human Rights Organisation) had not a word of condemnation or remorse for this exercise of ethnic cleansing. The Human Rights lobby that has been so shrill and vocal on other issues kept a deafening silence on this one. It was indeed a great pity and exhibition of rank hypocrisy and double standards. There is crying need for us to sensitise the world's conscience on this issue of the ISI's ethnic cleansing in Doda-Kishtwar and earlier in Kashmir. The ISI bosses who ordered this ethnic cleansing must one day be brought to trial for crimes against humanity. Crimes as serious as genocide and ethnic cleansing can hardly be overlooked. Radovan Karodzic, the Serb leader of Yugoslavia is currently being tried by a war crimes tribunal in Hague for the genocide and ethnic cleansing of the Muslim Serbs. Why should the ISI bosses not be targeted for the same crime?

Premature Withdrawals: A cursory look at the history of operations in the Kishtwar hinterland indicates that whenever a semblance of normalcy had been restored by concerted CI operations, we tended to misread the situation and withdraw troops in a very premature fashion. This often led to tragic consequences later. The troop withdrawals were done by harried commanders and staff facing a serious overall shortage of troops and resources. These withdrawals however led to a serious dilution of the CI grid which emboldened the terrorists to stage massacres. It also gave them needless reprieves and allowed them to regain their balance and reorganise themselves in these gap periods. The worst part was the disruption caused to the intelligence grid. Withdrawal of troops endangered the local sources and informants they had cultivated in the area and these were usually victims of terrible reprisals by the terrorists. It is incumbent on the troops to safeguard their sources and shield them from such reprisals.

The clear lesson learnt is that in areas where we are gaining success/ the upper hand, it is imperative that we retain the CI grid and maintain the pressure *for a minimum of two to three years after normalcy has been restored.* This will ensure that there are no premature withdrawal and relapses in the insurgency situation. Possibly our strategy should be to focus on such areas where terrorist morale/tanzeems are crumbling and gradually roll back the arc of Pakistani-sponsored terrorism in Kashmir. This roll back strategy of reinforcing success will be taken up in more detail in the succeeding chapters. In CT operations, what happens (in terms of attrition on terrorist tanzeems) is important. What is equally important is *what does not happen* (i.e., no terrorist atrocities or ethnic cleansing, etc.). At a macro level, the same syndrome of premature withdrawal of security forces is being repeated in the whole of J&K as an insecure Chief Minister has been tom tomming calls for the withdrawal of the Army and a dilution/partial removal of the Armed Forces Special Powers Act (AFSPA) from specified districts in J&K. 2014 will see a withdrawal of US and NATO forces from Afghanistan and hence a new surge of infiltration of J&K as surplus Taliban cadres are diverted eastwards. In such a situation lowering our guard by removing the AFSPA would amount to opening the gates for the huns. Similar is the even more sinister demand for disbanding the VDCs. Is it the aim to facilitate terrorist massacre of the minorities?

CHAPTER 5

Sector Commander Kishtwar: Energising an Organisation

Reception

HQ CI Force Delta had organised a very structured reception for me. This included an exhaustive briefing by the Staff at the Force HQ. In the evening I met the GOC Maj Gen (later Lt Gen) Mohinder Singh of the Punjab Regiment. He had been the Brigade Commander during the Charar-e-Sharif episode and was a very experienced officer in Counter Terrorist (CT) operations. I was a little miffed when he told me, "Your sector is letting grass grow under its feet." The sector had inflicted some 34 kills till then but for the last two months it had apparently gone into a shell. Whether it was a normal "maize phenomenon" (a seasonal degrade caused by the Maize crop in J&K that grows almost 10-12 feet high and severely curtails visibility. Chances of collateral damage rise in this period and hence troops consciously curtail their operations till the crop is cut) or something else was difficult to say at that stage. I assured him I would look into the matter and limber up things at the earliest.

The next day, I left with my star plates on. The thought of sneaking in on my new command, with the fear of Improvised Explosive Devices (IEDs) writ all over my convoy was not one which enthused me overly. Accordingly, I had brushed aside my DQs sage counsel to travel incognito on the IED prone roads. In fairness to my staff officer, I must add that he was not exaggerating. Just two weeks ago, my course mate, Brig Bobby Sital Shergill had assumed command of 7 Sector RR. His vehicle was ambushed and blown off by an IED within a week of his arrival. He and his Commanding Officer, both had died on the spot in this ambush which had actually been laid for the Commanding Officer (CO). With this somber thought at the back of our minds, for comfort, we set off from Batote. The main issue however was one of symbolism and sending the right message to one's command. In those days a pernicious practice had started of senior officers travelling incognito in civil clothes and civil vehicles to avoid being targeted. This sometimes went to ludicrous lengths and sent a very bad signal of rank cowardice to ones troops. Since I was required to get an organisation operationally limbered up, I had to be careful of the kind of message I was sending to my command on arrival. We turned off National Highway (NH) 1A to NH-1B. We drove past Doda and by lunch time reached Thatri. This was the HQ of 26 RR.

Col Anil Khosla, the CO gave me a preliminary briefing. The unit was affiliated to the Kumaon and Naga Regiments. The secondary Arm Affiliation was with the Mechanised Infantry Regiment. One good feature was the Special Teams. The CO had raised three Special Teams based on the Regimental Affiliations. The Kumaon Team, the Naga Team and the "Kavach" (Mechanised) Team had gained good results in operations. In the context of the Polygot mixtures that the RR units were, this was a good device to generate small team cohesion and effectiveness. All RR COs who invested in creating such quality teams usually did well in combat.

Overcoming the Morale Problem

Briefing over we went to the Mess for lunch. I scanned the faces of the officers there. It was frankly disconcerting to see grim and downcast faces. "When did you last go on leave?" I asked the young Captain next to me.

"Eight months ago, Sir." I was shocked and turned to the CO for an explanation. It is an unstated dictum in the RR (and for that matter for any unit engaged in active operations), each man must get a break after every 90 days in combat. This is not an arbitrary figure but one arrived at after considerable analysis of data from World War-II, Korea and some more recent conflicts. The CO hastened to explain that the officer was attached for a disciplinary proceeding and as such his leave had been stopped by the Force headquarters. When I enquired about the nature of the problem, he told me about the "Massacre in Navapachi Post" that had taken place a year and a half ago.

"What was this Captain's role in that affair", I enquired.

"He was then the Regimental Medical Officer (RMO) Sir. He was sent in to treat the injured civilians. That is why he is an essential witness."

The young RMO turned to me in desperation. "Sir, my mother is very sick. Could I kindly go on some casual leave?" I looked at him and felt moved. "Send him on casual leave. I'll speak to the GOC," I told the CO.

The young Company Commander who was at the centre of this media storm was sitting opposite me. Gloom and despair was writ large on his face. He had finished his RR tenure but was stuck here for the past year and a half. Along with him were attached one JCO and nine boys. The summary of evidence was dragging on and on, as the civilian witnesses were refusing to testify.

"What happened", I asked the erstwhile post commander.

"Sir, It was the Id of 1999. Large crowds had gathered for celebrations at Navapachi."

A source came and informed the post that a group of terrorists had entered the fringe houses of Yordu village across the Maru River. They were planning to attack the company post. He sent a JCO led column to check out. They saw four suspicious strangers who did not belong to that village. The terrorists had probably hidden their weapons. So they apprehended them and started moving back to the post with them. As they approached a log bridge near the Navapachi village—a huge crowd assembled there. It began pelting stones and shouting slogans. The RR column was stuck. The only way across was over the narrow log bridge and through the crowd. As they were getting on to the bridge—the large crowd surged towards them. Some terrorist sympathisers and OGWs in the crowd now attacked them and tried to snatch their weapons and free the prisoners. A real melee started. In the violent melee scuffles led to shots going off. Possibly some terrorist who were merged with the crowd also opened fire. In panic, the JCO opened fire to save the lives of his men. In the confused melee, nine civilians were killed. There was a national furore. The then Prime Minister, Mr Gujral, himself flew down to Kishtwar to assuage the hurt feelings and offered a Rs 1.20 crore package for the development of these villages and compensation for the victims. The young major fidgeted nervously in his seat. Then point blank he asked me a question.

"Sir, what was expected of my men? Were we required to hand over the weapons and the prisoners to the mob? Would that have saved their lives?"

I looked at him but said nothing. For months thereafter, the young Major's question continued to haunt me. I could not shake off the hunted and desperate look on his face. What would have I done in his place? Navapachi was a heli-maintained post some three days march from the nearest road head. On that day the terrorists had mingled with the crowds and were shouting pro-Pakistani slogans from the mosque. Maybe it would have been more mature not to have launched the operation that day. What would the men have thought of their Major then? He was from the Armoured Corps and keen to prove his mettle in a combat environment. Not going out to check information about terrorists in the vicinity of the post could have given a wrong message in a combat zone.

"Anyhow, having launched the operation, what would I have done on the log bridge", I asked myself. As I lay on my bed in Kishtwar that night, with my arm over my face, I tried not to think of that young Major. I also tried not to think of my family. But the Major's dejected face continued to haunt me. What would I have done in his place?

The answer came to me with astonishing clarity the next morning. I would have opened fire in self defence. For if I had not, I would have been accused of the military disgrace of losing my weapons.

The CO had told me that the presence of these unfortunate undertrials in the unit was taking a toll on the morale of his men. Each day they saw them stuck behind in a field area, one and a half years after their three years term of duty in J&K had ended. Their leave was blocked and at the mercy of the Judge Advocate General (JAG) department of the army who were so well-versed in the fine print and nuances of the law. The process of the enquiries and trial sometimes becomes worse than the punishment itself. I thought long and hard over the incident. If I was serving in 26 RR and watched these Navapachi lot day in and day out in their misery, would I be much enthused to prosecute vigorous CT operations, where so many things could go wrong? If you killed a terrorist all glory would be yours. God forbid, if you killed a civilian by mistake (and most encounters are over in fleeting seconds), you could be attached here for years after your tenure got over in the field area. Your leave would be stopped and the mental agony and torture of an extended court of enquiry followed by a court martial would be your fate. Would you be very motivated then to prosecute vigorous CT operations, where if anything goes wrong, you would be left in the lurch and be taken over the coals? I asked myself the question. "Would you still prosecute counter terrorist operations with your heart and soul? Come what may, I could not force myself to answer in the affirmative.

People who have not served in CT operations in their lives have no idea of the agonising decision dilemmas that the troops in the field face. They have only seconds to decide and that decision could make the difference between life and death or military disgrace. Let me elucidate. A patrol is waiting in ambush outside the maize field at 0530 hours in the morning. The maize grows 10-12 feet tall in J&K. It is freezing cold and the teeth are chattering. Suddenly the men notice the maize shaking and swaying. What could it be? Terrorists armed to the teeth or some village women coming for their morning ablutions? The soldiers raise their weapons and wait tensely. They finally see three tall men in *phirans*. They can see their arms protruding under the Phirans. What are they carrying? *Kangris* (Wicker baskets with hot coals) to warm themselves, or AK-56 Kalashnikov rifles to commence shooting within seconds? These are agonising seconds indeed. If they open fire and kill civilians, they could be in serious trouble. If they don't open fire the terrorists could shoot first and they all could end up as dead or wounded. In such encounters, he who shoots first—usually kills.

We have a strong Human Rights lobby in our country. The media goes ballistic with a shrill outcry the moment any civilians are killed even by mistake. The West preached lofty sermons to us on human rights. However, thereafter the Americans were involved in major operations in Iraq and Afghanistan. There the American and British armies used every single weapon in their armoury (from B-52 Stratofortress bombers to F-16s and Warthog jet fighters, to Abraham tanks and huge 155 mm canons and rockets) against the people of Iraq or Afghanistan. Very strangely indeed there was no outcry in the Western Press then. It gave us an agonising insight into international hypocrisy. How there are patently different yardsticks for Human rights if the US or western (White Caucasian) armies are involved and how the scene changes dramatically if the Indian army is concerned? How sometimes atrocity accusations are standard psychological warfare tactics to degrade and disrupt the CT operations and give reprieve to terrorist organisations that are under tremendous pressure from the Security Forces in Third World countries? The shrill media outcry puts the Army on the backfoot, slows down its operations and takes the heat off the tanzeems.

Where human rights outcries stem from genuine compassion, they are laudable indeed. However, where they are a part of a well orchestrated psy-ops campaign by terrorist supporters and Over Ground Workers (OGWs) designed to hamper and slowdown Security forces operations, it is criminal for us to get duped and berate our own soldiers, who risk their lives in a thankless war—day in and day out. The pity is no one gives a damn about the human rights of soldiers in this proxy war. The even greater pity is that there are some foreign funded NGOs in India who have made it their business to berate our security forces and undermine the legitimacy of their operations via their shrill and strident propaganda

I decided to speak to the GOC about the Navapachi boys. The opportunity was not long in coming. We had the Civil-Military Liaison Conference at the Force HQ, a few days after I assumed command of the Sector. I met the GOC and he asked me, "So why are we not getting any results in 9 Sector for the last two months?"

"Sir, I am amazed that despite all these courts of enquiries and summaries of evidence the boys have killed 34 terrorists this year." I gave him the details. The General arched an eyebrow. I had touched a raw nerve. He himself had been the victim of witch hunts and courts of inquiries in the wake of Charar-e-Sharif incident. He was perturbed.

"But I have been pressing for the finalisation of this Navapachi inquiry for months."

"The civilian witnesses are not forthcoming", I informed him.

"Look, I understand," the General said, "I'm prepared to do the utmost but you have to do the basics of completing the inquiry process. Get the civilians to testify."

"Let me try", I assured him and emphasised that to get our operations going again it was essential that we sent a loud and clear message to the units. *Honest mistakes and errors of judgements in combat would be accepted.* We were not perpetuating a zero error syndrome or any McCarthy'st witch hunts by staffs seated in the comforts of their offices and pronouncing judgement on the troops in the field. As it happened subsequently, within a month we had killed five terrorists in a single encounter in Navapachi. The civilian witnesses needed no further persuasion. They recognised the winning side and deposed truthfully about what had happened. The case was later dismissed by a court martial.

All that however was in the future then. The organisation was still not aware of what had transpired between me and the GOC. There was an undercurrent of apprehension and a sort of being left to the wolves feeling. It takes a herculean effort to get things moving in such situations. I went around my units and companies, by helicopter first, then by road and then by foot. I used to come back drenched in sweat but within a month I had seen my whole area. There was a deafening silence on the operational front. There was not a single terrorist eliminated. Multiple operations were launched each day but they came back with the standard NTR (Nothing to Report). It was infuriating and agonising. One's professional reputation as a combat soldier was at stake. I had earned my VSM in Kargil in conventional operations. I had been at the receiving end of the Artillery, mortars, rockets and Air Defense guns. I had launched very successful fire assaults (with well over a regiment of artillery, a Light Battery and almost five platoons of 81 mm mortars) that bloodied and shook up the Pakistani units opposite us. However, that was a different ball game. This was a different genre of operations altogether, where I was yet to prove myself. I felt mortified and diminished professionally by this lack of tangible results. The most agonising moments were when one had to report personally each evening to the General on telephone. The best part was that he never said anything but that only deepened my sense of guilt at the lack of tangible results in our operations. All soldiers who have served in J&K and other operational areas would recognise this phenomenon of guilt—the feeling that as a self-respecting soldier you haven't earned your pay for the day. I pushed harder. We had a few encounters but we missed, we failed to convert the contacts gained into kills. This could endanger our sources. I was furious.

"Sir, the terrain is very difficult and broken, there is so much undergrowth," my COs and company commanders said by way of explanation

"All right then, the next time there is any encounter I would like to be informed at once, so that I can come and see things for myself. It will educate me about the terrain and our tactics", I told them.

"But Sir—your security", they remonstrated.

"Don't worry about my security. I have a platoon worth of escorts and will take care of myself", I countered. I was asking people to risk their necks. I felt it was essential in such circumstances for the Commander to visibly put himself at the same risk. Unlike many others I was moving around with my star plates and flag. I decided to go a step further and asked my escort convoy to move with the siren blowing. The wavering wail of the siren was in itself a psy-ops weapon. It had a visible impact not just on the locals but also on the boys (I also had to take the sensible precaution of personally drilling me escort convoy in counter ambush drills). I told them that by putting myself at risk I was creating targets for my escort, providing they were trained and drilled adequately to respond promptly and effectively to any terrorist ambush. My Deputy Commander and Staff were most dubious about these "shock and awe tactics" of the wailing siren but had little option. They registered their protests and were overruled. Every time I left the HQ they winced and prayed silently.

At the next three encounters, I landed up personally on the scene with my siren blowing. I was establishing a pattern but I felt that to get my units moving I had to do something drastic. I went to each company post and spoke personally to the men about the importance of our task and the need to inflict attrition on the terrorist leadership and rank and file. I emphasised the need to be proactive, to seize and retain the initiative. It was important to be proactive—otherwise we would invite attacks. I had gone to 5 Sikh LI. After a particularly strenuous climb I had gotten to one of their remotest company posts. I had just finished speaking to the men when we got a radio message. *Manzoora,* one of the most dreaded terrorists in that area had been killed. People were ecstatic. Manzoora had killed one JCO and eight soldiers of ours. He had given us the slip on numerous occasions. He was a loner and used to operate alone. He had been a guide for hunting expeditions and knew the forest trails here like the back of his hand. My predecessor Brig (later Lt Gen Gangadharan) had warned me about this man and felt it was the unfinished business of his tenure. Manzoora was an inveterate womaniser. 26 RR had just recovered his body. Col Sharma, the CO of 5 Sikh LI congratulated me personally. It was a kill we could be proud of. It happened to be the eve of Diwali and there was a festive mood all around. I felt greatly relieved and happy. I ordered them to bring the body to the road where I could see it for myself on my way back to the headquarters. My convoy reached the place where they had brought the body. He was a huge man—over six feet tall and heavily built; very fair but curiously his face had turned purple. There were no bullet marks on his body. I asked the officiating CO about it. He took me aside and told me frankly that they had not killed him. The husband of one of the women he had raped had mixed rat poison in his food. Obviously the chore of cooking dinner outside for Manzoora, while he raped his wife inside his own house had been too much for the poor man. Manzoora died a horrible death with that rat poison. That is why his face had turned purple. The husband had then dragged his body, left it in the Shamdalin mosque and made an anonymous phone call to the post. The troops had rushed out and surrounded the mosque. When they crawled in cautiously they found Manzoora dead already.

Hesitantly, the officiating CO asked me whether the unit could claim the kill. I gave him a blunt no and told him to reflect whatever he had told me accurately in the sitrep (situation report). He looked crestfallen. Manzoora was a big kill. He was the biggest catch and had eluded us for the past 8 years. All we had to do was to pump some bullets into him to ensure he was dead. We had been cheated of our kill only by a few minutes, he pleaded. They had not fired because it was the Mosque. I appreciated his concern but told him point blank, "We are not vultures or carrion. We do not eat dead meat. We will claim only those terrorists that we kill ourselves." So we refused to claim this kill. The situation report (sitrep) reflected it exactly as per details and whatever doubts my staff had on this score were brusquely put to rest.

For two whole weeks thereafter we had no kills. It was agonising. I got some 'I told you so' looks from my staff but the unit concerned took it in good spirit. I was now getting anxious for results. I now began to call the local Company Commander at Kishtwar to my office each evening for a personal update on the operations. The boy (Maj Lokesh) was from the Artillery. He was a good and spirited lad and had scored a number of successes in the past. He had some information. His source was a young boy barely in his teens. But he was good and had delivered in the past. Lokesh and his team put on terrorists' clothes and hid in a village in the Keshwan area. Their vigil of two nights paid off finally. The encounter began at around 0530 hours in the morning. The boy had taken them to a hideout in a Nala fork. Most terrorist hideouts near villages are in the forks of Nalas. The terrorists use them as a navigation aid. When they reached the hideout they found it empty. However when they looked up the same Nala, they found a small camp fire some 600 metres upstream in the dense jungle. The terrorists had shifted hideout. There were 5 terrorists there. The sentry had lit the fire to keep off the extreme cold of the morning. The encounter started close to first light. One terrorist was killed in the initial volley and two weapons were recovered. The other terrorists fled down the steep Nala. One of our boys was wounded in the firefight.

I got the news at about 0600 hrs. They were calling off the encounter. I was furious. "How many were they overall", I asked them.

"Five", I was told.

"Don't stop the encounter. I am coming with the reinforcements. We will evacuate the boy who is wounded." The whole Brigade camp was electrified. My convoy and escort were lined up. Capt Sukhjeet, a young lady Medical Officer was standing next to the ambulance and saluted me smartly. I looked at the slim and frail little girl. Being the father of a daughter of virtually the same age, I asked her to stay back. She was quite crestfallen, but I did not have the heart to take a girl into combat. The

Nursing Assistant accompanied us thoughtfully. They were more concerned about my getting shot up. My staff had called in the helicopter for cas evac (casualty evacuation). My convoy of jeeps sped out-led by the LMG mounted jeep, the Jammer vehicle, my jeep, the back up jeep, the Signals Rover and another escort jeep with Light Machine Gun (LMG) mounted. The Ambulance bought up the tail of the convoy. CO, 11 RR, in whose jurisdiction the encounter had started, met me at Bhandarkot. We sped off for Keshwan. Everybody expected me to watch the encounter from the road head. However, I had put on my jungle boots and insisted on moving up to the site. It was a stiff climb of some two hours. As we started on foot, the helicopter clattered up. We picked up excited terrorist communication on the radio. They were talking of the helicopter and one station was asking the other to open fire on it.

This put wings to our feet. Panting and gasping we almost raced up the steep slope on all fours. The sweat was streaking into my eyes. Fortunately, the helicopter touched down, picked up the casualty and clattered out safely. I was hugely relieved. CO 26 RR had also been informed of the encounter and had rushed up with his QRT (Quick Reaction Team). He also joined up and we had a formidable strength now available.

Cas evac out of the way I insisted we recommence operations to get the balance terrorists. Maj Lokesh's column was now coming down the Nala with the dead body of the terrorist and the recovered weapons. Seeing us the local Special Police Officers (SPOs) in the neighbouring village rushed forward greatly emboldened. One young lad, an SPO of just 18 years charged up the slope past us into the Nala. He had detected some movement there. A wounded terrorist was lying there on his back. The SPO made the cardinal tactical error of approaching him from the feet side. As he rushed pell mell, the injured terrorist picked up his AK and squeezed the trigger—he emptied a full magazine into the young police man who screamed and died on the spot. Our troops rushed forward. A fullisade of shots rang out. Then the rattle of the LMGs started. The terrorist's body was shattered with scores of bullets. His shin bone (Tibia—the strongest bone in the body) was smashed to pulp. When we reached the Nala, flies were buzzing in his mouth and gaping wounds. Locals also told us that a third terrorist was also killed but his body had been dragged away by some civilian sympathisers into the forest. We searched high and low, but when the operation ended, we had two bodies and three weapons. Both of these killed terrorists were foreigners. It had been an exhilarating and educative encounter and there was jubilation all around at this first operational success after months of futile jungle bashing.

Getting the first break took tremendous amount of effort and hard work. Once the initial inertia was overcome, the successes began to come in fast and furious. The very next day there was a major encounter near the heliborne post of Navapachi. Five terrorists (to include Parbat, the Deputy Commander of Lashkar-e-Toiba—LeT) were killed. We recovered 4 AK-47 rifles, one pistol and two radio sets. This encounter had a very salutary impact in this area. Civilian witnesses had earlier turned hostile and refused to testify for the Navapachi court of enquiry. The day after this encounter they had definitely identified the winning side. We flew in the officer recording the Summary of Evidence a week later. Over 50 civilians truthfully testified about the details of the Navapachi encounter and how our boys had fired purely in self defence when people (led by terrorists in the crowd) tried to snatch their weapons. We had hired a retired army lawyer to defend the boys. He rightly pointed out that there was no ballastics report to indicate whether the casualties were from our weapons or caused by the terrorists in the crowd. The boys had acted purely in self-defense. Gen Mohinder was as good as his word. The Court martial trial was expeditiously held and the charges of murder were subsequently dismissed. The happiest day of my life was when these boys were finally exonerated and went home on leave after months. Tears sprang up in their eyes and they thanked me profusely.

9 Sector RR never looked back in operations thereafter. The next year, in fact the boys went on to set a new record in the number of terrorists killed in a single year in the Kishtwar area. We were now on the roll. An important lesson learnt here was regarding the Commander and his Command. The grid biasing has to be positive in the senior-subordinate relationship. When Commanders push their subordinates for results in a situation of such high ambiguity, where several things could go wrong, the subordinate has to have the faith that if some honest mistakes occur in the heat of battle, the hierarchy will hold his hand. No results are possible in the absence of this mutual faith. This does not mean that indiscipline should be condoned on the battlefield. *The entire issue devolves upon our analysis of the intent.* That should be transparent. Was the intent right? Was it a genuine error of judgement in the heat of battle? That has to be viewed very differently from say a premeditated murder, rape, molestation or a case of stealing. A Commander has to be ruthless in curbing such latter incidents. Anything less than ruthless would erode the moral

fibre of the combat organisation. Honest errors of judgement in combat however are a different things altogether.

The Jama Masjid Episode

One of the most disturbing episodes followed in the wake of our initial successes in Kishtwar. It was a most sinister and chilling incident. For the last few days my staff and intelligence operatives had been uneasy. There was something in the air. We then received information that Mr Bashir Ahmad Kichloo, the highly influential local MLA had arrived in Kishtwar and was camping in the Dak Bunglow. The tall and lanky, elder Kichloo was politically very influential. Post the Navapachi incident my predecessor had sought his help to defuse the local adverse fallout. It was an odd coincidence however that lately whenever he had been around, the political temperature had gone up and the Army had had its share of problems. So his sudden, unscheduled visit from Srinagar did leave us a little uneasy.

That evening we received an urgent message from the police that some three- four terrorists had entered the Historic Jama Masjid Mosque in Kishtwar town. We were later told that possibly they were holding some people hostage. My first reaction was to ask my escort to line up and go and personally check this most unusual occurrence out. Terrorists had never before entered this historic Mosque—at least not with weapons. My Deputy and staff however came running to my office and implored me not to go. They felt in the recent past I had set up a very predictable pattern of personally reacting to all local encounters and rushing to the sites. This one could be a trap. I was initially inclined to go anyway, for I felt the staff were over-protective. As I got up to leave however- I felt a deep sense of unease—a tiny piping voice deep inside that warns all old soldiers of the imminence of danger. The intuition was so strong that I sat down and for some time got lost in deep thought. The last time I had felt it was before the Pakistani artillery shelling in Kargil. This voice had never failed me in combat and I asked my escort party to stand down. Something definitely did not sound quite all right here.

The messages from the civil administration increasingly became more frantic. We got reports that some shots had been fired at the mosque. I asked the local police to deal with it as the Army usually avoided getting involved in action in any densly populated area to prevent collateral damage. The next few messages were absolutely hysterical. The Green Jama Masjid, the most historic Mosque of Kishtwar—reputedly some 200 years old, was on fire. We were stupefied. Why on earth would the terrorists set the Wahabi Mosque on fire? There were many instances of them setting Sufi shrines on fire but there was no recorded instance of a Wahabi Mosque being torched. I spoke to the Sub Divisional Magistrate-a local state service cadre officer who belonged to the town. He was in sheer panic and apparently set upon by local mobs. They had overturned his vehicle and gheraoed his office. I asked him whether he had sent the Fire tenders. He said he had but the people were not letting them go through.

Why? I asked in absolute astonishment. The locals felt that he had inordinately delayed the fire tenders and were now not letting them get through. The Green Mosque was made largely of wood and was by now a raging inferno. We could see the orange glow over the night sky in Kishtwar. I asked my local Company commander to try and help with his water bowser but even this was not permitted to go beyond the main market square by the rampaging mobs who were now all over the town.

Just then my GSO-2 rang up in considerable alarm." Sir, please switch on the BBC channel". We flicked on the TV in my office. We were absolutely stunned to hear the anchor announcing in strident tones that the Indian Army had set the historic Jama Masjid Mosque in Kishtwar on fire and it had been reduced to ashes. The local Brigadier had personally led this operation. It went on to elaborate that some terrorists had taken shelter in the Mosque and the Army burnt down the Mosque to smoke them out. The historic Mosque was completely gutted.

We looked at one another in sheer amazement. Then the spate of telephone calls started.

What the hell was going on in Kishtwar? Where was the commander? We patiently explained that the army was nowhere near the scene and we had wisely refrained from going to even investigate. The GOC rang me up and I spoke to him in detail. He whistled thoughtfully when he heard our side of the story. I sighed in relief and was glad that for once I had listened to my staff and to that tiny, piping voice inside my gut. If I had ventured anywhere close to the Mosque, this would have turned out to be a right royal mess and would have put a rather pre- mature end to my command tenure in Kishtwar.

The next day I went to the Mosque. It lay in smoking ruins and the smoke was still flowing out of the embers. I walked up to the hereditary Imam of the Mosque. He was a local power centre in his own right. I expressed my condolences. He looked sullen and grim faced. I couldn't help asking—but why did the people stop the Fire tenders last night? We could perhaps have saved the Mosque or at least reduced the damage. He stared at me sullenly. Then he said in his soft urdu—*"Log jasbat men aa gaye the"* (the people had become very emotional).

I sighed and left it at that. Kishtwar was a difficult place to serve in.

Non-Initiation of Combat Operations (NICO)

A relative lull descended upon the battlefields in J&K with the offer of Non-Initiation of Combat Operations (NICO) by the government in November 2000. This was a sequel to the offer of talks by the Hizbul Mujahideen (HM), which had been promptly repudiated by its Supremo in POK—Syed Salauddin alias Yusuf Shah. The government made its counter offer—most of us in the field were a little dismayed. "Winter" is our traditional "operating season" after the Maize crop is cut. The foreign tanzeems refused to abide by this offer and the ceasefire of sorts became a non-starter right from the outset.

A rather unhappy incident happened thereafter. Lt Gen Nanavatty had taken over as the Army Commander Northern Command and was going around on his tour of visits to all Headquarters. He went to 16 Corps HQ and was briefed in detail by the then Corps Commander, Lt Gen Khanna. During the briefing he apparently told the Army Commander that as per their assesment no infiltrating groups from the Jammu area were using the Kishtwar route. Unfortunately, our inputs were to the contrary. We had interrogation reports of apprehended terrorists that clearly stated that they had infiltrated from the Samba area, and gone via Kishtwar to the Marwah-Warwan area. Dutifully, we had marked this route on our briefing slides. After the Corps HQ, Gen Nanavatty then visited my HQ at Kishtwar and was briefed in detail by me. I had no clue about whatever had transpired at Nagrota. Even if I had, I was still duty bound to give my honest assessment. I therefore sincerely put across an assessment of the infiltration profile which was at variance with the Corps staff perception. Both the Army Commander and Corps Commander said nothing then and heard me out patiently. That evening however, I got a call from the Force Commander Gen Mohinder Singh, he told me that the Corps Commander was in a towering rage. He was most upset that I had contradicted him. I was dumb founded. I had the original interrogation report with me—which had in fact been sent down by the Corps intelligence staff. The same was also corroborated by our local sources. I had just done my duty in putting it across and totally failed to see what was so amiss. Gen Mohinder sighed. He seemed to think that I had sealed my career and the Corps Commander was upset beyond redemption. Frankly it was my turn to feel outraged. It was my simple duty to present facts honestly as I knew them. If one was to be "sacked" for this, it was most outrageous. Tempers flared up on both sides and it led to a lot of acrimony. Possibly, I had longer to serve in the Army and the Corps Commander was posted out before he could do the honours to my ACR. News of this acrimony somehow seemed to have reached the Command HQ. Orders were thereafter passed down that whenever the Army Commander visited the Brigades and Battalion or below he would be accompanied only by one Commander up the chain. As a military professional, Gen Nanavatty was keen that his subordinate Commanders express views frankly and honestly and were not unduly pressurised by the intervening HQs to doctor views to conform to perceptions there.

CHAPTER 6

The Road versus the Hinterland Controversy

Maj Gen Mohinder Singh moved out on posting thereafter and was replaced by Maj Gen Mono Bhagat, PVSM in January 2001. Gen Bhagat had headed a very high profile UN Mission in Somalia—where his approach of winning hearts and minds made the Indian contingent very popular with the people. This provided such a sharp contrast to the American, European and Pakistani contingents however which were ham handed and totally alienated the tribal population. The Americans in particular, took heavy casualties. Fresh out of the Desert-storm triumph of Iraq, they did not want their image of invincibility to take a beating. The Somali clans were vicious and this UN Mission had later to be wound up. The forces committed were far too less to control the situation. There was much mutual recrimination. The US troops blamed the UN for its soft approach and hereinafter refused to put their forces under UN command. The Indian Air Force and Navy had to intervene to extricate the Indian contingent. In military terms this mission was a tragic failure. Somalia became a classic failed state, riven by warlordism and wracked by increasing inner conflict and later became a base for piracy in the region. It was an epicenter of collapse. Gen Bhagat's hearts and minds approach however drew very favourable comments from various quarters. It was such a marked contrast to the American, European or Pakistani approach to Low Intensity Conflict Operation (LICO). The US Army proved incapable of sustaining itself in an infantry predominant environment, where it could not bring to bear the armour, artillery and airpower at the lavish scales it had become so used to in Iraq. Without this luxury, it could not sustain its force commitments or accept very high casualties. Iraq had exposed it to the notions of casualty-less campaigns and Somalia proved too hot to handle. The disconcerting bottom line however was that in purely military terms overall, Somalia had been a disaster.

The lesson learnt was that "behavioural and cognitive" objectives in such conflicts are equally important. However, to be completely successful, they need to be backed by adequate and credible military force that can inflict salutary attrition on the armed insurgent groups. The two approaches have to be combined for victory. By themselves, neither of them alone can yield success.

Maj Gen Mono Bhagat had gained international renown with this operation and acquired a formidable reputation. He became the Military Advisor to the UN Secretary General, Kofi Annan, and was his right hand man. Age wise he was well-placed to be the Chief. His appointment as GOC CI Force Delta was therefore seen as a step in the right direction and we all eagerly looked forward to his coming. A Commander with a sterling reputation tends to draw more resources and attention to his sector.

The tall and silver haired Mono Bhagat had an impressive and telegenic persona and was well-regarded in the UN circles. He unfortunately came to the job with some deep set convictions that he had acquired in New York. He was somehow convinced that the Indian Army had gone berserk with the people of J&K, that its approach was very ham-handed and muscular. He could not be blamed for his impressions formed in New York, under the constant barrage of telematic assaults launched by the CNN to denigrate and demoralise our troops. The western media had painted the Indian Army as the villains of the piece and berated our Human Rights record in a most strident fashion. The same stridency of tone was conspicuous by its absence when the American Armed Forces unleashed their strategic and tactical bomber forces and their Armoured Divisions and heavy artillery against the insurgents in Iraq, while a totally captive and embedded western media cheered the assaults upon unarmed civilians. Mercifully, the western Human Rights sermons ceased soon thereafter. Even in the worst phases of the campaign in J&K, we had refrained from using our Air power, tanks and artillery against the terrorists in that state. Ours had been Infantry predominant operations—where our straight legged infantry had been able to sustain Counter Insurgency (CI) campaigns for close to two decades. We had stoically accepted casualties to save collateral damage to the civilian population. Had we been far too restrained? Had we let the western propaganda and TV orchestrated Human Rights campaign hamstring our operations and drag them out for years interminably? Where their own national interests were involved, other nations had unabashedly used brutal military force to quell civilian populations. The Americans had used overkill in Iraq and the Russians in Chechnya. The Pakistanis had pressed in Attack helicopters, artillery, tanks and bulldozers in Waziristan. The Sri Lankan Army had virtually waged war against the LTTE and won a clear and decisive victory. In our pursuit of principles, as opposed to realpolitik, had we been unduly soft? Or was ours a far better approach in the long term? Frankly, time alone would solve this conundrum.

My assignment at the critical desk of Director MO-5 at the Directorate General of Military Operations (DGMO) at the Army HQ had recently given me a somewhat bitter experience of another UN mission gone sour in Sierra Leone. MO-5 was a terribly busy appointment. We had just finished Op Vijay when we received the request for contributing troops to the UN mission in Sierra Leone. Op Vijay had totally disrupted our CT operations grid and taken the heat off the terrorist tanzeems in the hinterland. We needed every man possible to plug the gaps and restart CT operations with renewed vigour. Indian Infantry Battalions had their peace-field profile in tatters. Units that had done extended CI tenures in the jungles of North East and had just come for rest and refit in long awaited peace tenures, had to be diverted to J&K. Some families were breaking up as result of prolonged separation and accumulated stress. In such a scenario, to spare troops for Sierra Leone seemed like very uncalled for sacrifice to me. When I was asked to put up the case, I was aghast. I put across my views in a most frank and forthright manner. I highlighted the adverse peace-field profile of our Infantry and the need for additional troops in J&K. *I stated that Sierra Leone was likely to become a quagmire. It would lead to a situation of mission creep.* Having committed our troops, it would become a matter of prestige and we would be forced to send additional troops. With our own house on fire, it was something we could ill afford at that point of time. To make up for the manpower crunch in J&K we had just commenced raising some 35 additional battalions of the RR.

The counter arguments were that since the Force commander was to be an Indian General, our prestige was at stake anyway and that we should send a brigade worth of troops. The UN lobby at the Army HQ was aghast at my views. Pressure was put on me to change my noting but I refused to budge from my principled stand. My immediate superiors disagreed with me in writing and put in notings strongly countermanding my views. The DGMO (then Lt Gen NC Vij, who later rose to be the Chief), however, agreed with me in his noting on the subject. It became an unprecedented situation. The Vice Chief disagreed with me and the DGMO. The Chief was inclined to go along with us but great pressure was mounted by the Ministry of External Affairs. This was the Whitehall system of notings at its best and has traditionally enabled a thorough staff analysis of complex issues. Much to my chagrin, I was finally overruled and the mission was sent to Sierra Leone. Almost a Brigade group went. The clinching argument was that if we didn't take it, the Pakistanis would jump at the offer and earn foreign exchange. With so many foreign postings at stake,(and dollars to be earned as a service perk) all voices of caution were overruled.

The UN mission to Sierra Leone was tragically flawed from the outset. It had all the signs of mission creep. The force inducted under the Chapter Six (and a half) was inherently weak for a Chapter Seven Task and invited attack. One of our Gurkha companies was disarmed and taken hostage. The simple Gurkha troops were just too confused by all these sermons on becoming diplomats and keepers of peace. Simple soldiers needed clear cut and straight forward orders. Then they could do miracles with their *Khukris*. We had no business to put them in such an ambiguous and confused situation just for the sake of a few dollars more. It reinforced my unfortunate conviction that such anomalous military missions under the UN flag eroded the will to fight and blunted the natural aggression and killer instinct of our units. There was great embarrassment and panic. Additional troops and Special Forces had to be flown in to restore the situation. My baleful prognostications of mission creep had been proved to be correct. It vindicated my professional judgement. My GSO-1 and GSO-2 had in good faith advised me not to press the issue as they felt it could have harmed my career progression. I had stuck to my guns. The Sierra Leone mission was ill starred indeed. The Indian Force Commander developed serious professional differences with his Nigerian counterparts. We were asked to change him and we withdrew our contingent in a huff. That ended the saga of Sierra Leone. We were left nursing J&K—something that demanded all our attention and energies. Selection and maintenance of aim is a cardinal Principle of War. My GSO-I and GSO-2 walked up to me with boyish grins.

"Sir, you had the last laugh", they said.

But at what cost? The cost was borne by our country and the boys battling it out in J&K.

So, I had my personal reservations about UN missions. They are very good as a form of welfare activity for our troops—they earn them dollars and foreign jaunts. No doubt such breaks are needed. Professionally, however, they teach little. They only erode combat skills and dampen the killer instinct. *At times, they can impart a pacific perspective that can be misplaced on the battlefields*. China had till then hardly contributed to any UN missions. It still had a seat in the UN Security Council. Despite contributing thousands upon thousands of troops, we are still struggling for a permanent seat in that august body, till today. It was possibly this UN based perspective that unfortunately brought a different slant to the whole issue of CT operations in Delta force.

The newly appointed GOC of Delta Force called all the Sector Commanders for a conference. He was genuinely convinced that we were tormenting the hapless people of J&K and committing gross human right abuses and excesses. "These are my countrymen", he said, "I won't let you chaps ill-treat them."

Gen Mono Bhagat was very genuine and sincere about what he said. Unfortunately, to troops dazed by contradictory requirements of inflicting attrition on the terrorist tanzeems and getting kills and being bombarded by human right allegations, these good intentions (stated so sternly) were like a thunder clap. We, Sector Commanders, exchanged uneasy glances. Anyhow, we thought that he would soon become cognizant of the actual ground realities, once he got to see things for himself. Possibly the perspective acquired in New York would change as he oversaw the ongoing operations for himself. I had gotten the operations going after a great deal of effort and personal risk taking in 9 Sector and was worried about anymore cognitive degrades in the operating environment. I and the other Sector commanders therefore did not convey these strictures down to our COs. However, things took a somewhat unexpected turn.

Perils of a Staff Screen

I had to go on a leave for a month since my father was undergoing a major heart operation. The Non-Initiation of Combat Operations (NICO) being in force there was a significant lull in operations, Hence I was permitted the leave. The General in the meantime was informed by the staff that the Sector Commanders had not conveyed the full import of his strictures down to the rank and file. Gen Bhagat was upset. He then called all the COs for a direct conference at the Div HQ and gave them a piece of his mind. They were stupefied and amazed. While the conference was dispersing, one of the COs remarked bitterly, "*Chalo*, let's go back to our sleeping bags. They don't want us to operate here anymore. I'll be damned if I ask my boys to stick their necks out after this." His remarks were overheard by the Staff and dutifully conveyed to the GOC. He never forgave the CO for this acid comment. Unfortunately most operations ground down to a crawl after this and we went into a phase of almost zero results in our daily anti-terrorist operations in the area of CI Force Delta.

Personalities play their part in shaping operations, attitudes and opinions. The Col GS of the Division was a dynamic young colonel from the Armoured Corps. He was intelligent and well informed but somewhat abrasive. He had done a long stint as UN Observer in South America and had personally known Gen Bhagat from that tenure on. He therefore had his ear. He had arrogated to himself the maximum number of helicopter sorties and thus had the best heliborne perspective of the entire force area. Unfortunately, in a terrain where it takes four to five hours to walk up to a company post, the helicopter view alone can sometimes offer a terribly distorted perspective. He somehow convinced the new GOC that he had spent more time in the Force than the other Sector Commanders and was therefore well-placed to proffer advice over their heads. The staff has proximity to the Commander. The electronic principle of a triode operates in these matters—the grid voltage sleeve nearest the cathode has a disproportionate influence in causing voltage fluctuations.

The decision dilemma in Delta Force was simple. Earlier we had an additional Brigade allocated to CI Force Delta during Operation Vijay. This brigade was used to man the heights overlooking the national highway to Srinagar. After Op Vijay, to give relief to Infantry units, which had been constantly in the field, this formation had been withdrawn. The key task of CI Force Delta was to guard and keep open the vital artery of Jammu-Srinagar road (National Highway NH-1A). The question was what now? My friend Brigadier Shyam Narula—the Sector Commander in charge of this sector, rightly insisted that he needed additional troops. He was principally correct in his stand. The correct thing to do was to have thumped the table and asked for the additional forces. The Col GS now stepped in to suggest that CI Force Delta could manage the problem in house. All it needed was to withdraw one battalion from the hinterland in Kishtwar. In his judgement two battalions were adequate to hold 7,500 sq kms of the most mountainous terrain and that the terrorist threat was overrated there by the Sector. In inter- se prioritisation the vital road sector was far more important than the hinterland of Kishtwar.

It was my contention that the road needed a brigade worth to properly dominate the upper reaches and heights overlooking the road. It was the Staff view in CI Force Delta that these upper heights were not that important. They felt only an additional battalion was needed along the road to secure it adequately. With good Road Opening Parties (ROP) drills and close domination of the road, all would be well. To most of us, it seemed like a recipe for disaster. It made us weak both along the road and in the hinterland. The Col GS informed the GOC that 9 Sector Commander was obviously likely to protest against the dilution of his grid and the GOC would have to hold firm and bulldoze his way through to this DS solution and not let Commander 9 Sector get away with empire building.

When I returned from leave, my staff informed me of this development and I was aghast. Unfortunately, much water had flown down the Chenab in that one month. I wished I had been there in the initial discussions. It now looked like a fiat accomplis. What hurt me the most was that the new GOC had not even been given one detailed briefing by me regarding my Sector. It was unfair that the decision be taken in the absence of input from the field commander who was directly affected. The GOC's perspective was simple. His obvious Key Result Area (KRA) was the road. Mine was a peripheral sector. He felt I was just being obdurate and he would not stand by any empire building. He felt I was not cognizant or sensitive to the higher commanders perspective and was focussing too narrowly on just my sector. He wanted to close the deployment in from far flung places and focus on close protection of roads, key arteries and communication centres.

To my mind, this was being overly defensive. These distant populated base areas, though not in the immediate vicinity of the roads, towns or villages, provided safe bases and sanctuaries, which the terrorists used to rest, refit and train and plan and execute their forays in the lower valleys. They had perforce to be dominated and held. My theory was simple. The best form of defense is attack. *To protect the road it would be essential to attack those who were likely to target the road.* This translated into establishing a CT grid in the upper reaches of the mountains overlooking the road and conducting offensive CT operations in that area. That alone would protect the road. This is how the additional brigade was deployed there earlier. HQ CI Force Delta decried this attrition/body-count approach to defending the NH-1A. They evolved excellent SOPs for the ROP and went into great details and minutiae of close in protection of the road, search drills, IED and mine sweeps. An excellent quantitative analysis of road length and the rates of troops to the kilometer was done for road piqueting. Unfortunately, this overly defensive approach did not succeed. As most of us had feared, there were a series of IED attacks and ambushes on the National Highway 1A in the year 2001. These hit the media headlines and in the end the Indian Army was forced to deploy an additional Brigade to conduct offensive CT operations to deny the upper heights overlooking the road. Only once the terrorists operating there were put under pressure, did the attacks on the road cease.

All that however was many months into the future then. I was summoned to the Force HQ and told about the redeployment plans. I protested vehemently. I pointed out that NH-1B, the alternative road to Kishtwar and Anantnag which passed through my sector would become vulnerable. More than that, the demographic composition of the population itself was a major vulnerability. Kishtwar had 60 per cent Muslims and almost 40 per cent Hindus. There had been a number of massacres of the minorities in the past. Once the troop density was diluted these would start again.

Gen Mono Bhagat was in no mood to listen. His mind was fully made up by then. He told me he had already spoken to the Army Commander and the Corps Commander. They both agreed with him. I persisted with my protests. He was now visibly incensed. "I have heard about you. You are obdurate. You lack the vision to see the next higher commander's perspective. This redeployment is not negotiable. It is a term of reference. It has already been decided. I'm now communicating it to you. There should be no further argument."

I was quite upset. I came back to my headquarters and wrote a detailed DO to him outlining all the risks inherent in this decision. I again pointed out the likelihood of the massacres of minority community and vulnerability of NH-1B that would result as a consequence of the dilution of troop density below the existing three battalion levels in my sector. Whenever troops had been withdrawn from Kishtwar in the past, there had been minority community massacres in this area.

My written protest was also overruled. I felt it was my duty as the Commander on the ground to appraise my senior commander of my analysis of the situation in my area and provide all inputs that were essential to arriving at such a critical decision. Beyond that one had no option but to obey orders. I could not legislate as to how the Jammu-Srinagar Road

(NH-1A) should be defended. It passed through another Sector's area. I strongly felt that this redeployment of just one battalion was too little for the road and also served to unbalance my sector. We needed additional troops. I was not fully aware now of the overall constraints or compulsions of troop availability within the corps zone and had to carry out the orders as conveyed. Such decision dilemmas in actual combat zones are a very frequent and commonplace occurrence. There are never adequate troops for the plethora of tasks on hand. The troops to task and troops to space ratio is always skewed on the battle field.

CHAPTER 7

Ending Ethnic Cleansing: The Need to Deter

The denouement was not long in coming. Unfortunately, this redeployment coincided with a change in Pakistani thinking and tactics in the Proxy War. Robert G. Wisring, in his eminently researched book "Kashmir in the Shadow of War—Regional Rivalries in the Nuclear Age", has given a fascinating account of the track-two diplomacy that had taken place between India and Pakistan in the period preceding the Kargil Conflict of 1999 and immediately in its aftermath. Wisring has highlighted that nine rounds of backchannel diplomacy took place—two in New Delhi and 7 in Islamabad. Indian representative Mr R K Mishra held the secret negotiations with Mr Niyaz A Nayak (a former foreign secretary of Pakistan). During these talks, India proposed the LC as border whereas Pakistan dusted out the Regional Partition Plan of Sir Owen Dixon of the 1950s vintage. As per the Dixon Plan, J&K was proposed to be partitioned along the Chenab River as a natural dividing line. These talks were held between March-June 1999, and collapsed due to the Kargil Conflict.

Though the Chenab Partition Plan had died a premature death, it seems that the grandmasters of the Proxy War in Pakistan thought that one day India could well be coerced by the USA and other Western countries to accept this solution. The very fact that India had agreed to even consider this preposterous proposal worried the Military-ISI complex in Pakistan. They did not want a partitioned Kashmir. They wanted the whole state to control the headwaters of the rivers that irrigate Pakistan. To stall this scheme, they told their terrorist minions to set the stage for ruling out this option all together by carrying out a very thorough and premeditated ethnic cleansing of the Hindu minority from the trans-Chenab areas of Doda and Kishtwar. This would be a repeat of the highly successful ethnic cleansing of the Kashmiri Pandits from the valley. Once a mass migration of the Hindu minority started from the trans-Chenab area, it would automatically make this solution less practicable and palatable to the world. Ethnic cleansing, which was a crime in Bosnia, was apparently absolutely in order for J&K. It appears that after the Kargil Conflict, the Pakistani grandmasters of the jihad in J&K hit upon this tidy plan of ethnic cleansing in Kishtwar. They were ready to put this into action by 2001. This unfortunately coincided with the reduction of troops from the Kishtwar sector which opened up huge voids in our deployment.

It was in the meantime left to me to call my COs and prepare them for the force depletion in our sector. CO 5 Sikh LI was visibly crestfallen on leaving the supportive and enabling environment of 9 Sector RR and COs of 11 and 26 RR were doubtful about the dilution of force density in the area, which had traditionally been held with three to five battalions.

"There are two ways to protest", I told them. The standard Indian way of bitching and carping and adopting an "I told you so" attitude. There is the other Japanese way of protest. If the Japanese workers demand a pay raise and are refused by the management, they have a novel way of protest. They work even harder. They refuse to go back home that night and are still working when their bosses return the next morning. They thus shame them into a redressal of their grievances. We decided to emulate the Japanese way of protest and redouble our efforts.

In view of our force dilution, our only saving grace lay in being proactive and offensive. Keep hitting and keep him off-balance, I told them. Our survival now lay in this offensive strategy. Since force density was being increased in the other sectors, the terrorists were likely to get displaced into our area. We should therefore go all out to impose attrition on their tanzeem leadership and rank and file. That alone could keep him off-balance and prevent him from launching significant offensive action against us. The aim was to create situations for him faster than he could create them for us.

I had thought long and hard over this problem. I now had just 12 companies of the RR to keep under control an area of some 7,500 sq kms of the most rugged mountainous terrain. The answer was to rapidly focus resources in the area where major contact was gained. I thereupon started the strategy of focussing two to three companies (milked from both the battalions) in the area of major contact. This tactic was to pay handsome dividends later and served to save the day for us in the difficult months ahead. We were thus able to concentrate resources rapidly in the desired area and disperse them soon after without disturbing the basic grid. Heliborne operations would later enable me to react even in the remotest region with a modicum of speed and surprise.

My Battalion Commanders were worried about any collateral damage and associated Human Rights accusations, in case our offensive operations went awry. I told them to leave it to me. I would accept any honest mistakes where the intent was clear. I had given strict instructions against any rape, molestation or torture/ill-treatment of unarmed civilians or even captured terrorists. That was absolutely unacceptable. However, honest mistakes/errors of judgement in the heat of combat—in the course of legitimate operations, were a different matter all together. Civilians getting killed in accidental cross fire cannot be treated on par with intentional attacks or custodial deaths. I would stand by my troops in such former situations. The vital criterion was an analysis of intent. I had reached a happy rank and earned my flag and star plate and was willing to pay the price for the orders I had given. They had no need to look over the shoulders in this regard. Visibly relieved, they set off with a will. The new Corps Commander Lt Gen JBS Yadava had also taken over in the interim—his approach was far more aggressive and forthright. He had a great deal of CI operations experience in Punjab and J&K, and was therefore clear, unambiguous and very straight forward in his views.

"Don't tell me you have one arm tied behind your back. Go on an all out offensive against the terrorists; use both arms, both legs", he said.

It was rather heartening for the commanders and COs on the ground to hear such clear and unambiguous instructions. Our troops are largely simple peasants. They prefer simple and clear cut orders. CT operations took off in a massive way soon thereafter in the entire Corps Zone.

When he visited my HQ I had put across to the Corps Commander my apprehensions about minority massacres as a result of the force dilution. He listened to me thoughtfully. Then he said, "You are a keen student of Military History. I do not want you to adopt a classical Montgomery approach. Anybody can do a task if he has unlimited resources. I'm afraid our resources are not unlimited. I therefore want you to take it up as a challenge and accomplish more with less. This would mean the Rommel approach to leadership in the field."

I liked the cogent analysis and the way in which he put it across in a military historical perspective. I assured him that my Sector would take up the challenge. The key to our survival now lay in being offensive and continuously hitting out.

Ambiguity in orders is one of the major banes of CI/CT operations I distinctly recall a Simple Jat soldier had once asked me bluntly, "Sir what do you want us to do? When we kill terrorists we are asked a whole set of questions. When we don't kill terrorists, we are asked why not? What do our seniors want us to do?"

His anguish hit me hard. All Headquarters in the chain had issued lengthy lists of "donts". Where were the "dos"-clearly spelling out what had to be done? We had to protect the population and go for the terrorists. To explain things to my troops in as simple a manner as possible I thought long and hard and coined a slogan for the Sector in terms of "Dos". It was simplicity itself—

"Be Nice to the people—be Nasty to the terrorists"

That about summed up the essence of what the Army had to DO in such situations. Most problems occurred when this simple equation was reversed. I went back to that unit and asked for that plain speaking Jat soldier. I told him my expectations in terms of this Sector slogan.

"Is that clear and simple enough?" I asked.

He did not say anything but he and his comrades grinned from ear to ear in endorsement of our simple operational philosophy.

Frankly, to conserve troops for offensive action, for a time, we curtailed troops for ROP duties simply by moving supplies and routine movements in civilian buses and trucks which were not likely to be attacked by the terrorists to avoid hitting the civilians.. We specifically targeted the terrorist leaders. I gave each Post Commander a list of selected terrorist leaders in his area whom he tracked and was responsible to eliminate. Within a month we had scored some very impressive leadership attrition. Over the next two months we went on to eliminate 23 terrorists in our Area of responsibility. These included two District Commanders, three Deputy District Commanders and 5 Area Commanders. Over 30 per cent of our kills were command and control attrition. These have a far more disruptive impact than rank and file elimination. Leaders keep in their heads the locations of caches and hideouts and financial resources. These are not generally shared with the rank and file for the fear of compromise/ disclosure. So when a leader dies, that knowledge usually dies with him. It has not only an adverse impact on morale but also causes loss of scarce material and resources for the terrorist organisations. I told my boys to focus primarily on leadership attrition and the strategy paid off handsomely. Some of the key leaders eliminated included Paswan, District Commander of HUJI, Kari Hanzalla, Deputy District Commander JeM, Abdul Majid Dar, Deputy District Commander HM, and Shabir Lawe Deputy District Commander HM.

Death Watch. One of our prime targets in Kishtwar was Sarwar of the Harkat-ul-Jihad-e-Islami (HUJI). He was a very tall Pathan, reportedly over six feet two inches tall. He was known for his extreme cruelty and had skinned one of our sources alive for giving us information. He was a great womanizer. He had married a very beautiful girl in the Dugadda village. Then he left her for a 14 year old girl. When she objected, he beat her black and blue with his belt and almost killed her. Hell hath no fury like a woman scorned. His wife then began to give the Army information about his movements. We received information from her that he was coming to visit his mistress at Naidgam village. 11 RR launched an operation to get him. Unfortunately the boys opened fire prematurely and lost surprise. There was a fierce fire fight. One of our boys L/Nk Surinder Pal was badly hit. His arm was shattered by a burst of AK fire and his abdomen was badly torn up. In fact when they brought him down his intestines were hanging out. We could not fly in a helicopter at night. So we brought him down to the Kistwar. There was a civilian hospital there. They reached at about 0130h in the morning. I was informed that the civilian doctors were scared and refusing to come out at night. I was enraged and drove down to the Hospital myself. Our boys banged on their doors with their rifle butts till the civilian doctors came out rather resentfully. I was very keen that the boy be saved. So I went to the Operation Theatre myself to see them work on the boy. His face was ashen. He saw me and his face lit up with hope.

"Please Sir, Im terribally thirsty. Please ask them to give me some water. They are refusing to give me water."

"Give him water this very instant". I ordered the doctors. The Doctor pulled me to one side and told me that he had a severe abdominal injury and giving water was not advisable. They had put him on drip. The boy looked at me piteously. "Please sir Im dying of thirst."

I felt deeply moved. "Wet his lips" I asked the soldiers who had come with me. The boys put the water bottle to wet his lips but he snatched it desperately and drank a few gulps before we could stop him. Then he laid his head back on the pillow, gave me a look of deep gratitude and closed his eyes. I held his hand to comfort him. A little later he was dead.

He died virtually in my arms. I was most shaken by this one death. I still cannot forget the look of great and infinite peace on his face to this day. We got after Sarwar with a vengeance thereafter. Within a month we had killed him.

Ethnic Cleansing

The elimination of so many top leaders of the Tanzeems shook up the area. The impact was electrifying. Very soon the area was pacified and incident free. The Over Ground Workers (OGWs) were subdued and the people were happy. The terrorist response was anticipated but not in the form and scale as it happened. I had received vague warnings from some of my sources that something was indeed afoot and that the tanzeem leaders had been warning that they would personally teach me a lesson. I thought that possibly an attack on my Headquarters was in the offing and had my defenses strengthened and rehersals for local defense carried out.

On 27 July 2001, a group of foreign and local terrorists swooped down on four Hindu graziers in a remote pasture in Cherji and shot them down in cold blood. We had created Village Defence Committees (VDCs) in vulnerable Minority villages. Volunteers and ex-soldiers had been armed with vintage three knot three (303) Lee Enfield Bolt Action Rifles. These are single shot but accurate and sturdy weapons and capable of dropping a target almost at a thousand yards. As a result the number of attacks on villages had declined. In sheer and desperate defence of home and hearth—even the 303 Lee Enfields of World War One vintage proved effective.

The terrorists however studied the situation and found a loophole. Every summer the local Dogra graziers take up their cows and sheep and goats up to the higher pastures in the Alpine scapes where good grass and herbs are available. This also keeps the cattle from damaging the maize crop in the fields around the villages (where there is no fencing). These graziers in the upper Alpine pastures are usually located at 4-6 hours march from villages which are themselves some 3-4 hours away from the road heads. The terrorists struck in these remote pastures, which were beyond the beat of not just the police outposts but also the VDCs. The news trickled down to us after a lapse of almost 12-14 hours after the killing. By the time Police and Army teams reached the remote pastures, the terrorists had fled the scene a long time ago.

Within a week there was another massacre of Dogras at Tagud. This time eight Dogra men, women and children were slaughtered. There was an outcry in the press and sharp polarisation in the streets of Kishtwar. Communal frenzy started rising and it was clear that the situation could take a very ugly turn anytime. That seemed to be the precise intention of the jihadis.

The dead bodies of the massacre victims were brought to Kishtwar for cremation. Huge crowds gathered; there were slogans chanted daily. Then came the worst massacre of them all at Gulabgarh on 04 August 2001 on the eve of the Yakut festival which the locals celebrate in the upper reaches. Assistant Superintendent of Police at Kishtwar, Viplab Kumar, a very spirited young man, gave me the bad news. Some six hours from the Gulabgarh village, were the Alpine pastures of Paddar. A group of terrorists swooped down on the Dogra graziers in their Dhoks. They robbed them of their watches and ornaments. They were asked to lie down on the Dhok floor and were then shot in cold blood. 13 people were killed. Women and children were slaughtered ruthlessly. The news trickled down to the Police some 18 hours after the incident had occurred. This was the last straw. I rushed to the spot. The Governor of J&K (Ex-RAW Chief, Mr Gary Saxena) and the DG Police (Mr Suri) flew down there in an M-17 helicopter and were gheraoed by the irate Hindu mobs. I had to rescue them and escort them to safety. The local Rashtriya Swayamsevak Sangh (RSS) leaders insisted on getting the dead bodies down to Kishtwar for cremation. The Press was all over the place. All my baleful predictions had unfortunately, come true to a letter and one could only curse silently. I was deluged with calls from the Force and Corps Headquarters, and it was only with a very visible effort that I could control the urge to say, "I told you so!"

I got a direct call from Gen Nanavatty, the Army Commander himself. He was now seriously concerned about the fast deteriorating situation in Kishtwar. I thought long and hard over the problem. Our senior headquarters opined that defending the minorities was not our task. It was the task of the State Police. That was not very plausible. If the State Police could have handled it, why was the army required in the first place in J&K? *The Gen Petraeus and Kilcullen school of thought in CI operations lays heavy emphasis on protecting the population. Could we absolve ourselves of this task?* We had done so, in the valley and all the Pandits had fled, displaced from their ancestral lands forever. Should the same be repeated in Doda-Kishtwar? Could we simply disown some 40 per cent of the local population because they belonged to a particular denomination? Solutions were proffered of forming Dhok Defence Committees (in addition to the VDCs) and issuing radio sets to these remote hamlets and grazers in the Alpine pastures. All these were a pie in the sky and would take months to come. The Police just did not have the strength to defend each pasture, village and hamlet. That would still leave the isolated Dhoks undefended. No, we simply could not defend such a diffused and spread out population over hundreds of villages and thousands of pastures. The state Home Minister and the State DG Police landed up in Kishtwar in view of the public anger and I had to brief them in detail in my operations room.

Deterrence Theory. I went to the Chogan in Kishtwar where the corpses of the victims were being lit. 13 Funeral Pyres were blazing in the field and showers of sparks were rising skywards. The women wailed and the men screamed slogans. I came back quite ruffled. I thought long and hard. We could not defend each pasture but we could *deter*. That was the solution. I asked 11 RR and 26 RR to send one company each to Gulabgarh. I headed there myself with my convoy of some seven jeeps with my siren blaring. By evening some 30-40 military vehicles had trundled in the area. It was essential that this remote region feel the power and responsiveness of the state in terms of protecting the population. The Police also rushed in reinforcements. I had all the village Sarpanches and Panches collected and spoke to them.

"Even in a Jihad, the Holy Koran forbids the killing of women, children and the old and infirm. In all these massacres, women, children and the aged have been killed in cold blood. Is this jihad? This is *fasad*. We will not accept this. Whether it takes us one week, one month or one year, we will ruthlessly track down these mass murderers involved and make a horrible example of them. We will specifically hunt these criminals down. I just want you to tell me who they were."

My Company Commanders were very pessimistic about tracking down these killers—18 hours after the massacre. I held a detailed coordination conference at Gulabgarh with the COs and the column commanders. We studied in detail all tracks and trails that led to and away from the site of massacre. Columns were launched along all probable routes of escape. Ambushes were launched from the opposite direction to intercept any fleeing groups. We pooled in intelligence. Detailed interrogations of suspects and sympathisers revealed that the chief perpetrators of this massacre were Abu Ghulam, Abu Umer and Abu Musa of the Lashkar-e-Toiba (LeT). Abu Ghulam, in fact had sadistically played with his victims before shooting them in cold blood. He had forced them to lie down on the floor of the Dhoks while he stood framed in the doorway. As his colleagues divested the victims of their cash, watches and valuables, he had joked in a macabre fashion. He held up his AK and asked his terrified victims to say what it was. Then he showed the magazine full of rounds and again asked them to identify what that was. Then he laughed coarsely and sprayed bullets into the mass of old men, women and children till their corpses stopped twitching. One small boy got buried beneath the others and somehow survived to tell this grisly tale. There were two local Gujjar criminals who had acted as guides.

I was filled with cold fury when I heard the grisly details of the incident first hand from the villagers. War is dirty business but should we not leave the women and children out of it? I decided to camp in Gulabgarh and was there for almost a week. We launched a massive manhunt for these criminals. I told all my Company Commanders to pass the word around that the Army was infuriated and would ignore all other terrorist groups and focus all energies and resources on this particular bunch of criminals. I told them to tell all locals that we planned to make a horrible example of them. We announced huge rewards for any information regarding the whereabouts of these desperados. All these psy-operations worked very well. We had deliberately spoken in the presence of OGWs and sympathisers, who dutifully conveyed our messages to the perpetrators. Massive search operations were launched. The aim was not so much attritional as behavioural and cognitive. The aim was to send a loud and clear message to all terrorist tanzeems. The state would not tolerate such criminal behaviour and ethnic cleansing had to stop. *We would in specific, single out and target groups and individuals responsible for such atrocities.*

"Don't trouble trouble"—that was the direct message to these terrorist groups and the troops conveyed it with gusto. The large scale presence of troops in that area was a great morale booster for the minorities. They saw the large scale operations being launched and were convinced that the state would not abdicate its duties and abandon them to the wolves. It was fully resolved to protect its citizens—especially the helpless minorities and would not permit such barbaric acts of ethnic cleansing to go unpunished. Gen JBS Yadava, the Corps Commander was a great proponent of having the media as a major force multiplier. He had set up an ad hoc media cell headed by his Chief Signals Officer (Brig Lamba). This cell proved to be very effective. As a conscious media strategy it was decided to expose the jihadi designs for ethnic cleansing and mass murders in this area. Gen Yadava spoke to me on the phone. A helicopter load of media men from the print and electronic media were bought in. They helped to spread our message—"whether it takes us one week, one month or one year—the Army was resolved to track down and kill these perpetrators of genocide". My wife and children were pleasantly surprised to see me on the National TV hookup in channel after channel. NDTV, Aaj Tak, Star TV, Zee TV and our own Doordarshan were full of the images of the ethnic cleansing in Kishtwar and Gulabgarh. It had a tremendous psychological impact.

One of our very good Gujjar sources soon reported to us that the trio of terrorists who had done the massacre was now fleeing pell mell. Huge rewards were announced on their heads and they were looking crazed. They mistrusted their own shadow, mercilessly beat up any innocent civilian who even looked their way and never stayed in one place for more than two hours. We kept up the pressure. The troops killed five terrorists within a week in this chase. The newspapers were full of reports of a massive *crackdown* in the upper reaches of Kishtwar. I had denuded troops from other areas at considerable risk. But this focussing of resources paid off eventually. It had the desired psychological impact upon the area and more particularly, on the terrorist tanzeems, who had never seen such sustained and focussed military operations. The operating philosophy in J&K those days was based on small teams. This sudden area saturation mode came as a big surprise. My objectives were not so much attritional as behavioural and cognitive. There was no way I could defend every hamlet, Dhok and pasture. The effort to do so would be reactive and futile. It would only dissipate already scarce resources. They key lay in mobility—to concentrate vastly superior forces at the point of decision and carryout pinpoint targeting of terrorist groups involved in civilian massacres.

The aim was to overawe and visibly demonstrate the power of the state even in those remote areas. Earlier, in a rather warped concept of a secular approach, the Army had turned a Nelsons eye to these communal massacres and ethnic cleansings. The entire Kashmiri Pandit community had in fact been assisted to flee from the valley. It was felt that we could not defend them—*that the Hindu minority was a baggage on our operations and it was better that they simply flee and get out of the way. They were a vulnerability we could not defend.* The state thereby acquiesced in this ethnic cleansing by the terrorists. I failed to see the connection between accepting ethnic cleansing and seeming secular. We were there to protect Indian citizens—whether Muslim or Hindu or whatever. The argument that saving minorities was the job of the Police was a rather specious argument. If that was indeed so, then why were so many divisions of army troops required in J&K? The road NH-1A was more important and the minorities of Kishtwar could hang or flee or do whatever they liked, seemed to be the unfortunate upshot of this line of thinking. The Army refused to send anymore troops to this area. I was told to do the best that I could. Even though I was weak all over, at the point of decision, I concentrated almost one third of my force and it paid off. It was a leaf right out of Field Marshal Erwin Rommel's book, as the corps commander had said. Surprisingly, Mechanised warfare and guerilla warfare have a great deal in common. Both need great *mobility of mind and the capability to concentrate rapidly to deal a swift blow and then disperse equally rapidly*. I used the road network and motor transport to rapidly build up my strength in the area of operations, to track down the culprits. The media hype leveraged our response and magnified it greatly. It made it look even larger than it was and underlined the state's resolve not to take it lying down.

Within a month we had tracked these terrorists down to a remote Dhok (shepards hut) in the Tanta forests. This lay in the area of 26 RR, almost 46 kms away (as the crow flies) from the scene of the massacre. Radio intercepts confirmed that these indeed were Abu Musa, Abu Umer and Abu Ghulam. There were desperate calls to help this surrounded group as the Army was apparently baying for their blood. One intercept said frantically "do something, distract the Army, they have surrounded them." This confirmed to us that we had zeroed in on our quarry. The Dhok unfortunately was in a clearing in the forest. As our boys tried to close in, one of them got shot through his head. The bullet penetrated the skull and emerged from the rear. Amazingly, the boy was still alive. The CO rushed to the area and had it cordoned off. Dusk was descending and it was not possible now to get a helicopter to evacuate the boy. With a head wound, he would surely die unless evacuated promptly. The CO was worried sick.

There were two major constraints imposed on our operations in those days. One was the Human Right accusations degrade and the other was the fear of incurring casualties. Fear of inadvertent human Rights accusations slowed down the tempo of operations. 97 per cent of the Human rights accusations in J&K had turned out to be false when investigated by the Indian Commission for Human rights. Nevertheless such accusations certainly put the Army on the backfoot and slowed down the tempo of operations in that area. The second degrade was the fact that casualties to own troops were just not acceptable to the hierarchy. Though it was a most well-intentioned policy and was aimed at avoiding needless loss of life, at times, it was pushed to extremes and a lot of unwarranted pressure was brought on COs who incurred casualties. Where a casualty has occurred due to tactical ineptitude, negligence, apathy or casualness in operations, it is indeed condemnable and needs to be dealt with sternly. However, with the best of precautions, casualties do occur in combat as bullets are flying around. There are the spirited boys who are brave and take undue risks. Curbing their initiative amounts to slowing down of operations. What greatly raises morale and risk taking in such operations is the absolute certainty that if any soldier is hit he will be speedily evacuated and saved. That has the most miraculous impact on combat operations.

What is gallantry? Gallantry amounts, at times, to taking foolhardy risks in combat. This facet of military activity cannot be curbed on the plea of reducing casualties. All this amounted to asking for a zero error syndrome. The unit had taken a few casualties in the past few months and the CO was understandably under pressure and edgy. The target that day was of critical importance. I asked him to hold on and not lift the cordon. I moved forward myself with an ambulance to get a feel of the situation and evacuate the wounded boy at the earliest. We reached there late at night. We got the boy out and got back to the Battalion Headquarters. The Regimental Medical Officer (RMO) checked his bandages. He was still conscious. We put him in an ambulance truck with escort and sped him off the same night to Udhampur by road. He was safely with the Neuro surgeon before 0500 hours the next morning, was operated upon and survived miraculously.

The casualty saved, I turned my attention to the operation. As the boys tried to close in they drew a heavy volume of fire. Since there was little cover in that clearing—a frontal assault was likely to be suicidal and prohibitive in casualties. I asked the CO what he planned to do. His Rocket Launchers (RLs) were now pounding the Dhok. I asked him to stop wasting the Anti-tank or High Explosive ammunition. Past experience had indicated that RLs have little effect on Dhoks that are made of pine logs. In most cases our boys fired from too close to let the round arm. Even once armed, there was little impact of the High Explosive Anti Tank (HEAT) rounds on the solid mud and log construction that simply absorbed the HEAT jets.

The CO then sought permission to use the Russian Thermobaric flame thrower. The CO was somewhat apprehensive that there may be some civilians also in the Dhok. We asked him to use the loud hailer and ask the civilians, if any, to clear out of the Dhok as we were going to destroy it. There was no civilians there. The terrorists inside answered with a burst of AK fire and choicest abuse in Punjabi. The rocket Launchers had failed against that wooden log hut. The alternative of not using the Thermobaric weapon was to incur heavy casualties to our own boys in that open clearing without a stich of cover. The Terrorists who were holed up there were mass killers and likely to fight till the bitter end like cornered rats. I ordered the CO to go right ahead and assured him I would be responsible for any consequences thereof.

The boys complied instantly. The Thermobaric weapon is terrible. It creates an eight meters fireball with an intense heat of 1000° centigrade at the centre. The entire Dhok was burnt to ash. The bodies of the three terrorists were charred to cinder. As we could see, there were lines of grey ash where the hips, spine and legs of the terrorists had been. The AK-47 rifles' woodwork was completely burnt. So intense was the heat that the barrels were bent into the shape of a 'U'. I asked the CO to get plenty of digital photographs taken of the charred terrorist bodies and AKs as evidence.

That evening I summoned a meeting of all the Sarpanches and prominent citizens of the Gulabgarh area where the massacre had taken place. We deliberately called some OGWs and terrorist sympathisers.

"The Lord himself condemns those who violate his injunctions. The Holy Koran clearly prohibits killing innocent women, children and the aged and infirm, even in a jihad. Abu Musa, Abu Umer and Abu Ghulam did just that. Now see their fate."

I asked my staff to project the video images of that burnt out Dhok. They were somewhat apprehensive and tried to advise me against it. I overruled them. Our objectives in this battle were Cognitive and Behavioural. We had to deter because we just did not have the troops and resources to defend every village, hamlet, Dhok and pasture. So we had specifically targeted those who had targeted the minorities and tried ethnic cleansing in our area.

There was a shocked silence once the enlarged video images were shown on the 10 feet by eight feet screen. The OGWs were aghast. As expected they dutifully carried the message to their mentors. The Sarpanchas nodded their heads sagely. *That was September 2001. Till date, there has been no further massacre of the minorities in the Kishtwar area since then.*

No tanzeem ever dared again to repeat this ethnic cleansing exercise. Our deterrence strategy had worked. It was a very high risk gamble but it paid off. We had to save the people from this campaign of ethnic cleansing and could by no means have stood and watched as mute spectators. It was indeed essential and highlighted that to modify perceptions and change target behaviour, we sometimes needed to commit large force levels and launch high visibility operations. These must be accompanied with a concerted psy-operations campaign, both in the print and electronic media as well as by word of mouth through the sources and civilians..

There was a deafening silence in the whole of Kishtwar district after this operation. It had a visible and salutory impact. How palpable it was, was proved to us when Op Parakram started a few months later and one of our units had to move out of the area. We got radio intercepts of terrorist transmissions, "The Army is getting in trucks and leaving", one of them said excitedly.

"Whatever you do, don't kill the Hindus. They will return like mad dogs." His leader replied.

The point had been driven home. We had succeeded in deterring the terrorists from carrying out any further ethnic cleansing in Kishtwar. We had succeeded in modifying the target behavior. It was indeed the high point of our Counter Terrorist (CT) campaign and a matter of deep personal satisfaction.

I earned a great ally after that—the Army Commander Northern Command. Lt Gen Rustom Nanavatty, was a soldier with a sterling professional reputation. He was intelligent, very hardworking and highly professional in his approach. He could be ruthless with his pen and people feared him greatly because he was a stern disciplinarian and a first rate combat soldier. He was dead against any human rights violations or ill treatment of civilians. He was a very patient listener. He moved about a lot and was clear headed and straight forward in his approach. Gen Nanavatty was a professional soldier par excellence. I had seen Gen Nanavatty as a trim and Spartan major in 2/8 Gurkha Rifles. Later I had served with him at the MO Directorate, where he had been selected to head the Special Forces Cell. Frugal and spartan—Rustom Nanavatty was a combat veteran and a thorough bred professional with a very high standing in the Army.

He visited me at Kishtwar and was very pleased with our handling of the situation. I outlined to him our policy of defending the minorities by deterring attacks on them. He listened thoughtfully and endorsed the offensive approach totally. In any case, it was highly economical in terms of troops. If you focus your resources correctly you can pursue a highly offensive approach even in a situation of overall paucity of troops. From thereon, he took a personal interest in Kishtwar. After the concerted operations, the area was fast returning to normalcy and he was very pleased and readily forthcoming with additional resources and troops for my sector. It was one of the Black Zones that was evidently turning white and the development was obviously cause for satisfaction all round. As part of the ink blot strategy, he wanted the white or pacified zones to grow and expand. He subsequently allotted to me three additional battalions the next year to turn this area around completely.

CHAPTER 8

Heliborne Operations at Navapachi

The Navapachi post was located at six days turn around from our road ahead at Patimahal. It lay in the heart of the Dachin-Marwah region. This formed a huge "U" shaped glaciated valley. Through this gorge flowed the sacred Marud Vridha River, which is now called the Maru River by the locals. Surprisingly, the Rig Vedic Aryans had included this river in their Nadi Sukta (or Hymn to the Sacred Rivers). It was placed on par with major sacred rivers like the Ganga, Yamuna, Saraswati, Beas, Jhelum and Chenab, etc. The Marwah bowl is highly fertile and is famous for its Rice and Kidney Beans crop. There was no road to this area or electricity. It was at the end of a tenuous mule track. Beyond this lay the Sarkund Pass and further flowed the Warwan River, which flanked the sacred cave of Amarnath.

This area was wholly devoid of any military presence. The terrorists had therefore had a field day. They had burnt all government buildings, schools and graneries here—in fact all public utilities were razed to the ground. All government officials had fled the area and it had become for all purposes 'a so-called liberated zone'. In purely Maoist terms, it had become a classical base area, where the terrorists could retire for rest, relief and recuperation. They could establish their training camps and command centers and carry out their activities unhindered. What was the right course of action to hold such remote regions, which had no road links—only a tenuous mule track. The journey to and from Navpachi took six days (three days either way). Initially, we had lacked the troops and there was no option but to let things be. As the people protested, at the terrorists high handedness with the population and atrocities on women increased, there was an outcry of sorts and the government was forced to respond. A BSF company was located there to help the pitiful Police outpost. Their supplies came by road and mule track, and were prone to terrorist ambushes in the dense jungles along the track, which followed the course of the Maru River.

Finally, it was decided to establish a military outpost at Navapachi. A company of 26 RR was located here, which was totally maintained from the air by weekly sorties of MI-17 helicopters. This freed it from any long and tenuous surface link. The French Paratrooper General Henri Navarre had hit upon the same solution in North Vietnam in 1953. The roads to the remote provinces passed through dense jungles and were highly vulnerable and ambush prone. He had therefore established air maintained garrisons in remote areas. The most tenuous of these was the famous Dien-Bien-Phu. Unfortunately Dien-Bien-Phu turned out to be a military disaster. The guerilla war in Vietnam was then in the second stage and was just entering the third stage of regular or conventional operations. The Viet Minh (led by the famous General Vo Nguyen Giap) laid siege to the large air-maintained garrison of Dien-Bien-Phu. The Viet Minh had artillery and mortars and they launched all out attacks that led to the final capitulation of the huge French Garrison. It was a sobering historical precedent.

There was much debate about this heli-maintained post. Such heli-maintained posts are a huge drain on scarce helicopter resources. Ensconced deep in terrorist held area—was this post an operational asset or a vulnerability? The Staff at the Command and Force HQ felt it was a waste of effort and could prove to be a vulnerability. The Force HQ wanted me to close in my deployment and focus on the close in defence of NH-1B road and population centres. The GOC was most critical of my venturing out into remote areas in search of terrorists to kill. Now that my sector had been denuded of a battalion, he felt it was prudent for me to close in and focus only on the essentials. In effect, it meant adopting a wholly defensive and reactive stance.

I had examined the problem in detail. Navapachi formed a vital airhead deep inside what was virtually a "free run" zone for terrorists. With its large population and logistical support base, it was a classical base area in terms of Maoist theory. If held as an airhead by bold and aggressive troops however, it was a major asset. Under the new Company Commander it was proving to be precisely such a tangible operational asset. He had already used it as a base to foray around and kill a large number of terrorists. Withdrawal from this airhead would be a retrograde step. Should the terrorists decide to put pressure on it we could easily reinforce it in time by helicopters.

The J&K Police was seriously concerned about the prospect of any Army withdrawal from Navapachi. In fact, they had themselves launched large scale operations against the terrorists in Warwan. The Warwan valley lay at a days march from Navapachi. It had a series of villages along the Maru River tract, which had flanked the Caves of the Amarnath shrine. Therefore, it posed a threat in being to the Yatra. In fact, terrorists from the Warwan valley had struck the Yatra camps in the year 2001.

The Army Commander paid me a visit. He was keen to know my views about Navapachi. I pointed out to him the analogy of Gen Henri Navarre's solution of surface maintenance free posts in Vietnam. He smiled and pointed out that the airhead theory had resulted in the disaster of Dien-Bien-Phu.

"But there was a major difference", I insisted, "Here the terrorist movement is only in the first stage. They are not operating in large sized gangs that could pose a threat to a heli-maintained post. They don't have any heavy weapons or artillery for a conventional assault. On the other hand they tend to be lax while moving in such remote areas. Almost 30 per cent of the attrition achieved by us in this Sector in the last year was inflicted by this Navapachi post. Abandoning it would provide a classical base area to the terrorists to rest, recuperate and train. Navapachi has a population and resource base, which we cannot afford to let slip into the hands of terrorists."

That clinched the issue. The Navapachi post was retained and is still going strong. This airhead proved to be a valuable operational asset and in the years 2001 and 2002 it continued to inflict almost 30 per cent of the overall attrition in 9 Sector RR on the terrorist tanzeems. A number of senior terrorist leaders were killed here. Used aggressively, it was not a vulnerability, it turned out to be a huge asset.

In the end, the whole argument hinged on overall mindset and methodology of operations in this area. With the reduction in my force levels, HQ CI Force Delta was concerned and wanted me to adopt a purely defensive layout that focussed on a close in protection of the road and major population centers. They wanted me to abandon the remote Navapachi outpost and forays in other remote areas. On the other hand my key priority was to retain our offensive orientation and keep hitting out at the terrorists to keep them off-balance. Getting bogged down in a purely defensive stance would be a recipe for disaster in a situation of force depletion. The best method of defense is attack. An offensive orientation leads to lesser combat stress as the troops feel that they are in control of their lives and situation. They are not reactive and thus retain the initiative. *The whole trick is to create situations for the adversary faster than he can create them for us.* This was our central dictum in 9 Sector RR and we kept hitting out repeatedly. This gave us an impressive tally of Command and Control (C2) kills and kept the terrorist tanzeems wholly off-balance in our area. Getting bogged down in a defensive mindset would have demoralised the troops and let the initiative pass on to the enemy. I was glad that I was able to retain the Navapachi post.

I was particularly keen to retain the Navapachi post additionaly, because it served as a base for launching heliborne operations in the Warwan area. The problem with land forays into this very remote valley was that there was only a single track approach along the narrow valley. The moment our columns set out, the terrorists' early warning apparatus would get into action and alert them. We hit the thin air at the end of long and grueling forced marches. The only answer was heliborne operations.

Another such remote terrorist Base area was Bari dhok in the Gundoh tehsil bordering Himachal Pradesh. It was a broad Grazing ground deep in the mountains bordering Chamba. The approaches to it were along the narrow gorges of long and winding mountain nalas. News periodically came in of a large concentration of terrorists there. This was a difficult target and the only possibility lay in heliborne operations. These were not forthcoming. The new Police Chief in Doda-Kishtwar was SSP Ashkoor Wani, a very spirited local policeman. He kept coming to me with reports of huge concentrations of terrorists in Bari dhok and wanted to launch Joint operations. We just did not have the troops for such a large scale and complex operation. Once when I had gone for a spot of casual leave, 26 RR received inputs of terrorist move in the Bari Dhok area. Unfortunately the operation was launched in a half hearted and hurried manner with a single column under a JCO. This was too small a force to be pushed out so deep. It should have been officer led. This force was ambushed in the narrow gorge of the approach valley. The terrorists sprayed them with small arms and Under Barrel Grenade Launchers (UBGL). One boy was killed and two were wounded. Some seven others received light splinter injuries from the UBGL grenade launchers fragments. This created alarm in all HQs and a number of helicopter sorties had to be launched to evacuate the casualties. I was returning from leave and heard of this ambush at the railway station. I rushed to the Udhampur Military Hospital on my way up and met the casualties. The boys confirmed to me that the terrorist group was not very large and the UBGL grenades had done the damage in that narrow gorge. There was just one track to approach Bari Dhok and it was prone to ambushes throughout its length. The only answer at this long range was to launch heliborne operations and land directly on the target itself or behind it. The debate about addressing these remote base areas continued and the arguments usually grew heated and acrimonious.

Heliborne Operations in Warwan

As a prelude to the Amarnath Yatra, heliborne and ground operations were usually launched into the Warwan valley to disrupt the terrorist preparation for any action against the pilgrims. These had become an annual ritual that lacked any element of surprise. The terrain here was a perfect analogue of what we would encounter across the LC and we could gain valuable experience by conducting heliborne operations against the terrorists here. The problem was the lack of reliable intelligence about these remote areas. Any source operating on foot would take days/weeks to come back from the target end and by that time, the terrorist concentration could have easily shifted or melted away. These constraints had caused a number of earlier attempts at heliborne operations to fail.

I requested Gen Rustom Nanavatty that he must give us the freedom to fail. Only then could we gain experience and perfect the technique of heliborne operations. It was pathetic that despite all the years of CI experience in the North East, Sri Lanka and J&K, we had hardly any successful heliborne operations to talk of. It was a sad commentary on our professional abilities. 73 Mountain brigade had launched a major Heliborne operation called Op Kukhri in the Warwan area in summer. However the massive buildup for this operation had compromised surprise and the terrorists had melted away before our troops struck. We decided to hit the terrorist concentration in the Warwan valley at the height of winter, when they would least expect us to do so. The new version of MI-17 helicopters had come in (post Op Vijay) and this had a much more powerful engine. Gen Nanavatty allocated us three new MI-17 helicopters for this operation.

Those days, the Air Force used to insist that the target area be sanitised by ground troops *first* before our troops could be heli-landed. If a Dropping Zone (DZ) securing party had to be inserted by foot earlier, it would make the entire heliborne operations unnecessary. However, peacetime safety requirements inhibited our Air Force colleagues from carrying out such missions. This had proved to be the biggest dampener for heliborne operations in J&K. Fortunately by that time, Op Parakram had started and it was decided to give the peacetime safety requirements the go by. The Air Force was much more forthcoming now.

Slithering or Low Hover

Another debate in heliborne operations was whether to use slithering techniques or drop from the low hover. We carried out a number of trials and found that the low hover methodology was much faster and tactically better. Slithering requires much training and is preferable for night operations in plains or desert terrain. The helicopters cannot always maintain a steady height during the hover and keeps going up and down. This leads to injuries to the slithering troops. Slithering takes relatively more time and thus exposes the helicopter to ground fire for longer periods. We worked out our landing drills from low hover which is made safer in the snow. An MI-17 helicopter could drop16 armed troops in a matter of just 18 seconds. The troops were trained to exit from either corner of the open doors. They ran outwards on landing and took up positions for all round defence in a circular perimeter around the helicopter as shown in Fig. 6.

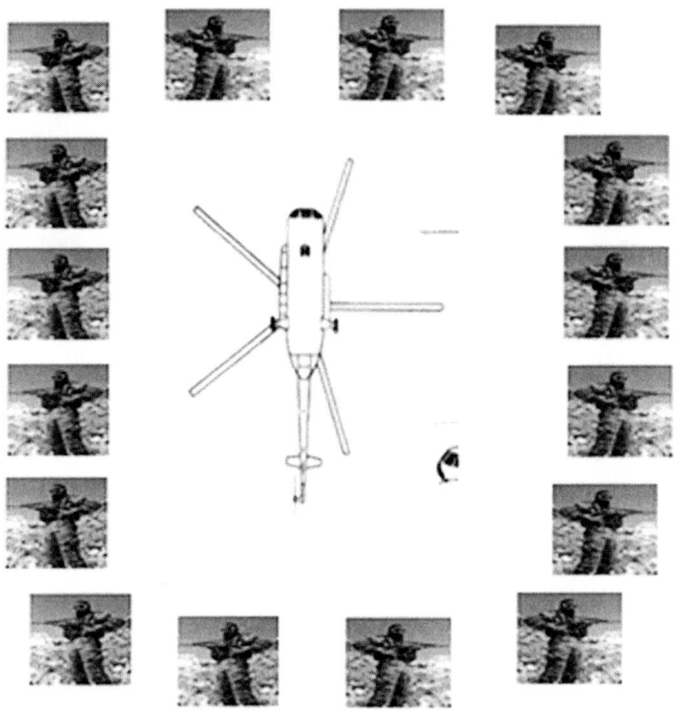

Figure 6 Perimeter around MI-17

In ground hover also permits the helicopter to present a much safer profile than for slithering and disgorges the troops in virtually half the time. To retain orientation, it is essential that the Officer/Stick Commander in each helicopter stands facing the door of the pilot's cabin and watches the terrain through window of the cockpit door. Otherwise troops tend to get disoriented on the target. We carried out a number of trials. One apprehension that arose was that the rotor wash would cause the snow to fly and cover the cockpit glass, thus obscuring the pilot's vision. To check this we carried out few low hover trials at the snow clad Kishtwar helipad itself. To our surprise, we found that the pressure of the rotor downwash caused the snow to melt and rise as water that simply washed the cockpit glass windows.

In December 2001, we decided to launch a company sized heliborne operation in Warwan. We had carried out three such operations earlier without success as the intelligence was poor/delayed. The Intelligence Bureau (IB) reported a large terrorist concentration in the village of Inshan and also that some surface-to-air missiles were cached there. This time I decided to accompany the troops for the helidrop. The MI-17 pilots were young and spirited. They were a little concerned about safety from ground fire in the Landing Zone, especially when they learnt of the presence of SAMs. However, when they learnt that the Brigade Commander was going himself, they felt much encouraged. We launched a total of five sorties that morning. I went in the lead sortie, it was an exilherating experience.

The MI-17 pilots initially flew high. As we reached the Warwan valley, they descended and almost flew at the tree top level. We reached the village of Inshan (where the terrorist concentration was reported). One helicopter went ahead of the village, hovered low and disgorged the troops in 18 seconds flat. The troops dispersed in all round defense positions as per rehearsed drills. My helicopter flew in the next. The landing in the snow was soft and easy. One column secured the helipad for the balance troops to fly in while the other rushed to check out the target houses. Unfortunately for us, the terrorists had constructed elaborate hideouts inside the houses and they hid inside as soon as they heard the rotor noise. We could hear them on our radio net, talking on their radio sets about our landing. The signal strength was high, indicating they were very close but we still could not locate them. One source had told us a place where he said a missile was buried. He had claimed it was a SAM (Surface to Air Missile). When we dug it out, it turned to be a 107 mm rocket (of the type that the Mujahideen had used for bombarding cities in Afghanistan). They had probably bought it here to extract its explosive for making Improvised Explosive Devices (IEDs). We were deeply disappointed. We carried out detailed search of the Inshan village but in the absence of any local sources, could not locate the hideouts. We decided to look for terrorist tracks in the snow but these were mixed up with the footprints of civilians. The local civilians were simply too terrified of the terrorists to venture any information. "You'll go away Sahib. What will happen to us then," they lamented.

The next day I sent out my troops to search the other villages. Surprise by now all had been lost and we did not hit anything. After two days we decided to change tactics. We staged an overt fly out but left two teams behind to hide in the jungles at night and lay ambushes on the tracks. An Afghan District Commander came sauntering on the track and was shot dead. We recovered an AK-56 assault rifle and a radio set along with pouches and ammunition. His diary revealed his identity and gave invaluable information. We then called off the operation and extricated the remaining two teams by foot. Overall five heliborne operations were launched by us in the remote Warwan area. We also tried the 'trickle' build up method of sending troops in over a period of time to Navapachi post as part of the regular maintenance sorties. We tried to swoop down on the Alti and Inshan villages in the Warwan valley directly on a number of occasions. These helped us perfect our drills for mounting such operations and landing from the low hover in remote areas. The problem in all cases was the availability of reliable intelligence of such depth areas. Possible solutions were using Unmanned Aerial Vehicles (UAVs) or small/clandestine surveillance teams to keep such target under surveillance and then direct the fly in to assured targets. In any case, there were very valuable lessons learnt in an extremely realistic setting. Professionally it was a most enriching experience.

CHAPTER 9

Advantages of an Offensive Mindset: The Kishtwar Experience

One of the first object lessons that I had learnt in live combat in Kargil was the need for an offensive mindset as the key to not just victory but survival on the battlefield. Apple Beeb, Swank and Marchand are the leading western authorities on combat stress. Their studies are based on extensive databases collected during the Second World War and the Korean War. They have noted that while physical casualties may be far higher in offensive operations, psychiatric or combat stress casualties are far lower in such operations (e.g., Attack, advance or pursuit). In such operations the troops *feel they are in control of their lives.* They have the initiative and set the pace of action on the battlefield. This results in greatly reducing the levels of combat stress.

Scientists had also noted the 90-180 days cycle of combat stress. 90 days of sustained combat will cause 50 per cent of the men in a unit to become dysfunctional. By day 180, almost 92 per cent of the troops would have become combat stress casualties. Hence, the criticality of giving each man in combat a break after 90 days, whether he asks for it or not. This is critical for recuperability and unit morale and cohesion.

Another important finding was that some men are intrinsically high stress levelers. Only 10-15 per cent of the men fired their weapons in actual combat in World War-II and in Korea. Significantly, it was the same 10-15 per cent men who kept firing throughout the duration of the conflict. Identifying and optimally utilising such men is the key to combat leadership.

These standard lessons on combat stress and its management had become starkly apparent to me in my very first combat assignment as a Battalion Commander in Kargil, where I led my unit for over a year, under heavy artillery, mortars, light weight air-defence bombardment and heavy small arms fire exchanges.

As our troops were moving in to take over their defences at Dalunag, a Pakistani soldier from the post overlooking ours had shouted, "*O Graeens! Humse panga mat lena. Tumhara fire ka hukum Dilli se aata hai—Hamara hamari jeb me hai.*" (O Friends! Do not mess with us. Your fire orders come from Delhi. Ours are in our pocket.)

It had led me to ponder deeply. In the days that followed I found 29 Baluch of the Pakistani Army playing merry hell into our unit. They fired wherever they felt like and in whatever volume they felt like. They used whatever weapons they wanted, wherever they wanted. We were under multiple constraints and had to seek permission and clearances all the way up the chain as the orders then were to avoid escalation. This left the boys demoralised, frustrated and confused. Why did we always have to tie our arms behind our backs and fight? This was not a crowd of misguided Indian citizens. These were troops of 29 Baluch and 3 Northern Light Infantry of the Pakistan Army firing from an area of intrusion. Why was the onus of restraint placed squarely on us in all situations? It was a highly damaging and ambiguous situation to place troops in on the battlefield. Two previous units that had served here had taken heavy casualties. One had to be withdrawn in less than four months. The next served for about 10 months before it was taken out of the area of intrusion. It was imperative that we change the rules of engagement here to reduce combat stress.

I raised the issue with the hierarchy with the utmost urgency. Fortunately the dispensation in the meantime had changed. The Brigade Commander and the new Divisional Commander were both very aggressive personalities. I made a detailed presentation and they agreed with me wholeheartedly. The restrictive rules of engagement were changed and I was given a freehand to conduct fire assaults as required thereafter. This caused a visible and dramatic improvement in troop morale and the boys did wonders. Thereafter, we dictated the pace of events and not the trigger happy troops of 29 Baluch. We acted to a central plan and design. One had learnt one of the cardinal lessons of combat. Never be reactive. Act. Make the enemy react. *Impose your plan on the enemy's plan.*

As a Brigade Commander therefore, I strove energetically to see that we retained the initiative at all times and the troops of 9 Sector RR maintained an offensive mindset. The best method of defense indeed is attack. Even when my force levels were reduced from three battalions to just two in Kishtwar, I decided to hit out proactively. I refused to pull in my deployment to a purely defensive stance designed to protect the communication centres and road arteries alone. We focussed troops and resources wherever contact was gained. We thinned out temporarily in other areas to fight a fluid and mobile battle, where we kept hitting the terrorists continuously. I laid major stress on offensive operations designed to inflict attrition on the terrorist tanzeem leadership and rank and file. My insistence on offensive operations paid off hands down. In the year 2001, even though we had just two battalions, 9 Sector RR had the highest tally of kills in the whole of CI Force Delta. In fact at 54 kills that year we had set an all time record since the raising of this formation. Never had so many terrorists been killed in a single year in the very difficult and mountainous terrain of Kishtwar.

The degree of difficulty of conducting Counter Terrorist (CT) Operations at these heights is generally not realised. The valley floors vary in altitude from 1,500 to 2,000 metres. The adjoining ridge lines rise steeply from 4,000 to 5,000 metres. Most operations required forced marches and climbs of 6-8 hours or more. Two, at best three operations per week can be exhausting for the troops. Add to these, the tremendous difficulty of evacuating casualties from these heights and one can form some idea of the degree of difficulty involved in operating in these extremely tough terrain conditions. The rates of attrition achieved in the flat valley of Kashmir are far higher. Troops can move for operations on road in Mechanical Transport. All operations in Kishtwar however were based on foot mobility over the most rugged and mountainous terrain in the world. Almost 60 per cent terrorists here were locals but unlike their valley cousins, a large number were former hunting expedition guides and trekkers. They were tough, fleet footed, experts at the mountainous trails and fairly good shots. They tended to operate in the valleys and lower heights. The foreign terrorists preferred to operate on the ridge lines of the Pir Panjals and other ranges. They depended for sustenance on the Gujjars and Bakkarwals whom they coerced into providing food, shelter, intelligence and women. I laid maximum emphasis on Command and Control attrition. Each unit was assigned its prime targets. Specified officers in the units specialised on a given terrorist leader in his Area of Responsibility (AOR). He maintained his tracking/movement map and the successive circles of his family members and friends and associates.

These were concentric circles. If he was a local, the first circle was his primary family unit—his father-mother, brother-sister, wife and children. They were unlikely to give information but knowing their actions was critical. In the second circle were friends, cousins and parmours. Sexual promiscuity is generally high in the hills and remote areas. The terrorists were inveterate philanderers and very promiscuous sexually. Sex was a great stress buster for them. As their so-called jihad progressed, they spoke less of their high fluting ideals and indulged more in rapes, molestations and extortions. *Criminialisation is the normal trajectory of all terrorist movements.*

When the first group of foreign terrorists came into the region, they were a great novelty. With their Karakul caps, long hair and cavemen beards—they gave the charismatic Che Guevara look. They claimed to be the liberators of the people and their Kalashnikovs were virtual phallic symbols. The local girls were swept off their feet by these guest Mujahideen who had come in from the mountain mists. There were a number of Nikahs (marriages) of local girls with these 'guest warriors'. To their shock and horror these girls and their parents realised that the Guest Mujahideens were there for two to three years tenure at best. After which, they just vanished into the mountain mists—never to return. The girls were left with fatherless children and unwanted pregnancies. The locals thereafter became very chary of these *nikahs*. The guest Mujahideens who came in later were quite frustrated. Their ISI handlers and former comrades had regaled them with tales of the beautiful Kashmiri women who were theirs for the asking. The situation on the ground however had changed drastically. The foreigners then started poaching on the married women as Nikahs with virgins were not popular anymore. This meant that the husbands had to stand outside their houses while a group of terrorists slaked their lust on their women within. This naturally became too much to take and overtime, intelligence began to flow in.

The Mujahideen justification for rape and using Kashmiri girls as comfort women was ingenious. "Do your duty by the Jihad. We have come to free you from the infidels.It is your duty to comfort the warriors." It was difficult for unarmed husbands to argue with the Kalashnikov of the terrorists.This led to unimaginable situations of stress in the rural communities of the hinterland. The family unit came under terrible stress. There were cases of psychiatric breakdown. And then the intelligence began to flow in. It came in fits and starts at first as fathers of daughters and husbands of gang-raped wives came forth to volunteer information about the terrorists—mostly foreigners, and we began to get a series of successes.

There was the case of a stressed out father whose daughters were regularly gang-raped by these thugs. He came to the post himself and wept before the company commander. He took our boys to the village and had them hide in homes on the outskirts. The moment the terrorists arrived in and were closeted with the girls, he rushed out to our boys. We killed that group of four terrorists in a clean and clinical encounter. There were many more such success stories as the terrorists fell from their self professed moral pedestal.

I had this fully exploited in our psy-op themes. We sent our Company Commanders from village to village—exhorting the people not to take the abuse of their women at the hands of the foreign terrorists, lying down. We scored repeatedly based on intelligence windfalls stemming from the terrorist exploitation of local women. It lent a degree of predictability to the terrorist actions. Our sources kept us informed of these terrorist liaisons and trysts with their keeps and this resulted in a number of successful encounters. In retaliation, the LeT and Jaish-e-Mohammed (JeM) tanzeems began to escalate actions. There were a string of attacks on the vital NH-1A. The withdrawal of the dual tasked formations after Op Vijay was keenly felt here. Unfortunately, Delta Force's solution of focussing on the road *per se* and leaving the higher heights undefended proved to be a tactical mistake. There were other high-profile terrorist strikes in the valley. The disruption of the CI grid during Op Vijay had led to this reprieve for the terrorist organisations in the hinterland.

However, what was worrying was that Pakistan-based tanzeems were widening their sphere of action into the Indian mainland *per se*. Buoyed by the 9/11 destruction of the World Trade Centre twin towers in New York, they began to hit symbolical targets all over India. There was an attack on the J&K Assembly first. This later culminated in the terrorist attack on the Indian Parliament and it was this final insult that set the cat amongst the pigeons. India responded with Op Parakram—a total mobilisation of its armed forces for war (as opposed to the partial mobilisation in Op Vijay). Our strategic reserves and dual tasked formations were once again moved up and even the Navy and the Air Force mobilised for a full-scale conflict. There was a great deal of ambiguity as to intent within the armed forces themselves. Was it a gigantic coercive exercise? Or was it mobilisation for a limited/full-scale conventional war to teach Pakistan a lesson? There was tremendous enthusiasm and excitement at the lower level as the buildup unfolded apace. The Rashtriya Rifles (RR) was mobilised for Rear Area Security (RAS) tasks once again. To strengthen the security of the vital artery of the Jammu-Srinagar Highway (NH-1A)—one of my units—26 RR was ordered to be redeployed for securing the route from Patnitop to Nagrota. Were we actually going to war? During the flurry of conferences, we put forth our point of view. Holding roads in some strength was essential but I argued that the RR troops were the most proficient in sub-tactical offensive actions like ambushes, raids or even the establishment of road blocks! This well-trained resource should be offensively employed to strike across the Line of Control (LC) and create problems for the enemy in his rear rather than be obsessed with guarding our own rear ad nauseum from an enemy Army virtually half the size of ours. There was considerable debate and excitement. There was also a tremendous flurry of activity. I was down for a recce of vital areas and vulnerable points we were required to assist in guarding, when I saw massive convoys of vehicles trundling out on the roads from Mamun and other military cantonments. Soon live mines were ordered to be laid. There was great excitement in the air. At last the Indian state had seemingly decided to teach Pakistan a lesson for its endless provocations of the last 30 years. The actions of the first month or two were credible and Pakistani President Gen Parvez Musharraf was forced to come on TV and denounce terrorism by his tanzeems. Thereafter, however, the impact of Op Parakram began to diminish very perceptibly. Pakistan undertook precautionary deployment of its own armed forces but appeared less than convinced of our resolve to commence limited/full scale conventional operations. Were we serious?

Orders were passed to add more credibility by ordering the laying of defensive minefields. Millions of mines were laid and we had to take many casualties recovering the minefields subsequently. It did not add to the level of conviction and was not credible action in terms of the cost-benefit ratio. The tremendous enthusiasm built up in the armed forces was soon frittered away as a purpose-less deployment went on and on interminably, leaving our troops fairly confused and frustrated.

In parenthesis, there was a school of thought that felt that in the initial month of mobilisation we had a window of opportunity to press in some actual action, but we lost it due to the tardy pace of our mobilisation. This school of thought averred that the political leadership had given the go ahead for a limited action but we were not able to exploit it as we were not psychologically prepared to act at that pace and tempo. 1971 had taught us the value of a slow and methodical build up.

Unfortunately that was no longer relevant in 2001. The world over, the trend was to go in for Rapid Reaction Forces of combined arms. The Air Force is best placed to react offensively in such a scenario, while retaining escalation dominance.

The other school of thought felt that we had not been able to summon the political will and the leadership failed to give the critical go ahead to the armed forces. Frankly there was a lot of skepticism that such a go ahead would come. Two decades of underfunding had eroded our conventional edge to a degree that it was not a viable option anymore. Nevertheless, to add some credibility to our exercise, some amount of limited action was most essential. Without that, the mobilisation became very prone to the law of severely diminishing returns. It once again took the heat off the terrorist tanzeems and gave them a breather in J&K.

At our level, we received orders for 26 RR to be diverted from CT operations to securing the NH-1A. My HQ was to set up a tactical HQ at Udhampur, with my Deputy to regulate the traffic flow on this artery. As the unit was mobilising to come down from its posts, we intercepted excited chatter on the terrorist radio network.

"The army is leaving", reported one terrorist.

"Whatever you do—don't kill the Hindus. That will make them mad. They will come charging back."

I listened to this terrorist radio transmission with very grim satisfaction. Our massive deterrence exercise to stop ethnic cleansing had succeeded. Its psychological impact on the enemy was clearly visible in this radio intercept.

We completed our redeployment in very quick time. I personally went over the entire stretch of the road from Patnitop to Nagrota and explained my concept to the CO and the Company Commander.

"*Attack those who are likely to attack the road*. Keep hitting out on the hill features dominating the road. Go for those who are likely to target this artery. *Kill them before they can come close.*"

CI Force Delta wanted us to focus on our Standard Operating Procedures (SOPs) for road clearance and close in protection drills. They were important of course but in a largely Dogra dominated area—an offensive methodology based on acquisition of early intelligence of threats to the road and hitting out offensively would be far more cost-effective. The men of 26 RR were somewhat crestfallen.

"There are no terrorists to kill here, Sir. We are being wasted on a purely defensive para-military task."

"A good battalion will squeeze the terrorists even out of a stone. Find them—wherever they are. Kill them before they can even think of targeting the road."I told them.

It was amazing, but that is the way it happened. A month later we picked up a radio intercept that a group of foreign terrorists had lost their way and were now in the vicinity of the Vaishno Devi shrine and the road—trying to find their bearings. I immediately picked up the phone and ordered the CO to go for this group. In a Dogra area, they would stick out like sore thumbs. I ordered the CO to throw everything—get in touch with the police, the ex-servicemen and go for this group. It took us two weeks of intensive searches and chases to pick up the trail. We coordinated with the police. CI Force Delta were worried that the road was being uncovered by these wild goose chases in the wilderness. But my instincts had not failed me. Two weeks later, we had surrounded this group in a cave near the Trikuta peak. Our troops made extensive use of rocket launchers and explosives. The trapped terrorists tried desperately to break out but were picked up and shot one by one in a remarkably clean operation. At the end of it, five foreign terrorists lay dead and their arms and ammunition were recovered. It was a precision operation for which kudos came from the Army Commander himself.

It removed all threat to the road. We held it open for the smooth flow of traffic for almost four months and there was not even a single incident on that road. The offensive way of road clearance had proved itself. It was an indirect and therefore a far better approach. However, I kept clamouring that my troops be taken off this defensive task and reverted to their primary role of counter terrorist operations in the hinterland. The battalions were accordingly restored to the CT grid and subsequently scored impressive successes in the Tanta-Halaran forest and elsewhere.

The Highest Award: Ashoka Chakra

On 22 October 2002, 26 RR received information that a very large group of 14 terrorists from the LeT and HUM Tanzeems had gathered in the Kaku village near the Tehsil HQ of Gundoh. A massive joint operation was launched with five coloumns of 26 RR, one from Police Special Task Force and one from the ITBP Battalion which had recently been allotted to me. The cordon around the Kaku village was in place by 0630h in the morning. The troops began the search. Soon contact was gained and a massive fire fight started at 0730h. Heavy fire was drawn from one house on the outskirts of the village. Maj Karthikeyan, one of our very spirited company commanders from the Armoured Corps, moved up personally and fired four rounds of the Carl Gustav Rocket Launcher. There was a sudden and deafening silence. A team of Two RR soldiers and two SPOs led by Nk Rambir Singh Tomar of 26 RR now was detailed to enter and search the house. There were four terrorists hiding there and a fierce firefight developed. One SPO was killed on the spot and Tomar was hit below the left eye. He began to bleed profusely. Despite his wound he charged in single handed, firing from the hip. A confused hand to hand fight started. The wounded Naik grappled with the terrorists and killed three of them and possibly the fourth as he was trying to escape from the house. Then he fell down dead. Nk Tomar was from the Bhind-Morena area of MP, fabled for its dacoits and outlaws. He was a very brave soldier and died like a true hero in this encounter but not before he had personally killed four foreign terrorists. He could easily have withdrawn from the encounter as he was seriously wounded but the brave lad pressed on the attack and eliminated all the terrorists holed up in the house. It was a superlative feat of raw courage, above and beyond the call of duty. He was posthumously awarded the Ashok Chakra, the nation's highest gallantry award for courage in peace time. The other terrorists in the village now fought furiously like cornered rats. The second in command of 26 RR, Lt Col Goel, a short statured but very intrepid officer who was much experienced in CT operations, now rushed out immediately with reinforcements. It was evident that the terrorists were trying to break out of the cordon and escape. With troops from three different units all blazing away in excitement, it became a very confused melee. For hours the furious gunfire echoed from the hills and it became very difficult to make out what precisely was happening. Some 20 more rounds of Rocket launchers were fired. We were worried about civilian casualties and collateral damage but luckily the intensity of the fighting had caused all the civilians to flee the village well in time. Finally the firing died down and an eerie silence descended on the area. Huge vultures began to circle the village. Thorough search operations were now commenced. Five houses in the village had caught fire because of the rocket explosions and columns of smoke had filled the air. No more terrorists bodies were found. The second in command, Lt Col Goel now decided to search the nala behind the village. Subedar Satya Prakash personally led this search. Two terrorists hiding in the nala now suddenly opened fire. Subedar Satya Prakash and another police SPO were killed in the firefight. The boys fired an RL and both the terrorist were killed. The body of one was almost torn to shreds by the blast of the Rocket and pieces had to picked up from a scattered area. It was one of the biggest encounters in the Kishtwar area and overall six Foreign terrorists were killed. Three AK rifles (two AK-56 and one AK-47), two radio sets and seven hand grenades were recovered. Major lessons were learnt. One was handling the information hunger of the staff. Though two official situation reports are issued each day (morning and evening), whenever a major encounter starts, staff officers at all level go berserk trying to gain minute by minute details on the phone. This disturbs the commanders and troops engaged in the serious fire fights. Often some radio operator starts a running commentary of the fight as he sees it from where he is located. There is a great deal of the fog of war—especially if more than one unit and the police are involved. Both our boys and the terrorists use AKs, so from the sound of firing it becomes very difficult to make out who is firing from where. Sometimes inexperienced Police SPOs and CPO personnel tend to fire wildly and there is serious risk of Blue on Blue casualties—especially if an all-round cordon has been established. It usually takes many hours before the situation crystallises in an encounter like this. So telephone commentaries on a minute to minute basis can add to the confusion and really disturb the commanders and troops in the field. I invariably used to go forward and try and see things for myself. Whenever deluged by calls from higher HQ staff officers, my instructions were simple—switch off the radio set to the rear and let the boys in contact focus on the fire fight. Information hunger in high stress situations like this is understandable but has to be managed. The very next day, news came in that the 11 RR battalion had scored again in Navapachi. Parbat Ali, a district Commander of the JeM and a Tehsil commander were killed and two weapons, a radio set and slidex radio codes were recovered along with a lot of currency.

The grant of Ashok Chakra (AC) to one of our NCOs, Naik Rambir Singh Tomar of 26 RR was a tremendous fillip to the morale of our formation. It went on to score a record number of kills that year. 11 Sector then had four battalions. It had scored some 38 kills. 4 Sector had 3 battalions and 42 kills. 9 Sector with just two battalions had eliminated 54 terrorists. Despite the odds in those difficult mountains, it had been a singular achievement and my heart went out to those boys who had sacrificed so much and striven so hard day and night in that most difficult terrain.

Miracle at Machail

One of the peculiar tasks that we had in the areas south of the Pir Panjals was to provide security during a number of local Pilgrimage yatras to remote shrines in the upper mountain reaches. Somehow, the Dogra community of J&K kept these yatras going throughout the two decade long Proxy war in J&K. One of the underlying purposes of the local people was to keep the faith in these remote shrines alive and even more to reassure these isolated Dogra communities that they were not alone and thereby prevent them from fleeing. One of the holiest shrines in my area was the Machel Mata temple near the Sapphire mines at Gulabgarh. This is where the largest massacre of the minorities had just taken place in August-September 2001. In that year a record number of pilgrims (almost 20,000 were expected to visit this shrine in August). To ensure safety of the pilgrim convoys, the Army was required to launch major operations onto the neighbouring heights to sanitise the area—while the Police was required to provide close in protection of the Pilgrim convoys and the foot marching columns. In view of the large scale massacres of the minority community that year, the threat was particularly acute. We pooled in a company each from 11 RR and 26 RR and sanitised the heights along the whole route. Our concerns were heightened when a record number of pilgrims actually came in that year to Kishtwar for the onward journey to Gulabgarh, from where the pilgrims would march on foot. I decided to carry out a helicopter recce of the mountains that overlook the Machail temple near the Padder gem mines. The area was so remote that helicopters fly here only in pairs. On 17 August 2001, two Cheeta helicopters flew in at Kishtwar to pick me and CO 11 RR for this recce flight. CO 11 RR had just come down after positioning his troops in Gulabgarh and was looking visibly tiered and drained out after his grueling climb. We took off and flew along the valley of the Chenab and then crossed the Gulabgarh confluence. The plan was to ascend up the mountains leading to the famous Umasi La pass (5342 metres over which Gen Zorawar Singh had led his famous expeditions to Ladakh) and scan the upper ridges and slopes for any sign of terrorist activities. As we were nearing Machail the helicopter began to wobble. It yawed to the left and right in a most eerie fashion. I thought it was because of strong headwinds but the yawing persisted. Both Rajesh and I exchanged uneasy glances. The pilot then turned to me and said

"Sir is there any place we can land?"

I said we could turn back and land at Gulabgarh where there were some school playgrounds.

"Sir", he said, doing his utmost to keep the panic out of his voice, "we don't have that much time."

Col Sahai now leaned forward. "One of my patrols had gone up to establish a base at Machail. I had asked them to mark an emergency helipad for casualty evacuation. It should be somewhere close by."

We all scanned the mountain slopes in considerable panic. The pilot located a small H marked with lime and Wheat flour that the boys had carried. Some isolated and tall pine trees were in the way but the pilots managed to touch both the birds down safely. We hurriedly got out of the choppers and the pilots literally mopped their brows. They took out their AK-47s for safety in this remote area where terrorists could be lurking around. It was a messy situation

"Sir the Governor of our chopper has packed up. A few seconds more and we would have come down like a stone" the pilots informed me with obvious relief. It was beyond any local repair and the only answer was for the second chopper to fly back and return with a replacement governor. The pilot offered to fly me back and drop me at my HQ enroute.

I refused. I haven't come all this way just to go back. You go and get the Governor, meantime I'll walk up to the Machail temple. The temple was some 30 minutes climb from where the Helicopters had landed. That incidentally was the day the final *Havan* of the Diety is performed. We started climbing up. Meanwhile hundreds of pilgrims had seen the two choppers land. Many locals had never seen a helicopter before and they all rushed down towards us, breathless with excitement.

"Sir this is indeed a miracle. This is the day of the final *Havan* that marks the culmination of this yatra. The Devi has brought you down for her darshan." They gushed excitedly. The crowds milled around the helicopters childishly even as the alarmed pilots fingered their AKs nervously and asked them to stay back.

The CO and I walked up to the Machail temple and had the Darshan of the Diety. Legend has it that Gen Zorawar Singh had built this temple when he was enroute to his invasion of Ladakh in 1834 and that he prayed here each time he attempted the crossing of the 5342 metres high Umasi La pass for the invasions of Ladakh and finally of Tibet. It is a small but beautiful temple and it was a glorious sunlit day in the massive mountains. We spent an hour there. Meanwhile the patrol from 11 RR fetched up to escort us. I was really overjoyed at this rather unexpected turn of events. A team from Doordarshan had come up on foot to film the pilgrimage and insisted on interviewing me about this miracle—as to how they said the Devi had not let us fly to the Umasi La pass without paying obeisance to her. The incident has since become a staple of the local folklore.

Meanwhile the chopper pilots had informed all HQs about our forced landing and there was great concern about my safety in this remote area where massacares had taken place recently. But it was a very pleasant interlude and one of my most memorable outings in Kishtwar. By the late afternoon the rescue helicopters landed with the replacement parts and we bid farewell to the crowds and took off for Kishtwar. It was quite an experience and has now become part of the local folklore as to how the Army Brigade commander trying to fly to the Umasi La pass was forced to land here and pay homage to the Goddess of the mountains at Machel.

Second tryst with Umasi La. In October 2001 we received alarming reports that a large group of some 200 terrorists had infiltrated via the Dras-Kargil area and were now coming via the Padam and Suru valley of Ladakh to hit Gulabgarh again. I immediately requested for a Helicopter recce flight and it was given promptly. I set out for the second time to recce the Umasi La pass and this time try and fly over the pass into the Padam valley across to pick up any movement of a large sized terrorist group. Co 11 RR again accompanied me and I do not blame him for being a bit apprehensive. Frankly, despite my outer sang froid, I was equally apprehensive after the last episode. The GOC had asked me to take no chances and the caution was well meant. There were no ground patrols in the area now to rescue us. It was a memorable flight. We reached the Gulabgarh valley and began to climb. There were strong winds near the pass. The helicopter engines seemed to strain every sinew but for some reason they could not climb up to the Umasi La pass. It was a formidable mountain scape of bare rocks and snow. Even as the helicopter engines strained, we thought of Zorawar Singh and his Dogra Army crossing this pass at the height of winter in 1834. It was indeed a hair raising feat especially in that era when there was no snow clothing and specialsed equipment. We had now climbed up to 15,300 feet. The pilots now requested permission to abort the flight and return to base. Having come so far I was very keen to cross over and look into the Padam valley for any sign of terrorist movement but the pilots felt it was unsafe and I had to go by their technical judgement. We turned back a 1000 or so feet from the Umasi La pass. On the way back we flew over the Hangshu La pass (4975 metres). This was on the sunfacing slope and all the snow had melted. The track to the Padam valley was clearly visible. There were no signs of any human beings around. It was a hair raising flight and frankly both

Sahai and I were really glad to touch down on terra firma and feel the earth under our feet. My soldiers said we should have landed at the Machail temple first, before attempting the pass but that was tactically not prudent in the changed circumstances. The difficulty that the Army choppers had encountered in crossing the Umasi La only served to highlight the feat of stamina and courage of the legendary Gen Zorawar Singh and his men, who crossed this formidable pass not once but five times and in the peak of winters.

CHAPTER 10

Winning Hearts and Minds

The people are rightly regarded by the Indian Army as the Centre of Gravity of our Counter Terrorist (CT)/Counter Insurgency (CI) Operations. This is the anchor premise in such situations. You have to separate the terrorists from the people and make a concerted attempt to win over the latter's sympathy and support. Only then will intelligence flow forth and will the security forces be able to operate successfully. One has to therefore not only know and master the geophysical terrain but equally understand and master the human terrain in one's area of operations.

I was under heavy pressure in my first year of operations and could not pay as much attention to civic action. The denuding of troops from our area had put us under considerable pressure and we were hard put to just manage our operations. The situation had become much worse after the massacres of the minorities had started in my area. Putting an end to the terrorist attempts at ethnic cleansing stretched us to the limit. However, by the end of 2001, we had managed to turn the situation around. Concerted operations to track down the perpetrators of such massacres ultimately paid off. We were able to eliminate this particular group of criminals and this sent a salutary message to the terrorist tanzeems in our area. The high visibility operations coupled with the media attention on this ethnic cleansing served to deter the tanzeems from any further such massacres, which alienated the civil population.

My GOC, Gen Bhagat paid the sector a visit. This time he came by road and spent some three days in my sector. I must say in fairness to Gen Bhagat that despite our initial differences on operational issues and methodologies—he was broad minded enough not to hold them against me. In fact, over the months his attitude softened and he became very nice to me personally. He realised that I was hard pressed in this sector and our retrieval of the situation after the massacres of the minorities (without asking for additional troops), pleased him greatly. He also saw the situation for himself in our area and realised the dire need to impose attrition on the terrorist tanzeems to pacify the area. In this, my sector was doing the best in his whole Force zone. In fact, Gen Bhagat was subsequently gracious enough to recommend me for the Sena Medal. This speaks volumes of the professionalism of the Indian Army where operational divergence of views is tolerated and commanders are broad minded enough to accept dissent on operational issues.

Each one of us, in our trajectory through our careers, acquires a great fund of experience that is unique to our context. Gen Mono Bhagat had acquired considerable experience in Somalia. His method of winning the hearts and minds of the Somali tribes had been eminently successful. He had carried with his Brigade well-boring machines and engineering equipment and struck sweet water wells in the Somali villages; constructed schools and hospitals and won the locals over completely. Hence, our troops in Somalia were rarely attacked by the Somali tribes and the Indian contingent area remained an oasis of relative peace amongst the severe turbulence all around. The American and Pakistani columns suffered heavily, primarily because they incensed the locals with their ham-handed methods.

Gen Bhagat had considerable experience of civic action and he now initiated civic action on a large scale in the Delta Force Area. We held a Prominent Citizens Meet where he addressed the citizens of Kishtwar. I was visibly struck with the quick rapport he established with the citizens. He asked them for any short gestation projects that they wanted the Army to do for them and the citizens came up with a number of innovative ideas. This way, instead of forcing unwanted projects on the civilians, he was adept at gauging what they wanted or needed and taught us to fulfil the local aspirations. I was struck by his positive approach towards civic action and the rapport he was able to generate with the people. So far, we had been overwhelmed by the pressure of the ongoing operations, and had little time or energy for executing any major Civic action projects. Now that the operational situation was under better control, I resolved to take up civic actions in a major way thereafter and gave my personal attention. Normally, these took the perfunctory form of building some playfields or sheds for bus passengers that largely remained unused. These were limited utility actions.

Gen Mono Bhagat taught us to think big in these matters. Accordingly, we focussed on building schools and hospitals for the locals as part of the Sadbhavna Projects. One of the first actions of the Foreign terrorists was to burn down all schools that were imparting secular, humanist and modern education to the children. The aim was to push an entire generation into the Madrasas so that they would be radicalised and brainwashed with the strident propaganda of the Jihad. Our first priority therefore was to rebuild the schools and educational institutions. We used the local labour and the local craftsmen and contractors, so that the funds made available for the projects were all spent locally and benefited the people in economic terms. As far as possible, we purchased the construction material also locally, so that the money would be pumped into the local economy. Health care was very poor in these remote regions and we focussed equally on building hospitals which would really help the local people. One of the better hospitals that we constructed was at Gundoh. We started it as an eight bedded hospital and then added an Operation Theatre (OT) to it and provided generators. It was a tremendous hit with the people of Gundoh and served to win over the population in that area that had grown quite sullen over the years. The civilians organised a major function for the inauguration of the hospital. The school children sang patriotic songs including Alama Iqbal's "*Sare Jahan Se Achha*" and everyone enjoyed the festive atmosphere. We had begun to build our bridges with the local people.

Navapachi Reconstruction

Our most ambitious project however was executed at the heli-maintained post of Navapachi. This is where the killing of nine civilians had happened some years earlier. The Prime Minister himself had sanctioned some Rs. 1.2 crore for civic action projects here. The problem was transporting the construction material over a mule track that took almost three days one way and entailed a six to seven days turn around. Ultimately, we pressed in additional Mi-17 helicopter flights to ferry in the material. We constructed a very well-equipped hospital and a school here and built shops for the families of the victims. We also created a Handicrafts Centre for the training of the local people in carpentry, electrification and allied skills. We distributed one solar lantern to each household in this group of villages. This was a most popular innovation and brought light to the lives of the people in these remote areas. The impact on the local population was highly positive and support for the terrorist tanzeems dried up greatly.

The Army thus showed to the people that it cared and would go extra mile to ameliorate their suffering and better their lot. It was certainly not an Army of occupation and its very presence boosted the local economy and these civic action projects gave the people much needed roads, schools and hospitals in the remote mountains. Depending upon local needs, at places we supplied pipelines to bring water to villages. One of the most popular program with the locals however were the Medical Camps and Veterinary Camps. Our Army Lady doctors were a tremendous hit with the local women folk. In J&K, the ladies are key opinion makers and getting them over to our side was vital. It is the women who suffer the most in any conflict—either as mothers, wives, daughters or sisters who lose their loved ones. Many of them were raped by the foreign terrorists and suffered inordinately. Our Army Lady Doctors were a big hit with them and served the most to create a strong peace constituency amongst the women folk in particular and the people in general. The Gujjars really welcomed the Veterinary Camps where their animals were treated free of cost. It is the Gujjars who were some of the worst victims of the Pakistan's proxy war. In the remote heights and pastures, the terrorists lived off them, usurped their animals and food and misbehaved with their women in the isolation of high pastures. This latter aspect was the most galling and led many Gujjars to provide information to the Army at great personal risk to themselves and their families. My heart really went out to these hardy people of the hills with gratitude for the tremendous support they gave for our struggle in J&K. Many of the sacrifices they made will go unrecorded and unsung because of the need to protect the identities of those who took such enormous risks for the national cause.

Op Sadbhavna served to build bridges of trust and understanding between the people and the Army. It also gave a chance to us to know our human terrain better and establish contact with those who risked their all to support the Army operations. Football or volleyball playing fields were not as popular a device but cricket was a craze in these parts, even in the remote areas and we often gifted cricket sets to the village boys and organised matches and tournaments.

Educational Infrastructure

One of the key areas of emphasis however was on rebuilding the educational infrastructure. In the initial phase, the terrorists had specifically targeted the schools and burnt them down so as to force the children to go to the Madrassas. We insisted that each company post should build/ adopt a primary school and each battalion a secondary or high school.

This would revive the framework of a secular, liberal and humanist education. We may have lost this generation to terrorist propaganda but we would strive to win back the generation next. Another popular device was to conduct tours for the local village children to the major cities of India to let them see the tremendous development that had taken place and interact with children in the mainland to deepen a sense of belonging to a great nation on the march.

Turning Black Areas to White

Kishtwar was slowly but surely being turned around by this combination of civic action and concerted action/operations against the terrorist tanzeems. At HQ Northern Command, Gen Nanavatty saw the rolling back of the terrorist tide. At the macro level, he decided to reinforce success and turn black (terrorist dominated) areas to white as part of an overall policy outlook. Where earlier, Kishtwar had been denuded of troops as a peripheral sector and resources focussed on to the road in a purely defensive stance—now Gen Nanavatty asked his staff to pull out reserve units from other sectors and give them to strengthen Kishtwar. A number of units that were being deinducted were now allocated to me for varying periods of time. The emphasis now was to maximise troop density in this area and accelerate the transition to peace and normalcy.

Accordingly, I first got a Madras Battalion and a Gurkha Battalion with a young and dynamic Commanding Officer (CO) Shokin Chohan and his highly motivated troops. Unfortunately, they were on their way out and just spent two months with me. Even then, they dominated the Khankudhar-Gulabgarh area effectively and greatly assisted in its pacification before they deinducted. Then I got two more battalions. These were also on their way out and hence were allocated for a period of a few months only. These were 21 Rajput and 12 Mahar. Both units on arrival requested me for a transfer of 100 odd AK-47s. The troops unfortunately had little faith in the 5.56 mm INSAS Rifle. The design philosophy of the 5.56 series of rifles was that it was preferable to wound an enemy soldier in a conventional war, rather than to kill him. A wounded soldier has to be evacuated, treated, rehabilitated and is therefore a greater liability than a dead soldier. The 5.56 bullet therefore was underpowered, especially when compared to the high lethality of the 7.62 mm AK-47 bullets. The INSAS had little stopping power. Many wounded terrorists managed to escape and this was frustrating for our troops. The INSAS was prone to stoppages and oil leakage. It used to overheat in situations of sustained fire. The plastic magazine was fragile and would become loose and fall and was prone to breakages, causing stoppages. The INSAS required considerable rectification for CI/CT operations. I transferred a 100 AK-47s each from my RR Battalions to these units as they were likely to stay for a few months. Similarly, the 9 mm Small Armed Factory (SAF) carbine was quite unpopular in CI/CT operations. It was prone to accidents and had little stopping power. Our 9 mm pistols were only decorative in purpose and hardly ever used in combat. It was much better to replace them with Machine Pistols (like the Austrian Styr) which only weighed 200-300 grams more and could do burst fire.

These units were only operationally under my command. I was not to report to the officers. The attitude of one of the COs was unfortunately coloured by this fact. He had his own peculiar ideas about operations here and was overtly defensive. He lacked experience in such operations but what was worse was his unwillingness to learn. I sincerely advised him not to get too focussed on the number of days/months he would serve under me—and whether these would qualify him to get a report from me or otherwise. I advised him to focus on the job at hand and do that with utmost sincerity. Such dossier minded calculations have a sad habit of going wrong. This was an operational area where his unit's *Izzat* was at stake and that was the right perspective to adopt. Attitudes are important in combat. In the months ahead, this unit got into five major contacts and firefights but failed to convert these contacts into actual attrition on terrorists. However, the boys of the unit were very good and sincere and the Company Commanders were quite keen and enthusiastic.

I remembered one early encounter that 21 Rajput got involved in. This was along the Chenab river enroute to Gulabgarh. The CO informed me that significant contact had been gained by one of his companies and a major firefight was on. I urged the CO to move forward with additional troops and ensure that the terrorists did not get away. To enable the new unit to get success we had given them sources of other units. Lack of success after contact was gained would endanger the sources who had provided the information.

The CO accordingly moved forward. The encounter had started in the late afternoon and by last light was still on. I advised him to cordon off the area of conflict. In the morning, I was told the encounter was still on, however, no success had been gained so far. I was a bit mystified—the terrorists do not hang around an area of encounter for so long unless they are absolutely cornered. I decided to move up and see things for myself. The CO had established his command post on the right bank of the Chenab from where we could clearly see the encounter site on the facing ridge line across the river. The firing was still going on in a desultory fashion. I watched the scene for half an hour. The bangs and crashes of AK fire echoed and reechoed in the valley. Then I was struck by something curious.

"Are you sure the terrorists are still there?" I asked him.

"Of course Sir. Can't you hear this firing?" He replied.

"Are you in radio contact with all your columns?" I asked.

"Certainly", he confirmed.

"Well, please make a net call and ask all your columns to stop firing."

He did so and soon there was a pristine silence all over the valley. The troops had been mistaking one another's fire to be the terrorist firing. This happens often to troops who are new on the battlefield. The CO was fairly embarrassed by the long silence. Suddenly we heard a loud burst of fire from one of the huts on the corner of the village where the encounter was taking place.

"See Sir, that's not ours", the CO said triumphantly.

I had been in too many actual firefights by now to know the difference.

"You have a Rocket Launcher detachment here?" I queried.

"Of course, Sir", the CO confirmed.

"OK. Ask them to fire but not on the hut—just a few metres to its south."

The boys loaded the round. The metallic bang of the rocket rang in our ears and a puff of smoke mushroomed on the ridge opposite—just a few feet from the hut from which the small arms fire had just come.

"Hey! Stop that! What are you doing? We are the Police!" A panic stricken shout from that hut echoed across the river. The local police post was not on our radio net and had not heard the order to cease firing. I and the RR boys broke into a huge grin.

But these incidents do happen in the initial stages while the newly inducted units are finding their battle legs.

"OK guys—you can call it off and take a break. I'm sure you have learnt something", I told them cheerfully. Terrorists, we learnt later had indeed come to that village the previous day but the unit had not been able to cordon them effectively or close in to fix the terrorists and gain tighter contact. The terrorists had slipped out at night but our troops had continued to fire at one another—mistaking their own fire for that of the terrorists. These are difficult operations and we learn only by experience.

From just two battalions, I now had four battalions in my area. Initially there were contacts and firefights as the units spread into new and hitherto unoccupied areas. However, the terrorists then found the increased troop density too high for their comfort and escaped into the neighbouring sector areas. This is called the displacement effect and is the physics of placing a huge rock in a vessel of water. But then, that precisely was the whole aim. Salutory attrition had already been imposed on the terrorists in the Kishtwar area by relentless offensive operations. The increase of troop density displaced the remaining terrorists and served to pacify the area completely. Peace and normalcy returned to Kishtwar and you could see it in the faces of people. The school children resumed their picnics to the more scenic spots. That was the intention of the higher HQs—to turn a Black Zone into White and the two additional units of 21 Rajput and 12 Mahar helped us a very great deal in achieving this happy end-state. This helped us to intensify the civic action and completely win over the population. The purpose of the deployment was not enhanced attrition but the protection of the population and the return of normalcy.

In the meanwhile the Command of CI Force Delta had changed once again. Maj Gen R S Choudhury of the Rajputana Rifles took over. He was very energetic and forceful and had extensive CT operations experience. He was a patient listener and very quick to grasp the essentials of the situation. We struck a very good rapport from day one and I found Gen Choudhury to be highly supportive of his subordinate commanders and their troops. He was offensive in his outlook and by that time an additional brigade was released to CI Force Delta (due to the additional troops inducted for Op Parakram). This was deployed on the higher ridgelines overlooking the National Highway—NH-1A; and its operations in the greater heights had a visible and dramatic impact on the safety of the road axis *per se*. All IED attacks ceased soon thereafter and the primary logistics artery was now far more secure. It needed this accretion of troops, for the National Highway was too vital to be weakly defended. Close-in protection and good ROP drills are not enough. The greater heights that overlook the road have to be physically held and vigorously dominated by offensive operations. That was the clear lesson learnt. My colleague, Brig Velu was the new Brigade Commander here. He was brave, physically fit and aggressive and soon sanitised the area. Traffic on the highway now moved smoothly, without hitches or IEDs or ambushes.

Jointmanship and Coordination. One of the major problems in such areas is the plethora of organisations that are operating in the insurgency ridden regions. Inter-organisational synergy and close coordination is vital for success in such tricky operations. The key organisation is the local police. Without their support one can do very little in these areas where most operations are dependant on the quality of intelligence. The best intelligence usually comes to the local police. Besides the Police used to attach their locally recruited Special Police Officers (SPOs) with the army units. These SPOs have rendered invaluable support to Army operations. They have the local language skills and the intimate knowledge of the local terrain and population without which it is virtually impossible to operate in such areas. The SPOs in fact formed the backbone of the intelligence networks that most RR units had established in that area. How good the intelligence network was, was largely a function of the quality of SPOs allocated to that unit. That is why it is very sad that Foreign funded NGOs have raised such a hue and cry against the Salva Judam raised against the Maoists in Chattisgarh. People not familiar with such operations simply do not understand the need for navigating the human terrain of these insurgency areas. This can only be done by locals who have the knowledge of the local language and dialects as also intimate, by face knowledge, of the local population. Taking away the SPOs is tantamount to badly sabotaging such operations. That is why the Indian Army subsequently raised its own Home and Hearth Territorial Army (TA) Battalions to recruit the locals to support our operations and also deny local manpower to the terrorist tanzeems (who try and recruit the local unemployed youth). I was very lucky in that Ashkur Wani, a feisty local was the SSP of the Doda-Kishtwar district. He was from the valley and had suffered personally in this proxy war. Many of his family members had been killed by the terrorists. He was personally very brave and deeply committed to the fight against the terrorists. He had a good intelligence net work and moved about a lot. Many people, including his IAS superiors, found him rather difficult to get along with. However, I made a concerted effort to establish good working relations and he responded very well. The ASP at Kishtwar was Viplab Kumar of the IPS. He was a very brave and physically tough officer who had personally led some very successful operations into the remote Navapachi region. I liked this young man immensely and had later recommended him for the Presidents Police Medal. I had two CRPF battalions with me. When I came in, relations had been somewhat strained and the units were not even on talking terms with us. My own brother in law had been a Commandant in the CRPF and I went out of way to reach out to these units. They responded very well to this initiative. Each month we had an Operations and intelligence conference at my HQ and I began to invite the Police SSP and ASP, as also the CRPF Commandants to these conferences along with the local Intelligence Bureau representative. We used to host lunch for them after the first phase of the conference (before we had our separate in house discussions). This went a long way to building bridges and establishing rapport and good relations amongst the multifarious organisations involved. This practice went a very long way towards generating the much needed synergy in our operations and served to avoid collateral damage and Blue—on Blue casualties that result if operations are not closely coordinated between diverse organisations. I tried to exhort the CRPF units to also undertake some offensive operations and inflict casualties on the terrorists. Mostly they were engaged in protective tasks like guarding government offices and installations as also bridges, etc. In this they did a yoemans job. They were however weak in offensive operations. Since I was short of Army troops in my area, I tried to persuade them to step in and fill the breach as it were. One unit did make a valiant effort and in fact scored an initial success by defeating a terrorist ambush where they killed two terrorists. Thereafter, however they seemed to go into a shell of sorts and despite my best exhortations and encouragement, failed to eliminate any terrorists. I was a bit exasperated as the boys were quite good and one Commandant in particular was personally a brave and steady officer. I tried to enthuse him to be more proactive. Finally, one day he requested me to come to his unit. He treated me with great courtesy and explained to me the limitations of his organisation. The CRPF constables serve till the age of 58. About half of his battalion was in the age group of 40s and 50s. In the very tough and demanding terrain of the mountains of Kishtwar, this was hardly the age profile for offensive operations that entailed climbing from valleys at the altitude of 6-7000 feet to ridges that were almost 14,000 feet or higher. In the RR battalions we had laid down that all the men would be in the age group of 30 and below. Besides, as per organisational procedures of the CRPF, they were required to work only in 12 hours shifts. With such a unionised working ethos, they were good for protective/defensive tasks but no short-notice offensive operations can be undertaken with such severe work culture constraints. I understood his problems and thereafter was very careful not to push these units beyond their intrinsic capacities. That is why, I feel that the later Kargil Review Committee decision to make the CRPF, the primary CI force of this country, was far removed from ground realities and does not take into account the inherent age profile constraints and working/operational ethos of these units that usually work in company sized packets and rarely as cohesive units. Very often the Commandant and the Battalion HQ are located several hundred kilometers away from the companies. The CRPF will have to change its age profile and be militarised in its operational ethos before it can be called upon to undertake such difficult offensive operations in adverse mountainous or Jungle terrain. Otherwise they will suffer heavy casualties (like they did in Dantewada). Towards the end of my tenure I was also allotted an ITBPF battalion. I found the hill troops much tougher and the ITBPF cadre officers quite motivated and enthusiastic. The senior IPS cadre officers with this force however, were quite obsessed with turf issues and resented being asked to operate under army formations. In an area where uncoordinated operations could lead to Blue on Blue casualties, this could be very dangerous and such needless ego hassles in a battlefield environment could be quite counter-productive. Despite these constraints we did manage to get joint operations going finally. One of the major advantages that the ITBPF battalions had was the Commandant's powers to recruit constables for his unit locally. This helped intelligence a lot but once again turf considerations came in the way of fully exploiting this strength. The clear lesson that emerged was the imperative need to infuse synergy and coordination and go out of the way to ensure good and harmonious working relations with the other organisations operating in a common area. This is a sine qua non for success and requires that we put aside our individual and institutional egos and subordinate them to the higher national purpose of fighting the terrorists and insurgents. The value of periodic coordination meetings of all organisations involved is inestimable and can help in pooling intelligence and sharing good operational practices.

CHAPTER 11

Operational Research and Statistical Analysis (ORSA)

The Russians had built up the greatest fund of combat experience in the Second World War or the Great Patriotic War, as they called it. Meticulously, they had recorded their combat experience not in semantic terms of verbiage, adjectives, and metaphors, but in statistical terms of ORSA. This enabled them to put it to excellent use in terms of the superlative engineering design of a series of very robust and effective weapon systems. The Russian Kalashnikov Assault Rifles (the world beater AK-47) that emerged at the end of the Second World War was based upon this vast database of statistical details on the performance of weapon systems that was gathered in the Second World War. This had helped the Russians to produce some robust and revolutionary weapon designs like the T-34 Main Battle Tank (MBT), the Grad Multi-Barrel Rocket Launcher, the 130 mm Field Gun and the legendary Kalashnikov Assault rifle. The Israelis have been equally successful at weapons innovation and design precisely because of such meticulously recorded statistical databases.

The Indian Armed Forces are one of the most combat tested forces in the post-war period. Yet, despite this vast experience, we have not been able to innovate or design good weapon systems to suit our context. The primary problem is our failure to translate our combat experience into such statistical databases on weapon usage and performance. In fact, we have even failed to record and write down our aggregate combat experience of various campaigns. Leave alone databases, we do not even have objective military historical accounts. A self defeating cult of secrecy has consigned our military lessons learnt to the deep steel vaults of the

MO Directorate. Individual officers are not encouraged to record their battle experience and pass it down to future generations of officers. Our military history examiners still prescribe exotic and foreign military texts for the promotion examinations of Indian Army officers. Fortunately, the first stirring of change came in the 1980s when talented generals like Gen KV Krishna Rao and Gen K Sundarji encouraged cerebration in the Army, It was in this period that combat soldiers like, Lt Gen Harbaksh Singh and others began to record their experience and we slowly created a body of military historical writings in India. ORSA Statistical Bases however still remains a glaring deficiency. Till we create such statistical bases on the usage of our existing weapon systems in combat, we cannot hope to innovate or create new designs suited to our circumstances.

ORSA in Kishtwar

One of the key life-saving innovations in J&K was a rough and ready Bullet Proof Patka (BPP) and Bullet Proof Jacket created by one of our Special Forces Officers "Karate Datta" (who later became a Maj Gen). This was badly needed to save lives in combat and was rapidly procured (largely from the Army Commanders' Financial Powers to supply to our troops in Northern Command). The BPP and Jacket however, were heavy and somewhat unpopular with the boys. To make them water proof, they were encased in plastic covers of camouflage pattern. This made the cover unbreathable and caused the troops to sweat excessively while climbing mountains—usually from valley floors around 5-6,000 feet to ridges, over 11-14,000 feet in height. Naturally, the boys preferred to move without these heavy jackets. The Army's response was to treat it as a lapse of discipline and threaten punishment/disciplinary action against those who did not wear these in operations. The jackets could certainly save lives. They were cheap and quite evidently, better than the nothing we had been making do with earlier. While our staffs and Ministry worked out the GSQRs, at least something was made available to the troops in the field. However, I tried the Bullet proof Jacket on myself and understood instantly what the boys were going through.

I applied my mind to the problem. I asked my staff for statistical databases on the location of fatal hits in combat in J&K. I was surprised to learn that despite years of operations, there were no such databases. This was outrageous. As per SOP, each Army doctor treating a casualty is supposed to record on a body diagram, the precise location of the gunshot wound. This was being done but the records were getting lost in our archaic manual filing system at the hospitals. I ordered my staff to create scanned computer databases of those body diagrams that indicated the precise location of all gunshot wounds suffered by our men in actual combat. Soon we compiled a reliable and exhaustive computerised database. We found to our surprise that over 32 per cent of the total hits had come in the region between the forehead (just below the BPP rim) and the upper chest (just above the upper edge of the Kevlar Frontal Plate in the Bullet Proof Jacket). As troops walked, the jacket used to sag—exposing the vital aorta arteries of the upper portion of the heart. This exposure resulted in near fatal hits. A surprising 24 per cent of the fatal hits were on the thighs. This indicated poor first aid drills and bandage procedures that caused our boys to bleed to death.In many cases I found the troops going into action without carrying the first field dressings and the bigger shell dressing bandages I ordered Battle Field Nursing Assistant Cadres to be run, to create additional well-trained Nursing Assistant pools in each unit.

It is amazing that it took the army so much time to introduce the Blood Coagulant Spray/Powders that the American/NATO forces were using in Iraq and Afghanistan. The BPJ had two plates—one at the front and the other at the back. These two Kevlar plates really added to the weight of the Bullet Proof Jackets (BPJs). We studied the database and found that only 7 per cent of the fatal hits had been sustained on the back. Most of the time it was our boys who were in the attacking mode and as such, all hits came to the frontal arc. The weight of the BPJ could be drastically reduced by doing away with the back plate. This reduced the weight by half. Some of the Kevlar material so saved could now be used to cover the upper heart region. Thus, ORSA helped us to redesign the BPJ to make it more effective and efficient. We submitted these findings to our higher HQs and they were enthusiastically taken up by them to effect design modifications. However, Army HQ decided upon bulk purchase and it took over six years to finalise the GSQRs. Ultimately, I understand, a modular design was accepted where one could add or remove the level of protection depending upon the nature of combat anticipated (e.g., in open or built up areas, etc.). This is where theory and commerce generally supersede practice.

In the interim, at our Sector level, we did not wait for the military bureaucracy to finalise its staff duty procedures. Based upon our statistical database—the boys in the unit came up with a simple and practical solution. They discarded the unbreathable and sweat inducing plastic cover and discarded the back plate. Unit tailors created a loose Gaberdine Cloth Bag that could be slung around the neck. The troops removed the Front

Kevlar plate of the BPJ and put them in these bags. This was a breathable harness and reduced the weight by half. Such innovations on the battlefield are life saving and must be encouraged by the command chain. It is part of the Indian system of *"Jugaad"* or innovation.

ORSA Applications

I did my best to spread this ORSA culture in our formation and generate large statistical databases on weapons usage. Thus, one of the most useful weapons in close-in combat, especially in built up areas and caves, was the Swedish 84 mm Carl Gustav Anti-tank Rocket Launcher. Mainly two types of rounds were used—High Explosive (HE) and High Explosive Anti Tank (HEAT) that uses a gas jet caused by the Munroe effect to pierce steel plates. The terrorists generally took cover in pine log huts and cement and brick buildings where the HEAT round had no effect whatsoever. As part of the after action reports I asked the units to record the effects of the various types of rounds on different types of targets, as also correlate them with the ranges of engagement. To our horror we found, many instances where troops in the heat of battle had fired off rockets at less than 30 meters. The minimum range required for the arming of the round is 30 meters. So this led to a lot of wastage of ammunition, which we were able to correct. ORSA was a sound methodology, which the Indian Armed Forces need to adopt in a very big way.

Another very effective weapon system was the Russian Thermobaric round, which was able to create a fireball of eight metres radius and burn the terrorists to death. Highly effective against terrorists hiding in caves and pine log huts—its use had a tremendous psychological impact upon the terrorists. They were terrified of it due to reasons of faith—where the burning of the body has severe religious connotations in terms of resurrection on the Day of Judgement. However, it had a delicate safety mechanism and the troops were rather nervous carrying it around for fear that it would accidentally get set off. We ran cadres in the units to familiarise the boys with this excellent weapon system and encouraged them to use it to full effect to exploit its tremendous psychological impact. It thereafter proved to be one of the most effective weapon systems in our inventory.

CHAPTER 12

Lessons Learnt

The long and arduous Counter terrorist campaign in J&K has reached a successful culmination in recent years. Pakistan had systematically maintained a force level of 3,500-4,500 terrorists in J&K every year, from 1990 onwards. Whatever attrition the Indian Army inflicted each year, was simply made up by Pakistan infiltrating fresh terrorist cadres across the LC. Gen Zia-ul Haq's injunction was to keep the pot boiling in Kashmir at precisely the right temperature. He was careful not to escalate beyond a point where the Indian tolerance threshold would be breached and India would react militarily across the LC. The Jihad had been carefully nurtured via the Jamat-e-Islami (JeI) cadres from the early 1980s onwards. Key Jamat leaders were called out to Saudi Arabia on the pretext of pilgrimages and then taken to Pakistan to meet Zia himself. They were cajoled and instigated into starting the Jihad.

The CIA's Jihad in Afghanistan provided the inspiration and resources for Zia's Jihad in J&K that was far closer to his heart. He clearly articulated to his Jamaat supporters that the jihad in Afghanistan was merely the smoke screen behind which he would seek to seize Kashmir by asymmetric assault. The Inter-Services Intelligence (ISI) had grown into a major tool of asymmetric warfare. It had insisted that all arms and funding for the Afghan Mujahideen would be routed through it. Gradually it began to skim off huge consignments of Kalashnikovs and Rocket Launchers for the tidy little jihad in J&K that Zia was hatching so carefully all through the 1980s.

The scale and scope of Zia's asymmetric operation can be comprehended once we realise that the Indian Army recovered over 80,000

Kalashnikovs in J&K over two decades of CT operations. These, quite obviously, were only a fraction of the arms pumped into J&K. Kalashnikovs do not grow in the Apple orchards of Kashmir. What India faced was a full scale asymmetric assault orchestrated in Pakistan Occupied Kashmir (POK) and Pakistan, along with several Harkat-ul-Mujahideen (HUM) camps in Afghanistan and the Af-Pak border. Starting from 1989, *over the next two decades, the ISI infiltrated over 40,00 armed cadres into J&K. Of these the Indian Army had been able to eliminate some 50 per cent or 21,047 terrorists. The bulk of the rest presumably were able to exfiltrate back to POK after completing 2-3 year tenures in J&K.*

The campaign in J&K can be divided into three clear phases:

- The Jammu & Kashmir Liberation Front (JKLF) phase from 1990-1996.
- The Jihad phase spearheaded initially by the Hizbul Mujahideen (HM), Harkat-ul-Mujahideen (HUM) and then the Lashkar-e-Toiba (LeT) and Jaish-e-Mohammed (JeM) from 1997-2003.
- The Post-LC Fence phase from 2003 onwards to the present—when infiltration was drastically curtailed by a physical and electronic barrier on the Line of Control (LC).

Let us analyse each phase in some detail.

The JKLF phase: Between 1990 and 1996, the JKLF (that ostensibly stood for *'Azaadi'* or independence for J&K), spearheaded the militancy. In actual fact, this was a cover for deniability by the ISI and the insurgency was actually spearheaded by the Jamat-e-Islami cadres. This insurgency had been meticulously and deliberately planned and prepared for in the decade of 1980s. *Yet the Indian media and the world at large have swallowed the canard that the insurgency was triggered by an alleged rigging of the elections in 1988. This is purely an optical illusion. Rigging or no rigging, the ISI had planned the insurgency and it would have happened anyway.* The ISI infiltrated some 18,000 armed cadres of the JKLF, HUM and Harkat-ul-Jihad-e-Islami (HUJI) in this initial phase from 1990-96. The Indian Army and the J&K Police Forces were able to inflict some 7,655 casualties on the terrorists in this phase. This roughly works out to a casualty ratio of 1:7 between the insurgents and Security Forces (SFs). Infiltration initially was in large batches of around a hundred and more each. As vigil was stepped up, the size of infiltrating columns declined steeply to 10 or less in each group.

The ostensibly secular JKLF carried out large scale ethnic cleansing of the Kashmiri Pandits in the valley. Over a 1,000 of them were slaughtered in cold blood and hundreds of their temples and houses were burnt. Some 400,000 Kashmiri Pandits fled the valley to spend the next two decades in the refugee camps of Jammu and Delhi. They still have not been able to return to their homes. This has been one of the most sordid episodes of ethnic cleansing of an entire community, post the Second World War. It is a horrific crime against humanity. The pity is that to absolve itself of its responsibility to protect its citizens, the Indian state was complicit in this abominable conspiracy—complicit by its own conspiracy of silence that it threw over this horrible episode. The world, which raised an outcry over the ethnic cleansing in Bosnia and Serbia had nothing to say about the forced eviction of over 400,000 Kashmiri Pandits from their ancestral homeland.

This was a grim phase. The civil administration had disappeared at one stage—especially around 1992-93, when the JKLF campaign peaked. The civilians were badly demoralised and pessimisstic and felt we had lost J&K. This was when Gen VN Sharma, the then Chief of the Indian Army rubbished these suggestions. The Army intensified its operations and killed some 1,310 terrorists in 1993 and pushed up attrition levels to 1,596 and 1,337 terrorists killed in 1994 and 1995, respectively. With this cumulative attrition, the situation was brought under control and State Assembly and later Parliamentary Elections were successfully held in J&K in 1995 and 1996, to mark the culmination of this phase. The intelligence agencies had been able to comprehensively penetrate the JKLF and that had resulted in its heavy attrition. By now the ISI was thoroughly disillusioned with the Azaadi agenda of the JKLF and deeply mistrusted this organisation. It now overhauled its plans completely and from 1994 onwards, it began to induct the far more radical jihadi tanzeems like the HUM and later the LeT and JeM, etc.

The Jihad Phase: As stated, by 1994-1995, the ISI had decided to discard the JKLF and switch the Proxy war effort to a set of brand new jihadi tanzeems that were now out rightly fighting not for "Azaadi" but for merger of J&K with Pakistan. Pakistan had duly noted the pusillanimity of the Indian state in trying to hide the fact of ethnic cleansing of the Pandits. It now decided to give an outright communal and Islamist identity twist to the entire campaign. A massive infiltration effort from 1995-98 heralded this phase. In 1995, the ISI infiltrated some 3,200 terrorists. In 1996, it pushed in 3,230 and in 1997 some 3,186 armed terrorists. The highest number of terrorists were pushed in 1998, when they reached an astounding figure of 3,720. This was the phase in which the Gujral doctrine was being propounded and it clearly sent signals of weakness of resolve to Pakistan. Pakistan made an all out push as it were in its proxy war.

These were well-trained and highly motivated zealots. Mostly these were Pakistani nationals and Afghan/other volunteers. Some 60 per cent of the terrorists operating in J&K now were foreign terrorists. The ISI's "martial race" theory had found the Kashmiris as unfit to fight the Indian army. They characterised them as too flat footed and unreliable in combat against the Indian Army. The local content was therefore downgraded to just 40 per cent as the bulk of the cadres now pushed in were Punjabi-Muslims and Afghans. In this Jihad phase from 1997-2003, the Indian Army inflicted over 20,304 casualties on the terrorist tanzeems. (Fig. 5) This is the phase where the imprint of Gen Pervez Musharraf, the Commando General is seen so very clearly. With the coming in of the maverick Gen Pervez Musharraf as Army Chief, Pakistan had already raised the pitch in 1999 and provoked a Limited War in Kashmir. Post-Kargil he overthrew Nawaz Sharif and intensified the proxy war by extending it to the Indian mainland proper. These escalations just triggered the Limited Kargil War of 1999 and then the massive deployment of Op Parakram in 2000-01. He deliberately raised the ante by increasing the levels of infiltration and raising the targeting profile by attacking iconic targets. This deliberately pushed the Indian tolerance threshold. He made a dangerous gamble with Kargil and was surprised by the scale, scope and manner of the Indian reaction. After the coup, he had no further check of civilian authority and once again seriously escalated the situation in 2000-2001. This grim period almost brought South Asia to the brink of war, as India reacted with a total mobilisation of its armed forces. This coercive deployment was quite effective initially and American pressure forced Musharraf to recant on television. India needed to reinforce the deployment with a limited offensive across the LC in J&K. This did not come and the credibility of the entire coercive exercise was badly eroded. The clear lesson learnt was the need to employ Air Power to commence the conflict and retain escalation dominance. For this India needed to enhance its Air Power exponentially. However, the further massing of troops in J&K had a salutary impact on the counter terrorist operations. One can see a clear drop in the infiltration profile in the year 2000—when the level of infiltration came down to 2040.

The grimmest phase of this struggle came in 2000-2002, when under the professional leadership of Gen Rustom Nanavatty, the Indian Army inflicted some 1,520 casualties in 2000 and then a record 2,020 casualties in 2001 and 1,707 casualties in 2002 on the terrorists. In 2003, it inflicted 1,484 casualties on the tanzeems. This sustained cumulative attrition broke the back of the Jihadi terrorist tanzeems. Op Vijay had taken place in 1999 and Op Parakram in 2000-2001. The benumbing impact of the Kargil war had caused a steep drop in the level of infiltration. It fell from 3050 in 1999 to just 2040 in 2000. This highlights the impact of live operations on the levels of infiltration. Even though these operations had distracted the troops from their CT campaigns to regular operations—the massive increase in troop density in J&K *per se* had an inexorable impact and splintered the jihadi tanzeems. However there were no live operations during the Op Parakram deployment and we saw concomitantly, a sharp increase in the level of infiltration in 2001-2002 (when it reached record levels) The ISI found the troop density too high in J&K and also decided to shift the battle to the rest of India. (Fig. 3)

The year 2003 marks a significant turning point in the CI campaign in J&K. This saw the sharpest drop in the level of infiltration that fell steeply from a peak level of 3543 to just 1720. This drop in the level of infiltration could be attributed to a clear cut realisation on the part of Pervez Musharraf that the Proxy War in J&K was not winnable. Possibly it can be attributed to a significant increase in US pressure on Pakistan. 2003 was also the year when after Op Parakram a ceasefire was negotiated on the LC and the heavy exchanges of fire ceased. 2003 was also the year in which the ISI raised the Indian Mujahideen to gain deniability and spread the war to the Indian cities. The first batch of some 80 subverted SIMI youth was taken to a training camp in Baluchistan (as part of the infamous Op Karachi).

The next significant drop in infiltration comes in 2005 when the LC fencing was completed. It fell sharply to just 516 and has continued to decline since then. However, India's restraint in not crossing the LC during Kargil, had later emboldened Musharraf to really spike the infiltration effort in the years 2001 and 2002 when these rose to the levels of 3486 and then an all time peak of 3543 was reached.The lack of any real operations in Op Parakram had enabled Pakistan to raise up the level of infiltration to a peak. How successful was Indian coercive diplomacy in Op Parakram? It is still not clear. 9/11 however was a major game changer that made terrorism unacceptable globally. The threat of the outbreak of nuclear war in South Asia, forced the Americans to lean hard on Musharraf and make him turn off the tap of infiltration substantially. In 2003, the level of infiltration declined to 1,729 from the earlier peak figure of 3,543 armed infiltrators in 2002. It then fell sharply and perceptibly to 1,313 in 2004 and by 2005, when the LC Fence was in place—the infiltration figure had declined sharply to just 516.

The Impact of the LC Fence: Historically, the LC Fence had been first mooted in 1990-1991 by the Border Security Force (BSF). The Indian Army in J&K (under Lt Gen Zaki) was then heavily focused on fighting the JKLF in the hinterland. In fact, Gen Zaki insisted on keeping the LC quiet so that he could focus on the CI campaign in the valley. This generated a great deal of controversy and consternation in the Northern Command. The problem however was the overall severe paucity of troops. India could not simultaneously pursue a conventional conflict on the LC alongwith the CI campaign in the rear. The situation was partially rectified when Gen BC Joshi raised 35 Rashtriya Rifles (RR) Battalions for the conflict in the hinterland. He pushed hard and ensured that this raising was completed in just one year. This enabled the Army to adopt a more proactive role on the LC. The Indian Army was still hesitant about the fencing. It was convinced that the border cannot be hermetically sealed in this type of terrain and if the onus of stopping infiltration was to be accepted by the Army, it would be hard put to deliver. However, it made up by activating the LC and major skirmishes and heavy firing broke out all along the LC in the tenure of Gen Padmanabhan (first as a Corps Commander in the valley and subsequently as an Army Commander in J&K). The heavy level of fire exchanges did add to the degree of difficulty in carrying out infiltration.

To take the pressure off its beleaguered terror tanzeems in J&K, Pakistan had launched its major infiltration operations in Kargil. A brigade worth of the Northern Light Infantry (NLI) troopers were infiltrated under the guise of the Mujahideen in a vast unheld gap that would bring the Srinagar-Leh highway under the coverage of direct firing weapons. This forced India to pull out its 8 Mountain Division from Counter Insurgency (CI) operations in the valley, thereby disrupting the CI grid. However, the prospect of war also impelled India to rush in its reserve divisions into J&K. A conscious decision was taken after the war to raise 35 more battalions of the Rashtriya Rifles (RR). With this enhanced force level a concerted campaign was unleashed from 2000-2003 and a record level of attrition was imposed on the terrorists. Op Parakram led to another massive increase in troop densities in J&K and these played a significant role in breaking the back of jihadi tanzeems. This is when Pakistan found the troop density far too high in J&K and decided to spread the terrorist war to the cities of mainland India. The Indian Mujahideen was raised in this period and the first batch of 80 trained in Baluchistan, not so much in the use of small arms but in fabricating Improvised Explosive Devices (IEDs) from commercially available chemicals like Ammonium Nitrate, Hydrogen Peroxide and Niogel Slurry. US pressure on Pakistan also intensified in this period and forced it to seek deniability in terms of shifting the effort on to the indigenous Indian Mujahideen cadres.

It was in the tenure of Gen NC Vij as COAS that the decision was taken to speed work on the Line of Control (LC) Fence, and create not just a formidable physical barrier but a significant Electronic Wall to stop infiltration.A determined effort was made by pooling in the entire engineer resources of the Army. By 2005, the LC Fence was complete and the infiltration figure fell sharply to just 516 from the previous year's 1,313. Thereafter, it has shrunk to an insignificant figure of just around 200 and less each year. The fence therefore was a significant degrade on infiltration across the LC. It proved to be a game changer—even as it had done so earlier in Punjab. Not only did it stop the turnover of terrorist cadres and seriously impede infiltration, it seriously curtailed smuggling of vast quantities of arms and ammunition into J&K. *The stoppage of arms and ammunition proved to be one of the key components of the defeat mechanism in J&K.* We had seen this earlier in Punjab and then again with the LTTE in Sri Lankan campaign. The Indian Navy's Campaigns (Op Tasha and Op Swan) had served to seriously curtail the LTTE's operations and staying power

The Impact of Night Vision Devices: Another important facet was the extensive use of Israeli hand held Thermal Imaging devices by our troops ahead of the LC fence. These virtually turned night into day and helped us to lay very successful ambushes ahead of the fence. Most of our kills in counter- infiltration therefore came not on the fence but ahead of it where we used to send out small ambush parties every night. The only constraint was the short life of the battries that had to be repeatedly sent for recharging.

9/11 Impact—The Al Qaeda's mass casualty attack on the Twin Towers of World Trade Centre at New York was a major turning point in the history of terrorism *per se*. The United States reacted viciously at the global level and initiated the Global War on Terror (GWOT). This was a paradigm shift of sorts and put Pakistan under tremendous pressure from America and the world. Almost all terror attacks across the globe could now be traced back to the jihad factory established on the Af-Pak border belt. This was the time when India also upped the ante with its large scale coercive military deployment for Op Parakram. This cumulative pressure forced Pakistan to back down. From 2003 onwards, we see a major drop in the infiltration levels to less than half of what it was in the earlier years the fence seriously curtailed ammunition supply; and was therefore a major cause of the final and decisive defeat of the proxy war.

Thus, this combination of global and local factors served to decisively defeat the Pakistani Jihad in J&K. The GWOT caused a global aversion to the use of terrorism *per se* as a policy tool. Pakistan came under considerable international and US pressure. On the ground, the Indian Army was able to erect a virtually impregnable land barrier that seriously disrupted the flow of infiltration and above all arms and ammunition supply to terrorists. The overall terrorist force levels in J&K fell to just around 300 and subsequently down to below 200 odd. Most of these cadres remained dormant and were just trying simply to survive.

The Intifada Phase: This was the time when Pakistan realised that it had lost the Jihad in J&K. Militarily it had been defeated by a significant enhancement of the Indian defensive posture on the LC coupled with intensified and concerted operations in the hinterland. The ISI now changed tack. It desperately tried to give the impression of a major Palestinian style Intifada in the valley. The tack it tried was blatantly communal. It made a major issue out of the shelters being constructed for the Amarnath Yatra pilgrimage. A Muslim Gujjar had discovered this holy cave of the Hindus and the annual Yatra was a part of the syncretic tradition of J&K State. The Jamaat cadres (with liberal ISI funding for stone throwing) now tried to give it the colours of an emotive Palestinian style Intifada—or popular uprising.

The Indian State was caught by complete surprise by this drastic change of tactics. The Police and Para-military forces geared for an armed insurgency, took time to adjust to the altered paradigm and failed initially to deploy non-lethal responses. Police stations were set on fire and several hundred policemen injured in heavy stone pelting. However, the establishment soon got over its surprise, used dye markers to identify and imprison key ring leaders instigating the riots and curtailed the flow of finances for organised stone pelting. In two years, this Intifada phase also petered out and the state returned to near total normalcy. Tourists returned in their thousands. However, the real measure of normalcy is not so much about tourist footfalls as the final dismantling of terrorist training camps—36 out of the original 42 are still functional and thousands of Pakistani terrorists are ready to infiltrate across at an opportune time

Meanwhile in 2007/2008, the ISI switched the war from J&K to the Indian metropolitan cities like Delhi, Mumbai, Ahmedabad and Bangalore, etc. It now factored in the imperative need for deniability by using the local Indian Mujahideen (IM) cadres. Mostly these were SIMI students and did not use small arms or military grade explosives but commercially available chemicals to make low grade IEDs. These however were used in tandem to cause fairly high casualties in crowded Indian cities. However, within a year, despite attempts to politicise the issue, the IM organisation was seriously disrupted and penetrated.

26/11: This was when Pakistan tried to revive the flagging spirits of its jihadi tanzeems by launching a terror strike via the sea coast in Nov 2008. It is noteworthy that by then the entire Indian land border from Kashmir to Kutch had been fenced. In fact, the well lit fence could now be seen clearly from outer space and figures prominently in the satellite photographs as virtually a wall of light. The Lashkar-e-Toiba (LeT) carried out meticulous ground reconnaissance through David Coleman Headley (a US double agent) and then struck via the sea through a hijacked Indian fishing boat. It was a firearm cum explosive vector attack. The LeT, an India centric Jihadi organisation was losing recruits to the Pakistani Taliban and others tanzeems that were active in Afghanistan against their ally, America. It had to do something spectacular to raise the morale of its cadres and ensure it remained relevant in the Anti-India Jihad. Hence 26/11. The 10 LeT gunmen held the city of Mumbai hostage for three days in which they grabbed the global media eyeballs and reduced the Indian state to a pathetic spectacle. The Indian response was rather confused and disjointed initially. It was only the heroism of the National Security Guards (NSG) that finally enabled the elimination of these criminals.

The overall response, however, was rather disjointed and confused. The local Army Garrison was placed under command of the Police and was placed in the outer cordon and asked to await the arrival of the NSG from Delhi. This was an unprecedented and unheard of situation of Army troops being placed under command the local police! Mumbai was a peace station far removed from the killing fields of Kashmir and unfortunately, none of the senior commanders in the local and regional command had any experience of live operations and tamely accepted this preposterous situation. The National Security Guards (NSG) also manned by Army troops, took its time to react. Some media reports indicated that the then Home Minister wanted to fly in at the head of the rescue posse from Delhi and for reasons of sartorial elegance, he could not be unduly hurried or rushed. Even once the NSG mobilised and came in from Delhi it took far too much time to flush out the 10 armed gunmen. This was primarily due to lack of contact intelligence that could have been provided by local troops if they had been permitted to move in. This however detracts not a whit from the bravery of the NSG boys, but the glaring fault was that the local Army Garrison was not used to locate and fix the terrorists. The even greater pity was that India took no steps to even threaten retaliation on

Pakistan for an attack, in which 166 citizens were killed and over 700 wounded. It refused to mobilise its armed forces or in any way raise the costs for Pakistan. All that India did was to bleat helplessly to the USA to put pressure on Pakistan. The US in turn put amazing pressure on India not to react in any manner. Their concern was not with the loss of Indian lives but their ongoing operations in Afghanistan.

The Indian state thereafter, seemed more keen to mitigate and staunch the outrage at home so that it could somehow resume negotiations with Pakistan (under concerted American pressure). All in all, it was a sad and unedifying spectacle that showed up an aspirant global power in very poor light. Though a lot has since been done to coordinate, synergise and speed up responses and strengthen coastal security—the primary problem is India's totally defensive and reactive mindset. India will have to raise costs for Pakistan in response to any such future mass casualty terrorist strikes. A purely reactive and defensive approach can be an invitation to more such strikes and unending loss of lives unless deterrent costs are imposed by either military, quasi-military or non-military means. No war in human history has been fought purely with shields. We need a shield coupled with the sword of retribution. *'He who tries defending everything—defends nothing'* is an old adage. The Chinese are more forthright. *'Only a fool or complete madman will adopt passive defense forever'*—Mao Ze Dong had said this so aptly. The Indian state unfortunately put its faith in the US assurances and its own and Pakistani courts. If we had any illusions left on this score they should have been rudely dispelled by the visit to India of Pakistan very garrulous Interior Security Minister and his outlandish and insensitive statements in New Delhi in December 2012. In the year 2013, we have seen a determined Pakistani effort to raise the level of ceasefire violations by almost 80% and the levels of infiltration equally sharply. There have been a series of rather serious and provocative incidents on the LC. In one two Indian soldiers deployed near the LC were beheaded, sparking outrage in India. This was followed a few months later by a Border Action Team strike that led to five Indian soldiers being killed, sparking another bout of outrage across India. The 2003 ceasefire now seems to be in tatters. All this points to the paradigm shift in the very nature of security in South Asia that will come about in 2014 after the US and NATO troops withdraw from Afghanistan. Will it lead to an all out drive by the ISI to reimpose the Taliban in Kabul? Will that in turn be followed by a major push by Pakistan to reopen the Kashmir dispute by another spike in the levels of infiltration? Will the China-Pakistan combine make a deliberate bid to weaken and erode India's position in J&K?

Macro Lessons Learnt: The Indian Context

The Indian state's response to insurgency and terrorism has been largely defensive and confined to one's own territory. It has relied upon a manpower intensive approach as opposed to the technology and firepower intensive approach of the Americans or Russians or for that matter the Chinese, Pakistanis, Sri Lankans and others. Though by and large this manpower intensive approach has served India well, our overall results have been somewhat mixed. We were decisively able to defeat the insurgents/terrorists in Mizoram, Punjab and Tripura, as also more recently in Assam. We got useful support from neighbours like Bhutan and Bangladesh. However, China and Pakistan have consistently provided sanctuaries, arms and financial support to our insurgents/terrorists and the Indian state has failed to dissuade/deter them by raising costs for such support. This is a serious failing that India must overcome, if it is to curtail the repeated occurrence and scale of such conflicts within. It will have to raise costs for external sponsors/abettors of terror or be prepared to take losses ad nauseum.

Though the insurgency in Nagaland and to an extent in Manipur has been contained, it sputters on largely as low grade extortion rackets. The problem in Nagaland is the splintered nature of the opposition that is divided on tribal faultlines and hence no one group can deliver peace (as had happened in Mizoram). Assam has proved the value of supportive neighbouring states like Bhutan and Bangladesh. The same cannot sadly, be said of Pakistan or China, which are now trying to arm and support the Maoists in their unending quest to destabilise the Indian state. The campaign in J&K has succeeded in pacifying the border province with a combination of effective border sealing and intensive operations in the hinterland. However, out of 42 trans-border terrorist training camps, 36 are still active and current Army force levels in J&K will have to be retained till such time as these are dismantled and the threat in being recedes completely. Otherwise there could be unwelcome regression in the security situation—especially after 2014—when the US-NATO troops leave Afghanistan; and Pakistan has surplus Taliban cadres to redeploy in Kashmir.

Issues for Debate

Gen Rustom Nanavatty, India's former Northern Army Commander and one of our most experienced combat veterans, has raised some key issues in his Thesis on *'Joint Civil-Military Doctrine for Internal Armed Conflicts'*, which merits wide ranging discussion and debate. Some of these are discussed in the succeeding paragraphs.

Legal Framework: Troops must never be committed to Counter Insurgency/Counter Terrorist operations without adequate legal cover and safeguard. In India, we have enacted following legislations to deal with such a situation:

- *Unlawful Activities Prevention Act* (1967, amended in 2004)
- *Armed Forces Special Powers Act* (11 September 1958). This is an important enabling legislation for the military to act effectively. It includes the power to declare an Area as disturbed. This then empowers the army personnel to:
  - Arrest suspected persons without warrant; to search person's, premises and vehicles and seize banned items.
  - It permits them to use force against those who resist apprehension/arrest to the extent of causing death.
  - It empowers them to destroy hostile premises/fortifications.
  - Finally it protects them for acts done in good faith (except with prior permission of the central government).

Many Human Rights organisations have termed this act as draconian and in recent times there has been an orchestrated outcry against this Act by foreign funded NGOs trying their best to slander/demonise the Army and de-legitimise its operations. This outcry is wholly unwarranted. The Act is not draconian. The US PATRIOT Act is more stringent in many respects and even allows search of premises without knowledge of the suspect/accused as also roaming interception of his electronic/computer mail. The AFSPA merely gives the Army the basal Police powers and protection under Sections 76, 79, 80, 96 and 106 of the Indian Penal Code.

The Army cannot realistically be expected to function without these legal powers in an environment where the local Police and Central Police Organisations (CPOs) have already failed to control the situation. The Armed Forces Special Powers Act (AFSPA) has enabled legitimate Army operations against insurgents/terrorists and helped to keep the country safe from such foreign inspired separatist forces. It would be highly counter-productive to cave in to the pressure of foreign funded NGO lobbies on this aspect. Recently, the Chief Minister of J&K himself tried to shore up his waning popularity by striking rhetorical postures against the AFSPA. He asked for its revocation from selected districts (including Srinagar). The Army has rightly advised against such partial revocation as the precedent of Imphal in Manipur, indicates that these areas became safe sanctuaries for terrorist groups on the run. Dilution of Security Forces presence in Srinagar for populist reasons has already led to ambush of an army convoy in which 8 soldiers were killed.

Besides, the factual position is that though the local terrorist groups have been brought under control, the terrorist camps across the LC are still functional and there could be a spurt in infiltration to revive the terrorist tanzeems anytime. Besides, the Army logistical convoys to Kargil and Leh have to pass through these areas and the road arteries have to be secured against terrorist attacks on Army vehicles and personnel. This necessitates the provision of legal cover under AFSPA. The recent terrorist ambush of an Army convoy passing through Srinagar has vindicated the Army stance. The rhetorical anti-Army stance of the state government has made Srinagar the safest sanctuary for terrorists to operate unchecked. This is a dangerous and counter productive development. Srinagar is the key centre of gravity in J&K and must be strongly held. Unfortunately, pandering to populist pressures has made it the weakest area where most of the recent terror strikes have begun to occur.

Diluting this act itself is a worse remedy. There is no way Magistrates can be found to accompany each Army column or clear operations in advance due to the time and space constraints of the terrain. Besides, what may be permissible in the termination phases of the insurgencies in North East and J&K cannot be applied as a norm to the start of a vicious insurgency in Maoist held areas.

Conflict Management versus Conflict Resolution: In Mizoram, Punjab and Tripura, the Indian Army/SF were able to achieve decisive outcomes in as much as significant attrition was imposed upon the insurgents/terrorists, there was a public surrender of weapons and the insurgents joined the democratic process. The same has not occurred in Nagaland and Manipur where despite the Shillong Accord, no closure has been achieved because of the fractured nature of the opposition. In Assam, the on again, off again "spurt" nature of our operations needlessly prolonged the conflict. In Nagaland, the opposition splintered along tribal faultlines and there was no one single group to engage in peace talks. The same is the problem in Manipur.

A perusal of the Indian Army's official doctrine for Counter Insurgency operations indicates a pessimistic approach that says that the Indian *Army can at best manage the situation so that talks are initiated with the insurgent groups*. It does not even attempt closure or conflict resolution. *Recent events in Sri Lanka and elsewhere indicate that such conflict resolution is possible and the Security Forces must set their aims somewhat higher*. At the very least, the level of attrition imposed on the insurgent/terrorist organisations must be of such a salutary nature that the government can then talk from a clear position of strength or an outright surrender of weapons can be negotiated to enable the disgruntled groups to rejoin the democratic mainstream.

Proportional Force versus Minimal Force: Most of our official pamphlets on Aid to Civil Authority are reprints/carryovers from the colonial period of the British Raj. It must be borne in mind that the British Raj largely faced a Non-Violent Freedom Movement based more on fasts, Satyagrahs and mobilisation of unarmed crowds. This could be easily managed by mere show of force (flag marches) or minimal use of force—by lathi charges/sporadic fire aimed to wound and not kill unarmed civilians and disperse agitating mobs. Post-independence, the levels of violence have unfortunately, risen exponentially. The Indian nation state has faced violent tribal insurgencies in the North Eastern states where Assault Rifles, Machine Guns and Rocket Launchers have been used. In J&K it became a virtual Proxy War and over 80,000 AK-47s were recovered by the Indian Army over two decades. Rocket Propelled Greanades (RPGs), and machine guns have been liberally used to militarise the conflict in J&K and IEDs were used to cause heavy casualties to personnel, vehicles and equipment. The Maoists have similarly militarised the conflict and are using IEDs in a very lethal manner. *This significant militarisation of such internal conflicts call into serious question the pre-independence notion of using Minimal Force against heavily armed and well trained terrorists.* The problem now is facing highly militarised groups operating in a guerilla mode with lethal small arms and rocket launchers/mortars being used quite liberally in tandem with very high powered IEDs that can destroy Armoured Mine Protected Vehicles. In such a lethal environment, the concept of Minimal Force is badly outdated and now needs to be replaced with the concept of using *"Proportional Force"*. The LTTE in Sri Lanka had graduated to a full fledged conventional military force that launched brigade/divisional sized assaults and fought pitched battles. Quite obviously, the Sri Lankan Armed Forces were compelled to retaliate in a conventional manner with their airpower, artillery and tanks. The results were a decisive outcome and a defeat in detail of the LTTE with the elimination of V. Prabhakaran and the entire command hierarchy in a full-fledged and bloody conventional war.

As the levels of militarisation rise in the Indian Internal Security context, it would be essential to transit to a regime of using proportional force and not just minimal force. The Maoists have already raised a People's

Guerilla Liberation Army (PGLA) that operates in platoon and company sized groups and is now reportedly graduating to Battalion level organisations. It has shown the capability to focus up to a thousand to five thousand cadres in set peace operations that include attacks on remote small towns and prisons. In such situations, confining the Indian response to small arms alone may no longer be viable or advisable. In remote areas (like Dantewada forests in Chhattisgarh) where chances of collateral damage to the civilian population are minimal, we could consider using Attack Helicopters and area weapons to inflict attrition on the heavily armed insurgents and minimise casualties to our troops. The state's response has to be carefully calibrated and in many cases will have to graduate to Proportionate Use of Force. This is the most important lesson learnt and the Indian state can now ignore it only at its own peril. Extreme notions of populism have hampered the state's response to escalating levels of Maoist violence in Central India. *The pity is that decades of experience in Low Intensity Conflict Operation (LICO) has been forgotten and stood on its head as the Police and CPOs now take on concerted CI/CT operations in dense jungle terrain. This was heretofore only done by the Army. The Police and CPOs, who previously only undertook defensive tasks, are now being militarised for this new and very ambitious role. This calls for an across the board transformation of their operational ethos, organisations and culture.*

The palpable worry is that by the time our Police and CPOs are fully militarised, the Naxal menace may have graduated to a level that is beyond their capacity to handle. *In overall terms of Cost-Benefit Analysis at the national level, it can be asked as to what would have been more cost-effective—Raising some 3-4 lakh more of CRPF units or raising 5-6 Light Army Divisions*, which could have been used against the Maoists initially; and then would be available for use against China or Pakistan in a situation of external aggression.

Internal Security: Primary or Secondary Role?: This now brings us to the seminal question. The Indian army considers conventional conflict against external state actors as its primary role and internal security as its secondary role. In fact, *there is a pernicious and increasingly vocal school of thought that this secondary task detracts from the readiness of the Army to train for its primary role. This is a seriously flawed argument usually put out by officers who have managed to avoid combat duty by constant postings to peace stations.* It is noteworthy that in the Kargil War, 8 Mountain Division was taken out of CI operations and thrown straight into regular operations against the intruders. The historical fact is that the 8 Mountain Division did much better than 3 Infantry Division, which had solely been deployed in a conventional role. Units in such non-active environments tend not to train as much as they should be doing. LICO situations provide excellent training and live combat experience under realistic settings. *The PLA of China and the Army of Vietnam grew out of guerilla outfits, which had engaged in LICO operations for decades; and had become combat hardened.* The less said about the performance of the peacetime trained 4th Red Eagle Infantry Division in the 1962 War, the better. Equally the performance of many formations based in the Punjab in 1965 (and free to train for years for their operational task) was less than optimal at the start of that conflict and many peacetime units took days to find their battle legs. Peacetime armies usually are the antithesis of a wartime Army. As the late Army Chief Gen BC Joshi used to say, "there is no better training ground than a live CI theatre, where bullets whiz past your ears." Troops and commanders who have not heard a shot fired in anger take some time to adjust to live combat and find their battle legs. This can be disastrous in short duration, high intensity conflicts and local wars that will last from two weeks to at best a month or so.

The PLA of China has four major tasks. These include defense against external aggression (conventional operations) as also Internal Security. All tasks have equal weightage. There is no gradation of primary and secondary. With the onset of the nuclear age, the simple fact is that 98 per cent of the time militaries will be engaged in the low intensity operations of Internal Security nature rather than in shooting conventional conflicts. Hence, this entire mindset of the Indian Army needs to change. It would be far more likely to engage in LICO than regular conventional operations. Hence, to label the most likely contingency of employment as a secondary task detracts from the seriousness with which armies must prepare for this level of combat. This mindset needs to change and Internal Security must rapidly be made one of the full-fledged tasks of the Indian Army—not just a secondary and avoidable role. This new found zest for peacetime soldering alone must be curbed.

The unfortunate fact is that in its quest to fight regular wars, the Army may end up unprepared for the LICO it will actually be called upon to fight far more often. An absence of operational challenge corrodes good units and leads to an atrophy of their combat skills and sub-unit cohesion. Given the nuclear overhang, our political leadership seems most unlikely to give the go-ahead for regular conventional operations either against China or Pakistan. The Proxy War in J&K and the Insurgencies in North East have largely petered out. Hence the Army has not faced any operational challenge for quite some time (almost two decades). A peacetime syndrome seems to be setting in where spit and polish and non-essential trivia start taking precedence over professional training. The strong officer-men bonding, which comes automatically in such combat environments and the mutual trust and confidence, tends to erode in long spells of peace. We had clearly seen this before the 1962 war. We have lately seen some regrettable instances of deterioration of officer-men relationships in a few isolated units. Sans a challenge from the operational/combat environment the fighting spirit of the units erodes and decays.

Not employing the Army in the intensive CI operations against the Maoists in the dense jungles of Central and Peninsular India is a serious mistake. The solution of militarising the Police and CPOs will take far too much time and simply compound the mistake. Traditionally, armies use LICO as Combat Laboratories, where troops are blooded and units/ subunits achieve far greater cohesion and bonding. Such experience is invaluable in high intensity operations. The Chinese Army that hit us in 1962 was combat hardened. It had fought the Chinese Civil War, the Korean War and an eight year long campaign against Khampas in Tibet. The results were there for the world to see. Fortunately, this well learnt lesson stood us in very good stead in the Wars of 1965 and 1971; and some three decades of LICO thereafter in the North East, Punjab and then J&K. This went a long way to enhancing the Indian army's combat experience and professionalism. Two decades of an absence of challenge has served to dilute these aspects. The Lessons are patent and obvious.

ORSA Approach: We urgently need to adopt an Operations Research and Statistical Analysis (ORSA) approach to recording our war fighting experience. This will help us to optimise our weapon design and make improvements related to our own operational context. Combat experience is the most valued assets of any armed forces but can be exploited only if it is recorded systematically.

Infantry Predominant Operations: The Indian model of LIC based on infantry predominant, small arms based operations has worked quite effectively so far. However, under the pressure of Human Rights lobbies we have strangely begun to resile even from our minimalist use of force levels. This is a dangerous trend and must be arrested. The Indian state cannot resile from minimal levels of force usage that have worked in the past. Universalism and Pacifism cannot be pushed to absurd levels that undercut our state sovereignty and ability to defend itself against asymmetric attacks.

Proactive Approach: Our lack of military capacity has prevented us so far from going across the LC/IB to raise costs for the sponsors of terror across our borders. This has condemned us to a totally defensive and reactive posture for over three decades. We must build up our air power and UCAV resources to retaliate and raise costs for Pakistan or any other nation that tries to promote asymmetric operations in our territory.

Use of Air Power: The Americans have made extensive use of drones and Armed UAVs in counter terror operations. Air Power will have to be used offensively to raise costs for states sponsoring terrorism/insurgencies in our country. Air power can help us to inflict costs while retaining escalation dominance.

Premature Withdrawal of Forces and Enabling Legislations: Few people understand that Low Intensity Conflict take 20-30 years on an average to play themselves out. Application of controlled violence to avoid collateral damage to civilians by itself, serves to stretch the campaigns out for decades. At the first sign of success there is a populist clamour by local politicians to withdraw the Army and curtail use of AFSPA. In most cases, this sadly premature removal of forces usually leads to a resurgence of the insurgents/terrorists. Populist moves by the Omar Abdullah government have made Srinagar the most conducive place for terrorist operations against the Army and the police. Such populism is dangerous and counter productive but is increasingly becoming the norm in a situation where politicians focus on short term gains at the cost of long term sustainability.

CHAPTER 13

Demographics as Destiny: The Road Ahead

In conclusion then, it is essential that we look ahead into the future to anticipate the type of conflicts we will have to fight. Most Armies end up preparing to fight the last war and are caught wholly unprepared to fight the wars that are actually forced upon them. Visionary organisations therefore must anticipate change and prepare to fight not in the past but in the future that is to come.

A key to the shape of the future environment is provided by the demographics of the population of the key countries that drive the global economy and hence shape its power equations. One of the key drivers of the national security process is the aspect of demographic growth. Unfortunately, so far security analysts have given it minimal attention. The graphical analysis is critical to India's future (see Fig. 7).

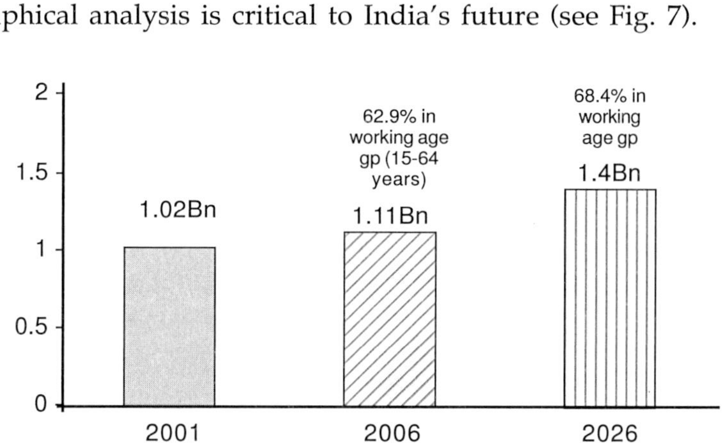

Figure 7 The Demographic Youth Bulge

Demographic Dimensions of Internal Security

India today has a population of 1.12 billion. Of this some 62.9 per cent are in the working age group. Today, in fact, India has one of the youngest populations in the world. Almost half of India's population is below 25 years of age. The median age of the Indian population today is just 25.9 years. Contrast this with the ageing populations in the other major countries. In China, the median age currently is 34.2 years, in the USA it is 36.9 years and Japan is worse off with a median age of 44.6 years. By 2026, India will have a population of 1.4 billion and will overtake the population of China. 68.4 per cent (or nearly 70 per cent) of this huge population will be in the working age group. India will then have the youngest population in the world. Considering the size of our population then, nearly 70 per cent of 1.4 billion would translate into the need for creating some 483 million new jobs in India by 2026. Now all the jobs in the public and private sector (including the unorganised private sector in India that includes the gardeners, dishwashers, sweepers, etc.) is just around 450 million. Hence by 2026, India would have to skill its population in a major way to get gainful employment for the huge numbers of additional youth who will enter the job market each year. It would have to generate some 450-480 million additional jobs by 2026 to absorb the expanded work force. A failure to do so would lead to huge number of unemployed youth and that could, in turn, set the stage for bloody revolutions and upheavals and great systemic turbulence in society. Unfortunately, *our economic liberalisation so far, has created the miracle of jobless growth.* Most of the jobs have come in the urban services sector that leaves the vast rural populations untouched. Indian agriculture just cannot absorb more people and as such India will have to industrialise rapidly or find some other means of generating employment. Doles cannot take the place of regular employment. Such doles lead to deficit financing and steep inflation and have really prevented India from focussing on creating badly needed infrastructure. Future industries should preferably be manpower intensive ones like ship-building and not those that lend themselves to automation (like our automobile industry). Cutting manpower and downsizing to have lean-mean organisations could prove to be a particularly disastrous idea in the context of the Indian democratic polity and its youthful demographic profile. Demographics therefore define our destiny.

India therefore is at the point of a paradox. If it could skill its population, like the tiger economies of South East Asia did in the 1960s, it could really become a breakout nation. If it fails to create the requisite number of jobs—Maoist violence may then just be the thin edge of the wedge. Youth bulges like the one India is now undergoing, have often coincided with bloody revolutions in the past in Russia and France and with Islamic extremism in the Middle East. However, it equally presents a significant opportunity for growth—providing we can skill our population and unleash the dynamic energies and potential of our youthful population.

This is what Nandan Nilekani and the Indian Prime Minister have been harping upon for quite some years now. Precious little however, seems to have been done so far to address this grave problem. Even more than Obama, it is the Indian PM who should really be counting every new job that has been created in India. Unfortunately, our colonial era mindsets impel us to simply ape the west and act as if what is good for America, is best for us. This is a seriously and tragically flawed approach. What suits America or Europe, may simply not be relevant to the Indian context. Thus, just a two decades ago, the Indian management sector was abuzz with slogans and clichés imported from the USA—like *"Downsizing"* and having *"lean and mean organisations by shedding the flab" of manpower*. Thus, Luce informs us in his immensely readable and insightful book, "Inspite of the Gods" that in the 1990s the Tatas steel plant in Jamshedpur was producing just one million tons of steel and employed some 85,000 people. By 2005 it was producing 5 million tons of steel but had cut its work force to almost half—just 44,000 people. Tatas Steel turnover had increased from just 800 million dollars in 1991 to 4 Billion dollars by 2005. Tata officials were then talking in terms of reducing the work Force at Jamshedpur down to just 20,000 and by automation, jack up production to 10 million tons of steel annually. Thus, Tata Steel, like many other Indian MNCs, transformed itself from a labour intensive Company that was supplying low grade steel to the domestic market in 1991, to a capital intensive company that now supplies world class steel to top of the line Automobile companies in Japan. *This economic expansion in India has almost entirely been in the capital intensive, and not in a labour intensive direction.* That may be good for the corporate sector profits but this simply fails to address our acute employment generation problem. Instead of alleviating it, it just makes it worse compounded. Such an aggravated lack of employment in a situation of a demographic youth bulge, could spell a collective disaster for India and lead to violent and bloody revolutions that could seriously damage or derail our economy and the MNCs that are now doing so well. This normative future is not a distant lode star. It could happen as early as 2020 and even earlier. We have to go for job creation on an emergent basis. Otherwise the violence of the Maoists would merely be the trailer for a scenario script that would be far more violent and worse. Rapidly skilling our young population is a primary national security imperative. it is in this context that our failure to truly indegenise our Defense Production is doubly dangerous. Not only does it erode our strategic autarky/autonomy. Off-shoring defense sector jobs to the USA, France, Russia or Israel could become a particularly disastrous course of action in a situation of a youth bulge in our population. If we are able to skill our people, a great future awaits us—if not the portents are grim. India today is on the point of a painful Paradox.

Organised and Unorganised Sectors. The peculiarities of the Indian demographic and employment scenarios must be well understood before we address the dire implications. Less than 7 per cent of India' dauntingly large workforce is employed in the formal economy, (which India calls the organised sector). *This means only about 35 million people out of the 450 million employed in India have some modicum of job security. The rest make up the seasonal army of mobile casual farm workers, running small shops or street side stalls, making incense sticks and Bidis, driving rickshaws, working as watchmen, gardners, maids or mechanics in small town garages.* The problem is really compounded by the fact that India has some of the strictest labour laws in the world. This makes it virtually impossible to sack an employee. Companies therefore prefer to hire temporary contract labour or outsource work to small unaudited outfits in the unorganised sector so that they can circumvent the tough labour laws. It is these underlying factors that push the bulk of the workers (almost 93 per cent) into the unorganised sector

Let us see the organised sector in some more detail. Of the 35 million Indians in the organised sector some 21 million are directly employed by the Government (armed and police forces, railways, bureaucracy, Public sector units, etc.). 14 million are employed in the organised Private sector and of this only 0.25 per cent (or just one million) employed in the IT sector. It is this small IT sector which (along with other services) now generates some 60 per cent of India's Gross Domestic Product (GDP). By 2005 India was employing just 7 million people in the manufacturing sector compared to more than a 100 million employed in China in low end manufacture.

Economic Phase Transitions: Skipping a Stage. China had transformed itself into the world's workshop. India, on the other hand, bucked the Steiglitz model of economic transformation, as per which countries evolve from an Agricultural economy, to industrial manufacture and finally move on to the Services sector. In the 1990s the Indian economy simply skipped the Industrial stage of manufacture and graduated to a service sector based economy where the services generate about 60 per cent and more of the GDP. The Indian economy thereby started resembling the post-industrial economies of Europe and America—without having gone through a full fledged industrial revolution in the first place. This unprecedented situation opens up a whole plethora of possibilities. India has bucked the standard Steiglitz model of development with its three successive stages that lead from an Agricultural to an industrial economy and then lead to a services cum Information Communication Technologies (ICT) based economy. India transited directly from an agricultural to a services economy, thus skipping the stage of an Industrial revolution that leads to large scale urbanisation. Has that been a good development or a bad thing? It has been good perhaps in ecological terms. Unlike China, India is relatively more stable ecologically—its rivers have not been totally poisoned and its ecology not ravaged entirely by industrialisation. In the bargain, however, India has lost some 100 million jobs that it needs so badly. Could India develop a unique alternative model of civilisational development? Could it base a new civilisation on a vast and completely de-masified power grid based on Alternative sources of energy—say a triad of Solar, Wind and bio-mass energy that powers each village individually, without needing the creation of huge and expensive conventional energy power grids that girdles the country at enormous cost of huge wastages. Could this demasified grid result in demassified manufacture in a whole series of SMEs? Could some 600,000 Indian villages be developed into Swiss style Cantons, where a more educated population would undertake local manufacture in terms of say watches, fruit canning/preservation and such—agro-industries based products that generate employment locally? Would that enable India to skip the need for catching up with an ecologically destructive industrial revolution? It needs a bold new vision but India must invest in creating infra-structure and give a major fillip to alternative energies and even large scale tourism that exploits India's Buddhist and historical heritage to create jobs on a very large scale. Most people may find this vision far too utopian and would insist that only large scale industrialisation can create the requisite number of jobs that India now desperately needs to employ its ever rising work-force. What must be very clear however, is the fact that—a future to create some 450 million new jobs by 2020 could lead to tragic consequences and large scale social turbulence and upheaval. India needs to more than double the number of jobs it has in the next two decades, that is India's foremost civilisational and security and developemental challenge.

Military Manpower Conundrum in India

The implications of India's demographic youth bulge have dire implications for India's military. Presently 50 per cent of India's population is under

25 years of age. It will grow even younger even as the population of China, Japan, USA and Russia will age further. Theoretically, India would therefore have the world's largest Recruitable Male Population (RMP) by 2025, when 68.9 per cent of its overall population of 1.4 billion will be in the working age group. China—during its civil war, with the GMD, its war with Japan and in the years of the Korean War, had fielded a vast Army of over 4.5 million men. It was a highly motivated military manpower which enabled China to face down and deter the technologically far superior forces of the USA and USSR. China became a significant military power of the world in this era, albeit, primarily a land power with little ability to project power and influence events far beyond its land borders. China's population has now begun to age. China however has carefully studied the changes in military technology and has been progressively downsizing its gargantuan Armed Forces. However a large portion of these were not de-mobilised but absorbed into the People's Armed Police (PAP).

Mao passed away in 1975 and Deng Xiao Peng became the new paramount military leader in 1978. He carefully drew up a virtual 50 years Perspective Plan for China's modernisation and rise to superpower status. He broke up Mao's Agricultural Communes and gave plots to the peasant families. They created an Agricultural Revolution that made China self-sufficient in food. This laid the basis for Chinas Industrial revolution. The disastrous economic collapse of the Soviet Union made China embrace capitalism with a vengeance. Deng turned China into the world's workshop for cheap, low-end manufacture. This generated over a 100 million jobs and gave a major export push to China's economy. What must be noted is the most deliberate manner in which China consciously postponed its military modernisation for almost two decades, while it deliberately gave priority to building up its economic muscle. During this period of economic consolidation, Deng Xiao Peng deliberately tried to defuse local and international tensions to secure for China a peaceful periphery in which to pursue its economic modernisation unhindered. Thus, China's economic modernisation had commenced in 1978 and her military modernisation was only spurred on in the 1990s by the shock of America's spectacular display of military technology in the First Gulf War. The RMA (Revolution in Military Affairs) left no option for China but to catch up rapidly. This seemed to confirm that the era of mass wars was over and wars could now be won from the air alone. It was all so much in tune with American Industrial buzz words and mantras about downsizing, shedding flab, and going for lean and mean organisations. The American Military actually started downsizing and soon paid the price for badly cutting the number of boots on ground in Iraq and Afghanistan.

The Indian Civilisational Trajectory

The Indian civilisation had come on the verge of economic collapse in 1990. With the eclipse of the Soviet Union, it had lost its source of very cheap, hi-tech weaponry. The Soviets had most deliberately subsidised the Indian military buildup against the China-Pakistan combine. The decisive 1971 Victory was due to this Soviet transfer of subsidised military technology. By the 1990s however, most of the Soviet era weapons of the 1960s and 1970s were due for turnover. The Soviet economic collapse at this juncture therefore hit India very hard. What was worse was India's own virtual economic collapse that resulted from the second oil shock of the Gulf War.

India had no option but to liberalise and decontrol its economy. Prime Minister Narsimha Rao and his economist Finance Minister Manmohan Singh unleashed across the board liberlisation and market reforms. India's economic reforms therefore started almost 13 years after the Chinese reforms had taken off in 1978. Much like China, the Indian nation state consciously postponed all its plans to recapitalise its military stocks of the Soviet era and focussed exclusively on economic consolidation just as China had done. The Indian Armed Forces were clearly told that they had no option but to wait till the economy revived and the country would try to secure a peaceful and stable environment by diplomatic means in the interim.

Major peace overtures were made to China and they did meet with adequate reciprocity and overly favourable response because China equally needed a peaceful periphery. Thus, Confidence Building Measures (CBMs) on the India-China border worked well and freed huge force levels on both sides. China's response to India's peace initiatives in the hindsight however, was far more complex and nuanced. Even as it thawed its own relations with India, it deliberately built up Pakistan as a nuclear, missile and conventional power and a counterweight to India. It also utilised this lull period to build its logistical infrastructure within Tibet to transform its capacity to wage war when needed. Not only was India denied a peaceful periphery, Pakistan (with generous help from the USA and China) acquired virtual conventional military parity with India. It used this parity to now initiate an Asymmetric assault in Punjab first and then in J&K in the 1990s and subsequently spread this to the whole of India. India was kept deliberately destabilised and tied down first in the Punjab and then in J&K.

Quite obviously, fighting this proxy war demanded great effort and resources from the Indian Armed Forces. The only logical solution was to raise costs for Pakistan by conventionalising this conflict. Unfortunately, India's indefinite postponement of its military build-up left the Indian Armed Forces with little scope to retaliate effectively across the border. The government deliberately underfunded military resources and supplies like ammunition, fuel oil and lubricants and spares that affected the Armed Forces' stamina to wage war in a meaningful manner. Indian Armed Forces were left with little option but to fight defensively within its own borders. It was reduced to a purely attritional and defensive approach in Indian territory. Despite this, by the sheer weight of numbers, India was able to wear Pakistani Jihadi Tanzeems steadily down. It shifted troops from the Chinese front to J&K and raised some 3½ divisions of the Rashtriya Rifles (RR) in 1990s and another 3 divisions worth of the RR post the Kargil Conflict. Thus overall, some Six Light Divisions were raised and two to three divisions transferred to J&K from the Eastern Front for the Proxy War in J&K.

Gen Shankar Roy Chowdhury, in his tenure increased troop levels in J&K and desperately requested for a speeding up of the military modernisation process. The Indian civilian leadership was adamant. The Finance Minister, Dr Manmohan Singh told the Armed Forces that they had no option but to wait. There was a school of thought that even though the hollowness in the Indian Army was alarming, the Pakistani Army was not in any better shape and that India could perhaps afford a short, sharp, limited war to deter Pakistan from its asymmetric adventurism. The collapse of the Soviet military-industrial complex had created huge problem of spares. India tried to obtain these desperately from Israel and Eastern Europe. China in the meantime simply body shopped for out of job Soviet scientists and engineers to get its own Military-Industrial Complex going. This was an opportunity to revitalise its own defense-industrial base that India missed completely.

The Gen Malik Era: Search for Quick Fixes

When Gen VP Malik took over the reins of the Indian Army, he was left with this unhappy situation of a complete resource crunch for military modernisation. The Indian civilian establishment was adamant that resources for modernisation would only be released once the economy grew sufficiently. This was also the era when western jargon and buzz words like downsizing and cutting flab were rather popular in the Indian context. The Gulf War had painfully highlighted the need for military modernisation and the Indian Army was desperate to get in force multipliers like UAVs, Attack Helicopters and Night fighting capabilities. There were simply no resources for these being released by the government.

Gen Malik and his staff now decided to work out some short term and expedient solutions around this modernisation cul de sac. One solution (that was initially hailed as brilliant) was the "we reduce military manpower and thereby bring down the Revenue Budget". Resources so saved, could be reallocated to buying capital equipment and military force multipliers like Unmanned Aerial Vehicles (UAVs), etc. Though on paper this solution looked quite innovative and brilliant, it had serious pitfalls and major practical problems. The kind of war that India was required to fight in the mountainous terrain of J&K was highly manpower intensive. Mountains simply eat up troops. We had transferred two to three divisions from the Eastern Front with China. These were not adequate to meet the huge need for resources in J&K. Gen BC Joshi had raised three divisions worth of the RR at a most impressive pace. Subsequently we had to raise another three and a half divisions of the RR. *What we needed desperately was more manpower, not less manpower*. Reducing manpower in such a situation of stretch could have spelt a disaster. The Infantry Relief Programme of the Indian Infantry was in tatters. Troops coming out from North East for rest and refit in peace tenures had now to be rushed to J&K, as the demand for more troops rose by the day. This was leading to a situation of great stress and strain for the troops—especially the very hard pressed Infantry component.

The New Army Chief tried to apply his theory with vigour. He asked for suppression of some 50,000 manpower from the Army. This was largely a notional theoretical quantification exercise. However, the aim was to probably pressurise the government to release resources for modernisation. The civilian response was somewhat bemused. "Look, if you need more resources—why don't you simply thump the table and ask for it—Why this linkage with manpower reduction"—was their natural query. This manpower suppression exercise now went to bizarre lengths. A whole army of manpower reduction specialists came up out of the woodwork—trying to find out ways and means to downsize units and reduce manpower in the Indian Army.

I was then posted as Director MO-5, the critical section that deals with force structure. I had very recent experience of combat in the Kargil Sector of J&K and had just experienced at first-hand, the way mountains simply eat up troops. In heavy fire exchanges, we had lost some six men killed and 21 wounded in my battalion alone—that had been the intensity of fighting. To evacuate each wounded soldier—we needed some 18 men in stretcher relays for 12-14 hours. One therefore needed every man one could lay ones hands on. Huge numbers of ambushes and patrols had to be sent out each night. Over and above this was the need to give everyone a break after some 90 days of combat. Leave Management itself was a nightmare. How could we think of cutting manpower in such a situation? I was aghast. Yet the whole Directorate General of Military Operations (DGMO) was in overdrive trying to somehow reduce manpower and thereby save and raise modern units. On the face of it, it was an unworkable theoretical exercise. I was fairly vocal in my practical apprehensions against these proposals. It was conveyed to the Chief and his displeasure was made known to us in no uncertain terms. "There are some people in the MO Directorate, who are trying to resist downsizing. It will be rammed down their throats", was the stern message.

I was called by my Additional Director General, a very humane, intelligent and cultured Maj General (later Lt Gen BS Thakur who rose to be the Vice Chief). He gently put across to me that there was hardly any point resisting this new trend as the decision had already been taken. The Chief wanted it—and we had no option but to comply in the military.

"Sir but Staff Analysis is equally the task of the MO—I'm sure we can convince the Chief of the unviability of this downsizing project."

He was a patient man but I seemed to be testing his reserves of patience. The gentleman, that he was, he sighed and said, "GD! I have been asked to tell you and your section to find out ways to do away with this list of units." He pushed the list across to me.

I looked at it and felt dismayed. It included units like Air Support Signal Units, Inland Water Transport (IWT) companies, etc. "Sir, we may not need the IWT companies in Bangladesh anymore, but we would need their trained crews and boats in the Andamans and the Rann of Kutch. We run the Air Support Signals units for the Air Force—just as they run the IL-76 Transport Aircraft for us. How would they respond?" I blurted out in genuine consternation.

The General sighed. He liked me but I was pushing the envelope a bit. "Well GD, I have spelt out the task for you. Keep me updated on what you do. That will be all."

I came back to my office and sat down in a daze. My GSO-1 and GSO-2, both intelligent and hardworking boys saw me and walked up to my table with concern, "Sir, you look disturbed. What is the matter?"

"Damn it! I am disturbed", and I told them of our task. I thought long and hard about the situation. Then I straightened up and asked my GSO-2 to take down a note from my side.

"May we have your views please on the proposal to downsize/ disband the following units?" Then I gave him a long laundry list of Directorates and Headquarters in the chain to address.

He looked up at me and smiled gently, Delaying is a standard staff tactic in such a situation.

"By the time this comes back we would both be posted out of here", I said brightly. That was April 1999. We did not disobey our orders. It was a rather high risk gamble but I was saved by the fast pace of events. I was saved in fact by the Kargil War that broke out within a month.

The MO Directorate was still working on proposals to downsize the Army when the news of the Pakistani intrusions in Kargil trickled in. We watched in horror as the red pins on the Kargil maps mushroomed by the day. We had been totally surprised. The situation soon took a turn for the worse. Casualties began to come down in a trickle first and then in droves. The Chief had gone up to the frontline. He saw the scores of wounded lying groaning, awaiting evacuation which was getting badly delayed. Quite obviously he was bloody furious.

"Why aren't they being evacuated", he demanded. He was informed that the MO Directorate had already issued orders for the disbandment of the Pioneer companies and the Mountain Artillery (MA) and General Staff (GS) Mule companies. These play a critical role in casualty evacuation—especially in a large scale conflict. When my section had been found dragging its feet on downsizing—another section of the MO had stepped in gleefully to score brownie points by doing away with what it felt were unnecessary logistics units.

The Chief came back in a right royal rage to the MO Directorate at New Delhi. Within half an hour, orders for the disbandment of the Pioneer companies and MA and GS Mule companies were cancelled forthwith. The moral of the story is we have to think before we act and "three bags full Sir" is no substitute for Staff Analysis in a professional Army. That mercifully was the last we heard of downsizing and cutting manpower flab.

I had sweet revenge after the war. A proposal had been sent to the Ministry of Defence for raising 12 additional battalions of the RR after the Kargil War. The then Vice Chief's office had been the most vociferous about downsizing. When asked by the Ministry about their change of heart regarding the new raising—they replied somewhat shamefacedly, "that actually we could make do with six battalions only and though we had asked for 12—we would be satisfied with just six." The Ministry sent the file back. I was now officiating as the Deputy Director General MO in place of my boss, who was on leave. I had served earlier as the GSO-2 with the then DGMO Lt Gen NC Vij (later the Chief). He had a soft corner for me and had given me the privilege of free access. I walked up to him with the file.

"Sir, the boys are under pressure—the peace—field profile of the Infantry is in tatters. Units coming from the North East for long awaited peacetime breaks have all been pushed into J&K. The entire CI grid has been disrupted in this war. We will need to resume operations with vigour. We will need far more troops, not less. This downsizing charade has got to end now."

His face turned grim but he registered every word I had said. He knew what I was saying was the god honest truth. He did not take a minute to respond, "Sit with the other sections; carry out an accurate appraisal of exactly how many battalions we need. Put it up to me at the fastest possible." Gen Vij was a man of tremendous energy and once he was convinced, he would pull out all stops.

We worked through the night, we consulted HQ Northern Command and came back with a reappraisal that said, "We need 45 Battalions not 12." Without batting an eyelid the DGMO signed the letter and asked me to take it up to the Ministry by hand.

It was the happiest moment perhaps of my military career.

I got a call from the JS (G) [Joint Secretary (G)] the next day from the Ministry. As the officiating DDGMO, I walked up to him to explain our altered stance. The JS (G) was a Sikh gentleman. He asked me for the reason for our change of stance and I took the liberty to reply to him in the vernacular.

"Mr Lalli, the unfortunate fact is that the dogs are barking in our cantonments."

His jaw fell with astonishment and his face changed colour. He stared hard at me and then asked me to explain what I meant.

I went over the details of our excruciating shortfall of troops; how the peace field profile of our Infantry was in tatters; how we would now have to resume the disrupted CT operations after the Kargil war, how we needed every man.

He listened to me with rapt attention, then nodded his head in vigorous agreement. "Col Bakshi, let me show you something in strictest confidence." He pulled out an Ministry of Home Affairs (MHA) file from his drawer. The CRPF had asked for over 180 Battalions and the BSF for 160 Battalions. So all the manpower saving we would do by asking for 12 and accepting six units would be well taken care of by the somewhat exaggerated demands of the CPOs. "Look Col, the money comes from the same central kitty. We have to decide as to what will be the more cost-effective option—45 of your RR Battalions or some 340 additional CPO Battalions, which are largely meant for static, guarding duties."

We got our 45 new RR Battalions through like a shot. They were in J&K within a year at the most and helped to turn the tide in 2000-2002 when we inflicted the highest levels of attrition on the terrorist tanzeems in J&K and broke their back. Since then, the strength of the Indian Army has been augmented by two more divisions for the North East and another Himalayan Strike Corps of two more divisions may get added in the years ahead. So much frankly, for that concept of downsizing in the Indian military context. Our American mentors in the meantime also learnt some rather bitter lessons in Iraq and Afghanistan about the dire need for boots on the ground and had to raise the strength of the US Army and Marines and resort to desperate measures like stopping troop rotation and turn over to create troop surges. The very energetic efforts of US Defense secretary Donald Rumsfeld to reduce the number of US troops in Iraq came back to haunt that Army. The dictum of the great captains of war like Marshal Napoleon are crystal clear—"God is always on the side of the big battalions."

India's security situation in the meantime has undergone another paradigm shift. Frankly, in view of the greatly enhanced threat of the Maoists in our rear—we will need 6-8 more Light Divisions of the Infantry in an urgent time frame. Downsizing is a bizarre solution in the Indian context of a youth bulge. Raising new Military and CPO formations will provide much needed jobs and help to control the rising new threat in our rear. What needs to be decided is the cost-benefit ratio of raising more CPO battalions (which will be of little use in a war against China or Pakistan) or raising Army Light Divisions, which would play a significant role in both conventional and internal conflicts.

Demographics therefore hold the key to our destiny. Despite all talk of downsizing—the Indian army will be bigger by some 10 divisions by the middle of this decade. We may have to add six divisions more. The Police and CPOs have already been expanded by some 300,000 men in India. That is the only way to create jobs for the rapidly expanding work force. Job creation would be the very key to our national survival and any failure to do so would only lead to internal chaos and instability. The menace of Maoism is merely a trailer of what could happen if we fail to generate jobs at the requisite pace.

The Path Ahead in J&K

Wahabi/Salafi School of Islam was employed by the ISI to subvert the syncretic Sufi form of Islam in J&K. There was a concerted attempt to stamp out the Sufi culture and even burn down its shrines (like the Charar-e-Sharif). This became an extension perhaps of the CIA and Saudi Arabia funded mobilisation for a jihad against the Soviets in Afghanistan. This backfired badly and singed the US itself in 9/11. It was one of the worst instances of blowback in the history of covert operations. Gen Zia-ul Haq's tidy jihad on J&K was a spinoff of the jihad the ISI waged in Afghanistan on behalf of the CIA. As a matter of fact, Zia tried to establish a new caliphate in Islamabad to destabilise the whole of Central Asia, Caucasus, Xinjiang and South Asia with a new ideology of militant mobilisation based upon an extremist interpretation of Jihad.

The Afghan jihad ended in the rise of the Taliban and the coming of Al Qaeda. The Americans were able to inflict a crushing defeat on the Taliban when it chose to fight like a regular Army in 2001. However, soon the Americans diverted their resources to Iraq and Afghanistan was left under-resourced and badly underfunded. The US failed to create a regular Afghan army till it was too late. Pakistan saw its opportunity and revived and sent in the Taliban now to wage dispersed guerilla warfare. The Jihad in J&K was an offshoot of this larger Afghan Jihad. Robert Gates, the then Director CIA (later US Secretary of Defense) had said that at one stage some 22 per cent of the terrorists operating in J&K had either come from Afghanistan or had been trained there.

The Indian Army has finally prevailed in J&K by a combination of effective border sealing to stop infiltration and manpower intensive operations in the hinterland to decimate the terrorist organisations. It has taken the Indian Security Forces some two decades to bring this terrorist jihad under control. However come 2014 and the American/NATO withdrawal from Afghanistan could materially alter the situation and lead to fresh spurts of infiltration. It is therefore highly premature now to treat the Jihad in J&K as history. Any dilution of force levels till 2015-2016 would be dangerous and invite the possibilities of a severe regression in the security situation in J&K. Thus, all the exaggerated hype to revoke the AFSPA and dilute the military presence as of now could prove to be highly counter-productive and destabilising. We need to consciously eschew such populist posturing on part of local politicians to seek cheap popularity by demonising the very armed forces that have indeed been the saviors of the state.

Education is the key to emancipation and the syncretic Sufi culture and tradition of Kashmir must be preserved in the face of the Wahabi/Salafi onslaught of extremism. There is no place for rabidly communal politics in a secular polity and as such the ISI orchestrated attempts at Ethnic Cleansing must be undone. The Kashmiri Pandits must return to their native lands and the Security Forces must ensure their protection. *The success of CI operations now is measured in terms of the ability to protect the population*. Merely creating kinetic events to impose attrition on the terrorist tanzeems is by itself not enough to win this type of a war. At its root lies the ability to protect the population from the excesses of the extremists trying to impose their medieval ideology upon a whole population in the 21st Century. The critical battle will always be for the hearts and minds of men and will be won or lost in the secular, liberal and humanist schools that the state sets up to skill the population and make it employable. The Jihadis had very specifically targeted these schools so that the children would be forced to go to Madrassas and acquire a medieval mindset. Even the curriculum of the existing Madrassas must be made more modern and scientific so that its students can get jobs to make a living.

We cannot prematurely let our guard down and fritter away the gains of two decades of operations in a bid to gain cheap popularity by first using and then abusing and demonising the security forces. The modern secular state will have to stand firm in the face of such divisive identity politics and revanchist agendas.

Above all, it must be remembered that J&K has three distinct regions—Ladakh and Kargil, the Kashmir valley and the Jammu-Doda region south of the Pir Panjals. The call for secession is largely confined to the densely populated valley where the Jamat-e-Islami (JeI) has been spearheading the struggle. It does not, by any means represent the views of the Shias of Kargil, the Buddhists of Ladakh or the Hindus of Jammu-Doda-Kishtwar, etc. The vociferous zealots of some five districts of the valley cannot speak for the vast regions of J&K that do not share this communal agenda. For, in the ultimate analysis, what is at stake in J&K is the Secular vision of the

Republic. At the time of partition, the forefathers of some 150 million patriotic Indian Muslims voted with their feet to stay on in a secular India rather than migrating to a theocratic Pakistan. Today, how can the Indian State afford to let the 5 million Muslims of the valley secede on the basis of a rabidly communal agenda? Should we let them go, what right would we have then to the loyalty of the 145 million balance patriotic Indian Muslims? The struggle is one of principle. Religion cannot be the basis of state formation. Else Bangladesh would never have separated from Pakistan. India simply cannot afford to let the valley go. Kargil, Ladakh, Jammu, Doda, etc. in any case have no desire to go. The voice of a few districts of the valley cannot be allowed to drown out the wishes of the balance state. Even in the valley, new Surveys of popular opinion have clearly established where popular aspirations lie. More than that, in election after election, some 70 per cent and more of the Kashmiri electorate have come out to cast their vote and strengthen grass roots democracy. The fate of not just democracy but the organised state itself is now in serious doubt in Pakistan. It is today 11th on the list of failed states and likely to sink lower in the years ahead. The people of J&K are not exactly stupid or blind to the developments taking place around them. By its deliberate and concerted investment in non-state actors as policy tools, the Pakistani state has shot itself in the foot. Its recovery will increasingly become more problematic. It may need to seriously worry about keeping what it has together, rather than trying to conquer new territories in J&K and Afghanistan. The world will seriously have to worry about what a fading nuclear armed state does in its dying throes.

The years 2014-18 could be crucial and critical for our Republic. 2014 will settle the fate of Afghanistan. That will have a huge downstream effect on J&K and the rest of India. The Maoist menace will have to be tackled decisively. India will also face huge external challenges from the China-Pakistan combine. We are entering a critical phase of our existence as a Republic. The choices we make today will decide the outcomes in the years ahead. Issues of Internal security will be even more critical than issues of external threats to India.

Issues of Governance

Issues of governance will always be critical to any analysis of our internal security. The very nature of our politics is now threatening our security as never before. The key issues are:

Fragmented Mobilisation based on Identity Markers: The first past the post system in our democracy allows a candidate to get elected on just 10 per cent of the votes in a constituency. Since 1990, there has led to an increasing focus on fragmented mobilization of targeted parts of the population on the basis of caste and creed identities. This emphasis on local identities in the place of emphasizing a pan-Indian national identity and national mobilization on issues of nation-wide concern is destroying the very idea of India. Crass identity politics has thoroughly splintered and divided our people along fault lines of caste and creed. The British colonial masters had not been able to so thoroughly divide the Indian people on the basis of caste and creed and ethnicity. This trend to emphasise local identity markers is having a serious impact on our Counter Terrorist operations. It is leading to a politicalisation of terror and a total demoralization of our security agencies. It has reached levels that are positively dangerous. This fragmentation trend could unravel and destroy our Republic. It must be reversed urgently if we wish to safeguard this nation state.

Electoral Funding: Our electoral funding system is seriously flawed. The basal lie on the permitted levels of expenditure and actual money spent in elections, is at the root of our Black Economy and the primal fountain head of all corruption. The levels of corruption have now reached such alarming levels that the legitimacy of the state per se has come into question. We need the most urgent reforms to stem this rot. It must begin with our electoral funding systems.

Erosion of Long Term Sustainability: The type of leadership that our current system of politics is throwing up is pathetic. The use of money and muscle power is leading to the criminalisation of politics. 30 per cent of our elected representatives are criminals or have criminal cases pending against them. Our identity politics is throwing up the Lowest Common Denominator in terms of money bags and dynasties enriched by decades of patronage and corruption. These are dominating our political discourse. There is a complete absence of visionary leadership and the entire focus is on quick, short term gains at the cost of long term sustainability. Coalition politics has dangerously weakened the centre in India and made policy formulation incoherent and dysfunctional. This needs urgent correction.

Erosion of the Political Economy: This focus on short term fixes and personalized gain has virtually destroyed our political economy. Competitive politics has led to the distribution of enormous doles and freebies/subsidies that have virtually destroyed our political economy. The MGNAREGA scheme cost us Rs. 1,40,000 crore. Some 30-40 per cent (14 billion dollars) worth has leaked out of the system. The spread of unearned largesse raised food inflation and money was wasted in simply digging/filling up ditches. No worthwhile infrastructure was created. The Food Security Bill will cost us Rs 2 lakh crores and torpedo what is left of our economy. The GDP growth rate has halved, inflation has doubted, the current account deficit is at a record 7 per cent of the GDP (we export $300 billion worth but import $500 billion- bulk of which is oil and gold). We have not been able to ensure energy security, or immunise ourselves to oil shocks. We have singularly failed to generate jobs. Our politics has virtually destroyed our political economy.

Reinventing the Republic: In sum therefore we need to reinvent the Republic. We urgently need deep and systemic reforms to cleanse our politics of the curse of identity markers and black money. This could entail a change to a Presidential Model from the existing West Minister Model and a transition from the Communism of Caste to the promotion of national talent and merit. Time is fast running out. We have reached a most critical stage of our history. We will either have to change or perish.

Post Script

As we go to the press, two aspects stand out starkly. The finality of the coming event—the US will withdraw from Afghanistan in 2014 and this momentous event is bound to cast its shadow all over the South Asian region. Pakistan's recent peace overtures are quite apparently designed to get a free hand on its western front- to decisively influence the outcome in Afghanistan. It quite obviously wants to hang Karzai and reimpose the Taliban in Kabul. For this it needs a temporary truce on its eastern front with India in 2014-15, so that it can deal undisturbed with Afghanistan and then turn around and send in thousands of out of job Taliban cadres into J&K and even the rest of India- for a final phase of the Gazhuwa—the civilizational conflict to dismember India. Hafiz Sayeed has been shouting this from the roof tops. Our amazing response has been to strive to conform to Pakistan's grand strategic design. So obsessed are we with the central idea of peace at any cost, that we seem to have lost our ability to define and safeguard our national interests. Most intelligent nations fight the war well away from their frontiers. Our natural response should have been to help the Afghan govt by giving it the heavy weapons it is desperately seeking from us. To the nations collective amazement, our Foreign minister feels it will annoy Pakistan and endanger the desperate peace process. Is that more important than India's national security interests?

The second natural response of any prudent power would have been to strengthen the defenses and security arrangements in J&K to deal with any resumption of the ISIs terror offensive. It is here that one is amazed to find that the state govts populist policies are doing their best (whether by design or sheer lack of vision) to dismantle the security architecture that has served us so well so far. There has been the desperate attempts to remove or dilute the Armed Forces Special Powers Act—the enabling legislation that helped the Indian Army to win the Proxy war in J&K. Srinagar, the key political centre of gravity in J&K has been denuded of the security forces presence to an extent that it is today the most vulnerable place in J&K. Army convoys are ambushed here and police picquets are regularly attacked. These most myopic and very short sighted populist measures have led to the killing of eight Army Jawans in a convoy passing through Srinagar. The state govt is squarely responsible for opening up this vulnerability in the key centre of gravity. We cannot afford to let some local politicians, wittingly or unwittingly, facilitate the resumption of terrorism in J&K because it ostensibly strengthens their bargaining power vis-a-vis the Centre.

Another very dangerous and destabilizing development has been the deliberate stoking of communal passions in Kishtwar. This has led to large scale rioting and arson in Kishtwar and the states Junior Minister for Home and the local MLA, Mr Sajjad Kichloo has resigned. Competitive politics of a very base kind are now being pursued in Kishtwar to disarm the VDCs that had been instrumental in safeguarding the Dogra community from the ISIs attempted genocide and ethnic cleansing campaign in the 1990s and early part of this century. In the face of a renewed Jihadi offensive in 2014, such a disarming of VDCs appears most sinister and tantamount to opening the gates for the Huns. Keeping in mind the certainty of the US withdrawal from Afghanistan in 2014, can we afford to dismantle our defenses before a deliberate resumption of such attacks? Time alone will tell whether this has been done by deliberate design or sheer stupidity and lack of vision. There is a clear and palpable need to be very vigilant and take all due precautions to see that the peace which was gained at such great cost is not disrupted once again by the ISI and its local Fifth columnists.

Select Bibliography

Books

Ahmad Rashid, *The Taliban: Islam, Oil and the New Great Game in Central Asia*, IB Taurus & Co. Ltd, London.

Air Marshal Mohammad Asghar Khan, *The First Round*, Oxford University Press, Karachi.

Barnett R. Rubins, *The Fragmentation of Afghanistan: State Formation and Collapse in the International System*, Yale University Press, New Haven, London, 1995.

Brian Cloughly, *A History of the Pakistani Army*, Oxford University Press, Karachi, 1999.

Brig Gulzar Ahmed, *Pakistan Meets India's Challenge*, Oxford University Press, Karachi.

Brig S.K. Malik, *The Quranic Concept of War* (with a foreword by Gen Zia Ul Haq), Wajid Alis, Lahore, 1979.

Brigadier A.A.K. Choudhary, *September 1965*, Oxford University Press, Karachi.

D.C. Sharma, *History and Culture of Kishtwar*, Chandrabhaga Publishers Kishtwar, 1995.

Dr Sukhdev Singh Charak, *Indian Conquests of Himalyan territories- Military exploits of Gen Zorawar singh Dogra*, Ajay Prakashan, Jammu, 1978.

Dr. E. Sridharan, *The India-Pakistan Nuclear Relationship: Theories of deterrence and International Relations*, Routledge, Taylor & Francis Group, London-New York-New Delhi, 2007.

Dr. T.V. Paul, *Asymmetric Conflicts: War Initiation by Weaker Powers*, Cambridge University Press, London, 1999.

Gen Mohammed Musa Khan, *My Version*, ABC Publishing House, New Delhi, 1983.

Gen Pervez Musharraf, *In the Line of Fire: A Memoir*, Free Press, Simon & Schuster, New York, 2006.

Gen Shankar Roychowdhury, *Officially at Peace*, Rupa & Co, New Delhi, 2008.

Hamudur Rehman Enquiry Committee Report.

Henry D. Sokolski (ed.), *Pakistan's Nuclear Future: Worries Beyond War*, Strategic Studies Institute, US Army, Jan 2008.

Jaswant Singh, *A Call to Honour: In Service of Emergent India*, Rupa & Co, New Delhi, 2006.

Kanti Bajpai (ed.), *Brass Tacks and Beyond: Perception Management of Crisis in South Asia*, Manohar Publishers, New Delhi, 1995.

Khalid Rehman, *The Jamait-e-Islami and National and International Politics*, Book Traders, Islamabad, 1999.

____, *The Future of Pakistan*, International Centre for Peace Initiatives, Strategic Foresight Group, Mumbai, 2002.

Lt Gen A.A.K. Niazi, *Betrayal of East Pakistan*, Oxford University Press, Karachi.

Lt Gen Atiqur Rehman, *Our Defense Cause: An Analysis of Pakistan's Past, Present and Future Role*, White Lion, London, 1976.

Lt Gen Gul Hasan Khan, *Memoirs*, Oxford University Press, Karachi, 1993

Lt Gen K.M. Arif, *Working with Zia*, Oxford University Press, Karachi.

Lt Gen Rustom K. Nanavatty, *Joint Civil Military Doctrine for Internal Armed Conflicts*, Centre for Land Warfare Studies, Knowledge World, New Delhi, 2013.

Lt Gen V.K. Sood and Pravin Sawhney, *Op Parakram: The War Unfinished*, Vision Books, New Delhi, 2003.

Maj Gen Shaukat Riza, *Pakistan Army – War 1965*, Oxford University Press, Karachi.

Maulana Abdul Ala Maududi, *Al Jihad-e-Islami*, cited in Pooja Joshi's *Jamait-e-Islami: The Catalyst of Islamisation in Pakistan*, Kaling Publications, New Delhi, 2003.

Paul Kennedy, *The Rise and Fall of the Great Powers*, Harper & Collins, New York, 2006.

____, *Preparing for the 21st Century*, Harper & Collins Publ (reprint), New Delhi, 2008.

Pooja Joshi, *Jamait-e-Islami: The Catalyst of Islamisation in Pakistan*, Kaling Publications, New Delhi, 2003.

Pushpinder Bedi, Ravi Rikhe, & Peter Stenison, *Fiza-Ya: Psyche of the Pakistan Air Force.*

R.S.N. Singh, *The Military Factor in Pakistan*, Lancers, New Delhi, 2008.

Robert G Wisring, *Kashmir in the Shadow of War: Regional Rivalries in a Nuclear Age*, ME Sharpe Armonk, New York, 2003.

Sadiq Salik, *Witness to Surrender*, Vikas, New Delhi, 1985.

Samuel P. Huntington, *A Clash of Civilisations and the Remaking of the World Order*, Viking Penguin Books (reprint), India, 1996.

Shuja Nawaz, *Cross Swords: Pakistan, its Army and the War Within*, Oxford University Press, Oxford, 2008.

S.N. Prasad and Dharampal, *History of Operations in Jammu & Kashmir (1947-48)*, History Division, , Ministry of Defense, Govt of India, New Delhi, 1987.

Stephen P. Cohen, *The Pakistan Army*, Oxford University Press, Karachi, 1998.

____, *The Idea of Pakistan*, Oxford University Press, New Delhi, 2004.

Walker Benjamin, *Foundation of Islam*, Harper & Collins, New Delhi, 1999.

Articles and Papers

A Study Report, *The Subtle Subversions: The State of Curricula and Text Books in Pakistan – Urdu, English, Social Studies and Civics*, Sustainable Policy Development Institute in Islamabad. By A H Nayyar, *et al.*

A.N. Verma, *Identifying the Nature of Current Terrorism*, Indian Defence Review, Jan-Mar 2003, vol 18(i).

Abha Dixit, *Soldiers of Islam: Origins, Ideology and Strategy of the Taliban*, Strategic Analysis, 11 Aug 2005 issue.

Ayesha Siddiqui's Article in the *Friday Times*, 12 Aug 2005 issue.

Bidanda M Chengappa, *Pakistan's Fifth Estate: Inter Services Intelligence Directorate*, Delhi Papers, Institute of Defense Studies and Analysis, New Delhi, Sep 2000.

Brig Ismat Saeed, *Strategy for Total Defence: A Conceptual Nuclear Doctrine*, Pakistan Defense Journal, Karachi, Mar 2000.

Col H.R. McMaster, *Learning from Contemporary Conflicts*, International Institute of Strategic Studies.

Scott, D. Sagan, *Inside Nuclear South Asia*, Stanford Security Studies, Stanford University Press, California, 2009.

Ejaz Haider's article in *Friday Times*, 12 Aug 2005 issue.

Farooqui Ahmad, "Failure in Command: Lessons from Pakistan's India Wars: 1947-1999," *International Affairs*, Vol. 78, No. I, Jan 2002.

G. Parthasarthy, "The Saudi-Pak Nexus," article in *The Tribune*, 11 Aug 2005 issue.

Lt Gen Sardar F.S. Lodhi, *Pakistan's Nuclear Doctrine, Pakistan Defence Journal*, Karachi, Apr 1999.

Mathew Clements, Article in *Janes Intelligence Review*, Jan 2009.

Michael Kreepon, "Nuclear Arms and the future of South Asia", *Joint Forces Quarterly*, Sep 09.

Moeed Yusuf, *India's Cold Start Doctrine: Explaining Pakistan's Stance*, Paper presented on Cold Start at US Naval Post Graduate School, Monterey, California.

P. C. Ramusma and M. Matellini, *Nuclear Safety, Nuclear Stability and Nuclear Strategy in Pakistan* (citing Lt Gen Khalid Kidwai).

S. Kalyanaraman, "Operation Parakram: An Indian Exercise in Coercive Diplomacy", *Strategic Analysis*, vol. 26, No.4, Oct-Dec 2002.

Shaikh Farzan, "Pakistan's Nuclear Bomb: Beyond the Non-Proliferation Regime", *International Affairs*, vol. 78, No.1, Jan 2002.

South Asia Terrorism Portal for data on Infiltration, Terrorist and security Forces casualties.

Sreedhar, "Pakistan-Taliban-Al Qaeda: New Trends in Terrorism and Violence", *Strategic Analysis*, vol. XXV, No. 9, Dec 2001.

Zafar Ali, *Pakistan's Nuclear Assets and Threats of Terrorism: How Grave is the Danger*, The Henry L. Stimson Centre, Jul 07.

Index

Afghan War, 25
Afghanistan, Soviet invasion, 41
Air Defence Gun, 24
AK-47 rifles, 69, 95, 114, 115, 117, 131
AK-56 assault rifle, 105
Al Qaeda, 46, 141, 166
Alama Iqbal
  Sare Jahan Se Achha, 122
Alni Ridge, 33
Amarnath, 98
Annan, Kofi, UN Secretary General, 75
Annihilate the enemy, 4
Armed Drones, 9
Armed Forces Special Powers Act (AFSPA), 58, 146, 147, 167, 171
Assam Rifles, 12

Bharat Ridge, 32
Bhot Kol Pass, 35
Black Economy, 169
Black Zones, 97
Border Security Force (BSF), 12, 53, 99, 140, 165
Brig Behel, 31
Brig Gangadharan (later Lt Gen), 31, 66
Brig Lamba, 91
Brig Velu, 127
Brigadier Shyam Narula, 79
British Templar Model of Malaya, 10
Buddhist period, 35
Buddhists of Ladakh, 168

Capt Sukhjeet, 67
Cassidey, Robert, 6
Central Intelligence Agency (CIA), 42
Central Police Organisations, 12
Central Reserve Police Force (CRPF), 12, 53, 128, 129, 165
Chandrabhaga, 28, 31
Charar-e-Sharif incident, 64
Chenab river, 31
Chhatru Nala, 31
China, 9, 154, 156, 158
  Civil War, 151
  Communist Armies, 1
CI/CT campaign in J&K, 3, 13-14, 44, 75, 86, 125, 139, 149
Civil-Military Liaison Conference, 64
Col Anil Khosla, 60
Col G S, 79-80
Col Sahai, 117
Col Sharma, 66
Combat in Kargil, 106
Command and Control (C2), 101
Communist Guerilla warfare, pattern, 2
Communist Party of India (Maoist), 4
Confidence Building Measures (CBMs), 159
Counter Insurgency (CI), 27
  Force Delta, 53, 78, 80, 108, 113, 127
  Operations, 45, 54
Counter Insurgency Force Romeo, 13
Counter Terrorist (CT), 27
  Campaign, 96
  Operations, 48, 55, 58, 62, 78, 136
  Operations in Kashmir, 18

Counter-Proxy War, 45
Counter-Terrorist campaign in Kishtwar, 21

David Galula, 3
David Kilcullen, 6
Déjà vu, 28, 44
Deng Xiao Peng, 9, 158
Dhok Defence Committees, 90
Dien Bien Phu, 2, 99
Directorate General of Military Operations (DGMO), 12, 24, 25, 76, 162
Dixon, Sir Owen, 83
Doctrinal Evolution, 1
Dogra Hindu, 21
Dogras, 19

Economic Phase Transitions, 156
Electoral Funding, 169
Erosion of the Political Economy, 169
Establish Secure Base Areas, 4

Field Marshal Ayub Khan, 40
Foreign Terrorist (FT), 46
Frank Kitson, 5

Gen BC Joshi, 15, 140, 150, 161
Gen Henri Navarre, 100
Gen K Sundarji, 132
Gen KV Krishna Rao, 132
Gen Malik, 160-161
Gen Mohd Musa Khan, 40
Gen Parvez Musharraf, 27, 46, 48, 111, 138-139
Gen Petraeus, 14, 21
Gen Shankar Roy Chowdhury, 160
Gen VN Sharma, 137
Gen VP Malik, 160
Gen Zaki, 140
    Era, 14
Gen Zia-ul Haq, 42, 43, 135, 166
Gen Zorawar Singh, 117-119
    Era, 35
General Henri Navarre, 99
Gens Giap, 2
Global War on Terror, 46
Great Patriotic War, 131
Green Jama Masjid, 70-71
Gulabgarh valley, 31
Gulf War, 159, 160

Hangshu La pass, 118
Harkat-ul-Ansar (HuA), 54
Harkat-ul-Mujahideen (HUM), 43, 136
High Explosive Anti Tank (HEAT), 94
Hindus of Jammu-Doda-Kishtwar, 168
Hizbul Mujahideen (HM), 45, 136
Human Rights (HR), 8
Human Rights Organisation, 57
humint, 7

Improvised Explosive Devices (IEDs), 59
Indian Air Force (IAF), 24, 74
Indian Armed Forces, 11, 15, 27, 131, 160
Indian civilisation, 159
Indian Mujahideen (IM), 143
Indian Penal Code, 146
Indo Tibetan Border Police (ITBP), 12, 18
Indus Water Treaty, 40
Infantry Predominant Operations, 151
Information Warfare (IW), 13
Internal Security, 149
Intelligence Bureau, 104
International Border, 41
Inter-Services Intelligence (ISI), 42, 43, 52, 57, 135, 136, 142
    strategy, 54
Intifada, 20

Jaish-e-Mohammed (JeM), 110, 136
Jama Masjid Episode, 70
Jamat-e-Islami (JeI), 20
J&K
    Proxy War, 116, 139, 160
Jammu and Kashmir Liberation Front (JKLF), 19, 43, 44, 45, 46, 48, 136, 137
Jammu and Kashmir Rifles (JAK RIF), 36
John Mc Cuen, 4
Julian Paget, 5

Kagune Gad, 31
Kargil Conflict, 25-27, 46, 53, 83, 139, 149, 160, 163
Kashmir valley, 32
Kashmiri Pandits, 19-21, 53

Khakri Ridge, 33
Khanku Dhar, 32
Khosla, Anil, 17
Kishtwar, 16, 17, 18, 31, 32, 34, 35, 37, 55, 56, 62, 72, 81, 87, 89, 96, 97, 108, 118, 127
Ethnic cleansing, 20
Korean War, 151, 158

L/Nk Surinder Pal, 87
Ladakh, 35
Laden, Osama Bin, 9
Lashkar-e-Toiba (LeT), 54, 90, 136
Line of Control (LC), 3, 26, 40, 110
Literature Survey, 3
Low Intensity Conflict Operation (LICO), 1, 74
Lt Col Goel, 114
Lt Gen Harbaksh Singh, 132
Lt Gen Hari Prasad, 13
Lt Gen JBS Yadava, 16, 85, 91-92
Lt Gen Khanna, 72
Lt Gen NC Vij, 76, 141, 164
Lt Gen Rustom Nanavatty, 18, 47, 72, 89, 96, 102, 124
Lt Gen S K Sinha, 13
LTTE, 141, 148

Maharaja Gulab Singh, 35
Maj Gen (later Lt Gen) Mohinder Singh, 59, 69, 74
Maj Gen Behel, 53
Maj Gen Mono Bhagat, 18, 74, 75, 78, 79, 81, 120-122
Maj Gen R S Choudhury, 18, 127
Maj General (later Lt Gen) BS Thakur, 162
Maj Karthikeyan, 114
Maj Lokesh, 67
Malaysia, 2
Mao Ze Dong, 144
Maoist Communist Centre (MCC), 4
Maru River, 31, 98
Marud Vridha River, 98
Maulana Abdul Bari, 42
Maulana Saidudin, 43
Military Operation (MO), 13
Mizo National Army (MNA), 12
Mizoram Accord, 12
Mobilise the Masses, 4
Mr Gujral, Prime Minister of India, 61
Mystic Ninth, 17

Nadi Sukta, 98
Naga Sen, 35
Nagin Sheru, 33
Nagin Shur Ridge, 32
Naik Rambir Singh Tomar, 22, 114, 115
National Highway, 15
National Security Guards (NSG), 143
9/11 Impact, 9, 110, 139, 141, 166
Non-Initiation of Combat Operations (NICO), 78
Northern Light Infantry (NLI), 25
NtR (Nothing to Report), 65
Nun Khun, 16

OODA (Observation, Orientation, Decision and Action), 16
Op Gibraltar, 40
Op Parakram, 27, 46, 47, 96, 102, 110, 111, 127, 138-140
Op Swan, 141
Op Tasha, 141
Op Vijay, 13, 24, 27, 46, 55, 56, 74, 79, 102, 110, 138
Operation Good Samaritan in the North Eastern stat, 8
Operation Sadbhavna, 8, 123
Operations Research and Statistical Analysis (ORSA), 12, 151
Order of Battle (ORBAT), 16, 28
Organised /Unorganised Sectors, 156
Over Ground Workers (OGWs), 8
Owen-Dixon Plan, 53

Pakistan, Proxy War, 83
Pakistan Occupied Kashmir (POK), 13
Para Military Forces, 12
People Friendly Operations, 11
People's Revolutionary War, 1
Peoples War Group (PWG), 4
Philippines, 2
Pir Panjals, 32
Prisoners of War (PoW), 41
Proactive Approach, 151

Psychological Tiring Out of Terrorists, 11

Rajesh Sahai (CO 11 RR), 17
Rao, Narsimha, Prime Minister of India, 159
Ridge Lines, 32

Saxena, Gary, Ex-RAW Chief, 89
Security Forces (SF), 44
Seek Outside Support, 4
Seoj Dhar, 32
Shillong Accord, 12
Sickle Moon peak, 31
Sickle Moon, 16
Singh, Dr. Manmohan, Finance Minister, 159
South East Asia, 154
Strategic Counter Offensive, 2
Strategic Defensive, 1
Strategic Stalemate, 1
Subedar Satya Prakash, 114
Surface to Air Missile (SAM), 24, 104
Sustained Force Committal, 11

Tagud Ridge, 32
Third World, 1
Thompson, Roger, 5
Trinquier, Roger, 3

Udhampur Military Hospital, 101
Umasi La pass, 117, 118
UN Security Council, 78
Unify the Effort, 4
United Jihad Council (UJC), 13
Unmanned Aerial Vehicles (UAVs), 9, 105, 161
US and NATO forces, 8
Use of Air Power, 152
US-NATO troops leave Afghanistan, 145

Van Tien Dung, 2
Vietnam War, 2
Village Defense Committees (VDCs), 16, 21
Vo Nguyen Giap's Viet Minh, 2

Wahabi/Salafi School of Islam, 166
War 1962, 150-151
War of Bangladesh, 28
Wars of National Liberation, 2
Warwan River, 98
Western Armies, 3
Westphalia Treaty, 9
What is gallantry?, 92
World War I, 21
World War II, 1-2, 60, 106, 131

2/8 Gurkha Rifles, 96
3 Infantry Division, 149
7 Sector RR, 59
9 Sector RR, 22, 53, 69, 80, 84, 100, 108
11 Rashtriya Rifles, 17, 87, 90, 115-118
26 Rashtriya Rifles, 17, 22, 62, 66, 84, 90, 99, 111, 112-116
35 Rashtriya Rifles, 15, 140
4 Red Eagle Infantry Division, 150
5 Sikh Light Infantry, 55, 66
5-6 Light Army Divisions, 149
8 Mountain Division, 149
12 Mahar, 124, 127
21 Rajput, 124, 125, 127
73 Mountain brigade, 102
303 Lee Enfield Bolt Action Rifles, 88